OPERATIC

Walter Bowart was
in 1939. He was aw
ism scholarship to the University of Oklahoma and has since worked as an editor, publisher and writer. His articles have appeared in many journals including *The East Village Other*, the underground newspaper which he founded in 1965.

Walter Bowart lives in Tucson, Arizona, with his wife and three children.

OPERATION MIND CONTROL

Walter Bowart

Foreword by Richard Condon

FONTANA/COLLINS

Published in the U.S.A. by Dell Publishing Co., Inc. 1978
First published in Great Britain by Fontana 1978

Printed in Great Britain by
William Collins Sons & Co. Ltd, Glasgow

This book is dedicated to those who are obedient to authority. May they follow in the path of Daniel Ellsberg, L. Fletcher Prouty, Victor Marchetti, John Marks, and George O'Toole, become responsible, and break free from the chains of command.

ACKNOWLEDGMENTS

From THE CONTROL OF CANDY JONES by Donald Bain: Reprinted with permission of Playboy Press. Copyright © 1976 by Playboy Press.

From "Assassination and Hypnosis: Political Influence or Conspiracy?" by Joseph L. Bernd: (Blacksburg, Virginia: Virginia Tech Pamphlet Series), Copyright © Joseph L. Bernd 1969.

From THE GARRISON CASE by Milton E. Brenner: Copyright © 1969 by Milton E. Brenner. Used by permission of Clarkson N. Potter, Inc.

From MARCH TO CALUMNY: The Truth About American POW's in Korea by Albert D. Biderman: Used by permission of Macmillan Publishing Co., Inc.

From THE SECRET WAR REPORT OF THE OSS by Anthony Cave Brown: Reprinted by permission of Brandt & Brandt. Copyright © 1976 by Anthony Cave Brown.

From pp. 219, 220, 223, 259 of PHYSICAL CONTROL OF THE MIND by Jose M. R. Delgado: Volume Forty-one of WORLD PERSPECTIVES, Planned and Edited by Ruth Nanda Ashen. Copyright © 1969 by Jose M. R. Delgado. By permission of Harper & Row, Publishers, Inc.

From THE CRAFT OF INTELLIGENCE by Allen Dulles: By permission of Harper & Row, Publishers, Inc.

From "Hypnosis: Its Tremendous Potential As a War Weapon" by G. H. Estabrooks with Leslie Lieber: Reprinted by permission of ARGOSY (February 1950). Copyright Popular Publications, Inc. All rights reserved.

From HYPNOTISM by G. H. Estabrooks: Copyright 1943, 1957 by E. P. Dutton & Co., and reprinted with their permission.

From THE REVOLUTION OF HOPE by Erich Fromm: By permission of Harper & Row, Publishers, Inc.

From NEW CONCEPTS OF HYPNOSIS by Bernard C. Gindes: Copyright 1951 by Bernard C. Gindes. Used by permission of Crown Publishers, Inc.

From BEHAVIOR MOD by Philip Hilts: By permission of Harper & Row, Publishers, Inc.

Interview with Albert Hofmann: From *High Times,* July 1976, pages 25, 28, 31. Copyright © Trans-High Corporation.

From "Science of Survival" by L. Ron Hubbard: Reprinted by permission of the Church of Scientology of California. Copyright © 1951 by L. Ron Hubbard. All Rights Reserved. Scientology is an applied religious philosophy. Scientology and Dianetics are registered names.

From R.F.K. MUST DIE by Robert Blair Kaiser: Copyright © 1970 by Robert Blair Kaiser. Published by E. P. Dutton & Co. Used by permission of the author.

From WERE WE CONTROLLED? by Lincoln Lawrence: Used by permission of University Books, Inc. (a division of Lyle Stuart, Inc.), 120 Enterprise Avenue, Secaucus, N.J. 07094.

From THE POLITICS OF HEROIN IN SOUTHEAST ASIA by Alfred W. McCoy: By permission of Harper & Row, Publishers, Inc.

From CIA: The Myth and the Madness by Patrick J. McGarvey: Copyright © 1972 by Patrick J. McGarvey. Reprinted by permission of John Cushman Associates.

From *Modern People*: © MODERN PEOPLE PRODUCTIONS. Used by permission.

From OPERATION OVERFLIGHT by Francis Gary Powers: Used by permission of Hodder & Stoughton.

From THE C.I.A.'S SECRET OPERATIONS by Harry Rositzke: By permission of Reader's Digest Press.

From *P.O.W.—Two Years with the Vietcong* by George E. Smith: Reprinted with permission. © 1971 Ramparts Press, Palo Alto, California. First published in *Ramparts.*

From OSS: THE SECRET HISTORY OF AMERICA'S FIRST CENTRAL INTELLIGENCE AGENCY by R. Harris Smith: Copyright © 1972 by The Regents of the University of California; reprinted by permission of the University of California Press.

From BRAIN CONTROL by E. S. Valentin: Copyright © 1973 by John Wiley & Sons, Inc. Reprinted by permission.

"I know of no safe depository of the ultimate powers of society but the people themselves, and if we think them not enlightened enough to exercise their control with a wholesome discretion, the remedy is not to take it from them, but to inform their discretion by education."

—Thomas Jefferson

"In the technotronic society the trend would seem to be towards the aggregation of the individual support of millions of uncoordinated citizens, easily within the reach of magnetic and attractive personalities effectively exploiting the latest communication techniques to manipulate emotions and control reason."

—Zbigniew Brzezinski,
National Security
Advisor to
Jimmy Carter.

Author's Note

This book is an exercise in citizens' intelligence. The author and the majority of those who've contributed to it are private citizens working on their own in a synergistic effort, without major funding or corporate support, without government privilege or "need to know," other than that need cited by Jefferson—the need for informed discretion in a democracy. Without the help of these many people, who, like the author, were motivated by shock and outrage that citizens have been so victimized by their own government, this book would not have been undertaken.

Thanks first to the victims of mind control who had the courage to come forward and tell their stories.

A number of professional people gave valuable technical assistance and patient explanations. My thanks to Harry Arons, Robert Brauers, Dr. and Mrs. Sidney M. Cohen, Dr. Remo Dicenso, Betty Dumaine, Dr. Milton E. Erickson, Morris Ernst, Bernard Fensterwald, George Griffin, Col. Laird Guttersen, Dr. Paul Henshaw, Edward Hunter, Hon. Louis K. Lefkowitz, John MacDonald, V. R. Sanchez, Alan W. Sheflin, Dr. Edgar Schein, Mrs. E. D. Yeomans, and Col. Joseph H. Ziglinski.

I received a great deal of assistance from a number of researchers and writers around the world. Thanks to Chip Berlet, Nancy Bressler, Jeff Cohen, Loren Coleman, Richard Crowe, William Grimstad, Paul Hoch, L. Ron Hubbard, Larry Lee, Charles Maierson, John Marks, David McQueen, Sandra Meiersdorff, Janet Michaud, Beverly Ogden, George O'Toole, Richard Popkin, Jeff Quiros, William

Stevenson, Scoop Sweeny, Harold Weisberg, David Williams, and Peter Watson.

Other valuable assistance was given by the following institutions and organizations: The Rare Books and Special Collections Division of Princeton University Library, Brain Mind Bulletin, Zodiac News Service, Freedom News Service, Pacific News Service, The Fifth Estate, Network Against Psychiatric Assault, The Assassination Information Bureau, American Society of Clinical Hypnosis, Sanity Now, Society for Clinical and Experimental Hypnosis, Center for National Security Studies, Group for the Advancement of Psychiatry, and the National Technical Information Service.

My understanding of the intelligence community was molded by exchanges with a number of intelligence and military people. They shall remain nameless. Special overt thanks to Colonel L. Fletcher Prouty, Michael Kradz and Alan Bell of Dektor Counterintelligence and Security, and Carl F. Boode of Desert Security.

Tom Miller gave me much of his time and expertise, as Director of Research and citizens' counter-intelligence agent extraordinaire. He gave me research and editorial assistance and encouragement. Above and beyond the call he patiently listened to the vent of all my frustrations over a period of years. His interest in the subject never waned, and research for his own book *The Assassination Please Almanac* (1977, Contemporary Books) uncovered leads for this one.

Kudos to Dr. Robert M. Thomson, Johanna Moore G., Martha Sowerwine, my mother Fenna, and my wife Peggy for their patience and support.

I owe a special debt of gratitude to Richard Condon, who gave me early encouragement and offered his valued commentary. And to my editors Wendy Broad and Cynthia Vartan who burned midnight oil to polish this manuscript.

Last and foremost I am indebted to my Enid High School journalism teacher, Miss Ruth Scott, who, twenty years ago, started me on the path of citizens' intelligence.

—Walter Bowart
July 7, 1977
Tucson, Arizona

Contents

Foreword

The father of Grock the clown, having had his legs broken in eight places by *his* father for professional reasons, broke Grock's legs in eight places to be certain that the child would grow up walking grotesquely so as to ensure his eminence as a clown. The act brought much pain and indignity forever but, Grock's father reasoned, was there not a wholly justifiable element involved? Was not the clowning tradition immortally enhanced by those unnatural legs?

As demonstrated inescapably by Walter Bowart in this book, our Father who art in the American secret police has endowed hundreds of scientists at American universities to unravel methods for fracturing American minds. That this research in so many great halls of learning has exceeded a cost of untold secret millions of dollars (the only yardstick remaining by which we are willing to measure anything) indicates that this Grockian entertainment being produced by our secret police is a matter of ambitious policy rather than the happenstance of cloak-and-dagger adventure.

In this book Walter Bowart has proven each step of this official, terminal, government anarchy, even though that appears to be a contradiction in terms. To alter and control human minds is the ultimate anarchy. What is offered by official apologists as a tribute to the needs of derring-do by romantic spies are acts of hatred and sadism against all people in an insane and degraded determination to extirpate conscience from society.

Walter Bowart underwent a long and expensive process to assemble the hard facts which comprise this book. Each document attesting to secret police intent had to be ferreted out of government archives by badgering persistence until, page by page, the information was released to him by his right under the Freedom of Information Act. The essence of that law seems to be that one need only write away to a federal agency for information about the general areas in which the citizen is interested. Not so. Walter Bowart needed to expend large sums of money to employ researchers in Washington and elsewhere in order to discover the precise *name, number,* and *description of contents* of each document toward which he was groping through black streams of informational darkness. Without this it would have been impossible to apply for the transfer of copies of these documents to himself for this book. He had to comb the United States for people from many walks of life who knew, vaguely remembered, or suspected that they had been under the mind control of secret police and military agencies, then had to backtrack again with information gleaned from them to labyrinthine research among thousands of federal archives.

Please keep fearfully in mind that the astonishing information published in this seminal work of investigative reporting, concerning avenues taken to decision and execution by our secret police to fracture or dissolve human minds, then to operate those minds as a small boy might operate a Yo-Yo, for purposes of counter-intelligence military "efficiency," and the destruction of democratic institutions, was drawn directly from federal records and from official laboratory archives of the highest educational purpose—as well as from the reviving memories of those who had already undergone the dehumanizing process.

The prostitution of the mind by our secret police preceded the murder of the mind. To attain the advanced techniques now available to "magnetic and attractive" political personalities, it was necessary to turn out the laboratories of science as a pimp turns out his heartless whores upon the winter streets; our hallowed educators, army and navy and air force commanders and personnel, the beloved medical profession, august and inspiring temples of the law, our esteemed statesmen, and all Americans living and dead. Each one of those groups is involved in this dismembering of the mind. Taxes and the collective conscience make the urination of the secret police upon the human mind possible. "Brainwashing" per se is no news to any of us. Controlled assassins are not known to us only through fiction. Advertising assaults on behalf of poisonous materials to induce us successfully to buy and consume are early on bastions of mind control.

No one—not anyone—needs theologians to answer the question: "Where does the soul live?" We know the soul lives in the mind because the soul is the mind in all of its unfathomably intricate individual conditioning. It is the mind of intent, of hope, of purpose, of achievement by the spirit beyond achievement by physical action. When Grock's father broke his son's legs in eight places there may have been alarm, on the one hand, that a man could do such a calamitous thing to his son but, on the other, the same people responded to Grock's genius to which those hopelessly deformed legs had contributed, and roared with laughter. That was the normal reaction when we were the audience and crazy-legs Grock was the clown. But Walter Bowart demonstrates to us in this book that we have become Grock. We are the spinning, hobbling, waddling clowns in the eyes of our vividly delineated secret police.

"Oh, no!" (Can you hear the outcry?) Oh, yes, writes Walter Bowart in this fearful record you now hold in your hands.

Apologists rush in, hired for all such occasions from everywhere, by the secret government crying out, "You are, as usual, like all of your exaggerating kind, making a mountain out of a molehill. While it may (or may not) be true that our secret police occasionally swing the sledgehammer on little minds, it is (or is not) being done as a patriotic act to protect our beloved people." They reel backward, hands clutching chests as the full realization seems to hit them. "My *God*! Bowart *cannot* believe that our government of the people, by the people, and for the people would use such loathsome forces against citizens. If such research were done (or was not done) then it would be for purely *abstract* research reasons—for the expansion of human knowledge."

Walter Bowart's book is also a freezing vision of the mutations of the aspirations of science. Scientists, educators, and their leaders, The Great Men, having stumbled upon the possibility of controlling the human mind, might well have withheld this knowledge from the secret police and brought it forward for all to share, would you not say? If the means are at hand actually to enter and control the mind—not through the far-off smoke signals of psychiatry and psychoanalysis—can we conceive of what might be found in terms of medical triumphs, the conquest of pain and of group hatreds, and mental energy released by unraveling the Gordian knots of mental perplexity to make one straight laser line that might then pierce the doubts and fears which beset each one of us? In terms of education light-years ahead of the educational means we presently employ, in basic and advanced learning of cultures, languages, and skills; in short, understanding each other across the face of the world, this development of Mind Control makes the invention of movable type seem like a primordial grunt from the shadows of a rain forest lost in time.

What has been achieved by the secret police in relation to mind control is scrupulously set down in Walter Bowart's extraordinary book. The question the book puts is this: do you wish this immeasurably important technique to remain as a weapon to be used *against* you and your children by what Bowart calls the cryptocracy, or do you wish to use it as a universal key to unlock a thousand new chances that your children will not be murdered in future wars?

In an epigraph to this book, Zbigniew Brzezinski measures the political probabilities of mind control use when he says, "exploiting the latest communications techniques to manipulate emotion and control reason." Today our secret police and our military establishment have demonstrated, in Vietnam and elsewhere (examined by Bowart herein), the powers to create assassins out of our children. The expansion of these powers, which are able to turn young men and women into murderous criminals at will, goes on unchecked by the oft-called "investigative" press, by "moral" leaders at the bar, in the pulpits, in high government, and on campuses. Yet the people they call the public have long suspected that it has become government policy to control minds. If there is general information abroad on this subject, then consider that which must be at the disposal of congressional investigating committees as they bugle their determination to control the powers of darkness within our secret police. Zombie is a quaint, old-fashioned folklore word but its meaning becomes obscene when our children's minds are being controlled by any one of dozens of federal secret police agencies. Have government agencies perfected methods sustained by the taxpayers to control the minds of the people who shot the Kennedys, Martin Luther King, and Orlando Letelier, the former Chilean economist and diplomat. Were the assassins programmed to forget they did it or were they programmed to do it? We may never know for they stand bewildered, idiotically grinning for the cameras. Have the technicians developed a model Giant, Economy-Size Government Assassin which can easily be turned out by the thousands?

The murders of a few hundred humans by a few hundred other humans is commonplace enough but, for the flavor of horror and terror, of endless nightmare rampant upon a landscape of what was once American democracy, consider this expansion of the Brzezinski epigraph which cannot be repeated often enough: "In the techtronic society the trend would seem to be toward the aggregation of the individual support of millions of uncoordinated citizens, easily within the reach of magnetic and attractive personalities, effectively exploiting the latest communications techniques to manipulate emotion and control reason."

The threatening state of American political leadership over the last fifteen years may seem to murmur that the "magnetic and attractive personalities" might rather not resist the destruction of democratic institutions by "effectively exploiting" these shocking gains into the control of minds. It might even be wise to consider Walter Bowart's real evidence herein, then to do what we can to protect ourselves if that proud right, with the love of freedom, has not been atrophied by "the latest communications techniques."

There is an alternative. We can all forever more be transformed into the image of Grock the clown.

Richard Condon
Kilmoganny, Ireland
31 May 1977

Chapter One
THE CRYPTORIAN CANDIDATE

It may have been the biggest story since the atom bomb. The headline, however, was small and ignored the larger issue. "Drug Tests by CIA Held More Extensive Than Reported in '75," said the *New York Times* on July 16, 1977. What it should have said is "U.S. Develops Invisible Weapons to Enslave Mankind."

The testing of drugs by the CIA was just a part of the United States government's top-secret mind-control project, a project which had spanned thirty-five years and had involved tens of thousands of individuals. It involved techniques of hypnosis, narco-hypnosis, electronic brain stimulation, behavioral effects of ultrasonic, microwave, and low-frequency sound, aversive and other behavior modification therapies. In fact, there was virtually no aspect of human behavioral control that was not explored in their search for the means to control the memory and will of both individuals and whole masses of people.

The CIA succeeded in developing a whole range of psycho-weapons to expand its already ominous psychological warfare arsenal. With these capabilities, it was now possible to wage a new kind of war—a war which would take place invisibly, upon the battlefield of the human mind.

"Literature always anticipates life," Oscar Wilde said. "It does not copy it, but molds it to its purpose." By Wilde's definition, then, Richard Condon's *The Manchurian Candidate* is literature.

Condon published his tour de force in 1958. It was the story of an American Army sergeant who was captured by the enemy during the Korean conflict and, in an improbable nine days, was hypno-programmed to murder on cue. The sergeant returned to the United States and was post-hypnotically triggered to kill by the sight of the queen of diamonds in a deck of cards. The sergeant automatically killed several people, among them a candidate for President of the United States. After he killed, his memory of the event was forever sealed by amnesia.

At the time *The Manchurian Candidate* was published, few people in the world, Richard Condon included, knew that total control of the mind was possible. Condon was writing fiction; he had merely read up on popular Pavlovian conditioning manuals and imagined the rest. He had no way of knowing then that mind control had already been the subject of eighteen years of secret research within the clandestine agencies of the U.S. government. The tricks of mind control he described were later employed (right down to the queen of diamonds cue) by the programmers of real political assassins who developed foolproof techniques for the control of thought, memory, emotions, and behavior.

The Manchurian Candidate brought the idea of "brainwashing" to public consciousness. Brainwashing is the use of isolation, deprivation, torture, and indoctrination to break the human will. But what the book actually described was something more than brainwashing. It was mind control: a total takeover of an individual's mind by someone else. The someone else in Condon's version was a mad Chinese psycho-scientist. Always the satirist, Condon brought the Fu Manchu myth up to date. But, ironically, the techniques he described were first perfected and used not by the Chinese or the Communists, but by the United States.

Condon's portrait of POWs during the Korean conflict went against the accepted scientific and medical opinion of the time, which held that a man could not be made to commit a criminal act against his own will or inner moral code by *any* known means. Although Condon's book was not completely on target about the details of GI mind control, he did accurately describe some of the motives, coercive methodology, and psychological results of real-life mind control.

The psychological techniques described in *The Manchurian Candidate* were to become a reality less than a decade after Condon saw his story set in type. As if Condon's fiction had been used as the blueprint, a group of hypno-programmed "zombies" were created. Some were assassins prepared to kill on cue. Others were informers, made to remember minute details under hypnosis. Couriers carried illegal messages outside the chain of command, their secrets secured behind posthypnotic blocks. Knowledge of secret information was removed from the minds of those who no longer had the "need to know"—they were given posthypnotic amnesia.

The ordinary foot soldiers who fought in the dirty, televised Vietnam conflict were released to civilian life without debriefing. For them there was no "decompression" from the rage of war. They were released with all the reflexes of trained assassins intact.

Those who had been conditioned in the black science of the war of torture, terror, and technology were debriefed with special attention. Their memories were so completely erased before they were turned out of the military that they returned to civilian life with only the minimum, fragmented knowledge of who they were or what they had done. The rest of their memories had been smudged or removed by drugs, hypnosis, behavior modification, conditioned reflex therapy, or some other evil wonder of mind control.

I encountered my first case of mind control in the midst of the Watergate scandal. A young man I'd known since childhood had returned from a tour of duty in the U.S. Air Force, with amnesia, remembering nothing of his service years, except having had a good time. He subsequently learned, through intensive private psychotherapy, that he'd been hypnotized and conditioned. His mind had been unmade, then remade: his mind had been controlled.

I was completely fascinated by his story, but naturally, in 1973, I thought it was an isolated, single event. Then, quite by accident, a few months later, I overheard another man in my hometown telling what was essentially the same story: how he figured he'd been hypnotized and had his memory erased at a "debriefing" prior to his separation from military service.

After hearing the second story I began to wonder how many more men had had their memories erased. I decided to run the following classified ad: "Researcher/writer interested in contacting anyone with knowledge of the use of hypnosis by the military, including ex-servicemen who have reason to believe they were hypnotized (or drugged) while in the service and subsequently exhibited signs of amnesia or hypermnesia (improved memory). All info held in strictest confidence . . ."

I placed the ad in *Soldier of Fortune* (a magazine which reports on the activities of mercenaries), a number of small publications aimed at hypnotists, behaviorists, neurologists, and other professionals, and popular magazines such as *Rolling Stone*. To my amazement, I received more than a hundred replies to the ad. Many stated that they had amnesia.

Ignoring the obvious crank letters, I followed up on the others and discovered that many men were unable to say just what had caused their loss of memory. In some cases, it was obviously a result of the trauma of war—what came to be called "the post-Vietnam syndrome." So I concentrated on those who had not seen combat but who either had high security clearances or were employed at the periphery of the intelligence services.

Letter and telephone exchanges narrowed the field down to eighteen persons who fit the pattern of the first two men who had reported their amnesia to me. All eighteen had had security clearances—and could only recall isolated events from their GI experience. I narrowed the field still further to those who remembered enough to have at least some idea, however fragmentary and incomplete, of what had happened to them.

Their stories were believable, but they shed little light on how amnesia had been induced and what behavior had been controlled. To answer those deeper questions I went to the libraries, and after two years of research I was able to find enough scientific reports and government documents to tell the whole story of what I call Operation Mind Control.

Though the documented trail of mind control extends back many decades, it was not always called by that name.

The church and the state have always engaged in psycho-theology and psycho-politics, the psychological manipulation of belief, opinion, and actions for political and/or religious ends. But the complete control of the human mind was only managed in the late 1940s. Therefore, my research is concentrated on the period from 1938 to the present, the period during which I found there was an effort made by the agencies of the U.S. government to develop sophisticated techniques of psycho-politics and mind control.

The objective of Operation Mind Control during this period has been to take human beings, both citizens of the United States and citizens of friendly and unfriendly nations, and transform them into unthinking, subconsciously programmed "zombies," motivated without their knowledge and against their wills to perform in a variety of ways in which they would not otherwise willingly perform. This is accomplished through the use of various techniques called by various names, including brainwashing, thought reform, behavior modification, hypnosis, and conditioned reflex therapy. For the purposes of this book the term "mind control" will be used to describe these techniques generically.*

Mind control is the most terrible imaginable crime because it is committed not against the body, but against the mind and the soul. Dr. Joost A. M. Meerloo expresses the attitude of the majority of psychologists in calling it "mind rape," and warns that it poses a great "danger of destruction of the spirit" which can be "compared to the threat of total physical destruction . . ."[1]

Development of mind control was accomplished largely through the efforts of individual psychologists, psychiatrists, and chemists, working in isolated conditions under government contract. Each researcher or research team was allowed to know only what he or she needed to know to accomplish his or her fragment of the research or testing.

* Various meditation groups use the words "mind control" to describe meditation, contemplation, and self-hypnosis; all these are usually harmless if not beneficial practices. These techniques might more properly be called "mind *self*-control," for the individuals who use them seek control over their *own* minds and bodies to obtain desired effects. The mind control examined in this book is the control of one individual's mind by another.

The contracts were let through a number of government and private agencies and foundations so that the researchers were, by and large, ignorant as to the intended use of their research.

While the CIA was a major funder of the mind-control research, virtually every major government agency became in some way knowingly or unwittingly involved. While I began my research believing that a "cult of intelligence" was behind the mind-control program, I found that there is, in fact, no single originating force, but several. The operation is too widespread and complex for it to be created by a "cult." If a cult there must be, then it is a cult within a cult, in an interlocking chain of invisible mini-governments with unwritten rules, unwritten plans, and unwritten loyalties. It is the plan of a secret bureaucracy—what I call a cryptocracy—which conspires against our laws and our freedoms.

"Cryptocracy" is a compound of *crypto*, meaning "secret," and *-cracy*, meaning "rule, government, governing body." The cryptocracy, then, is the secret government whose identity and whereabouts have slowly and reluctantly been hinted at by the Congress through its investigations into Watergate, the CIA, and the rest of the intelligence community.

While the CIA, near the top of the intelligence pyramid, has been drawing most of the fire, the evidence of a cryptocracy clearly implicates the National Security Agency, the Defense Intelligence Agency and its subsidiaries in military intelligence, as well as the civil service. The alliance extends even among private contractors and institutions and religious organizations. With Central Intelligence in the vanguard, the cryptocracy is composed of persons operating within the Office of Naval Intelligence, Army Intelligence, Air Force Intelligence, Department of Justice, Department of Health, Education and Welfare, Bureau of Prisons, Bureau of Narcotics, Atomic Energy Commission, Veterans' Administration, General Services Administration, National Science Foundation, and even major American corporations, especially certain airlines, oil companies, and aerospace contractors.

The cryptocracy invades the privacy of citizens and corporations. It meddles, often violently, in the internal politics of foreign nations, and has hired, trained, and equipped mind-controlled assassins for the murder of heads of state. The cryptocracy may have been involved in attempts to control U.S. elections. It may control key figures in the U.S. and world press.

The story within the story, I discovered, is an astonishing one of a psychological war waged by this U.S. cryptocracy against the American people. The scientific reports and histories place the story in time, and at the government's door. However, the literature of the cryptocracy ignores the very real human factor. There is no written record of the mental anguish, the torture to the soul that comes from loss of memory and the resulting identity crisis. That mental anguish is the human story of mind control.

The stories that follow are told by the failures of Operation Mind Control—failures because the victims remember *something*; for where mind control is successful there is no memory left.*

One of the characters in *The Manchurian Candidate* described his recurring dream that resulted from the suppression of memory. "It's not so much that I can't sleep. It's more that I'd rather not sleep. I'm walking around punchy because I'm scared. I keep having the same nightmare . . ." The nightmare Condon's hero described was actually the memory of having killed on cue. On stage, before an audience of Communist mind controllers, he strangled one of his fellow soldiers with a scarf, and blew out another's brains with a high-powered pistol at point blank range. Several of the men I interviewed had dreams which could have been written by Condon.

Tex was an army sergeant stationed in the Mediterranean area. He came back from service with amnesia. But in his dreams a vivid scene was replayed again and again: "In the dream my buddy—I know him real well, we've shared things together—my buddy is taken with his hands behind his back. I'm standing in rank in a line of other soldiers

* Due to editorial considerations, many of the stories I uncovered have been left on the editing room floor. Each individual in this book stands for and tells the story of many victims of mind control. In many cases the individuals I interviewed believed their lives or sanity would be in danger if their names were made public. I have honored that concern and have withheld real names and places when so requested. Except in these details, the first-person stories in this book are completely true.

and we are like a firing squad. I keep thinking I won't shoot my friend, I'll turn the rifle on the commander. But we don't have rifles.

"My buddy is marched into an open area in front of us with his hands tied behind his back. He is blindfolded and some Ay-rab is talking to him, or reading to him. Another Ay-rab comes up and hits him behind the knees with a rifle butt and he falls to a kneeling position.

"Then, while he's on his knees, one of the Ay-rabs takes a big sword and cuts his head off. His neck squirts blood, but surprisingly little . . . his head rolls on the ground. His face has a peaceful expression. His body twitches and squirms like a chicken. That's when I always wake up . . ."

So Condon was right. In their sleep, the memories of atrocities surface to vivid awareness among the victims of mind control. Night after night terrible images, suppressed by deeply conditioned responses, emerge as terrifying nightmares. Are they mythological? The stuff of dreams? Or are they recovered memories? Tex's dream is a mere fragment of more than 1,200 pages of such testimony.

Chapter Two
ONLY ONE MIND FOR MY COUNTRY

Through the gray waters of amnesia he drifted, coming back from blind coma. First the echoes, like electronically amplified voices speaking from a deep deep well . . . then, far off, the dim pink molecules of light . . .

David's body lay still in the military hospital bed. Only his eyes rolled beneath the lids. For several hours he lay that way, perfectly still—just eyes fluttering. The fluttering became more intense. Then his eyes opened.

"When I woke up," David said, "I couldn't remember anything. I couldn't remember how I'd gotten there or why I was in the hospital."

He asked nurses and aides why he was there. They told him he'd have to ask his doctor. When David finally saw him, the doctor said, "You tried to commit suicide."

That came as a great surprise to David. He didn't think he was the suicidal type. He asked the doctor *how* he'd tried to commit suicide.

"You took an overdose of Sleep-eze," the doctor told him.

David knew that Sleep-eze was a patent medicine, that it was related chemically to an antihistamine, and that it could produce drowsiness; but David also knew it was not nearly as dangerous as prescription sleeping pills. Although he began to sense that something was fishy, he did not challenge the doctor, nor did he let on that he suspected the story to be untrue. For the next several days he simply lay in the hospital bed puzzling over the odd chain of events that had landed him there.

I interviewed David several times over a period of two years. Each interview produced additional information as David's memory returned in fragmented, isolated bursts. The following is taken from thousands of pages of transcript and has been edited so that the tedious process which uncovered David's memories is absent. It is slightly misleading only in that David did not remember his story in one continuous sequence. Nor did the other victims quoted in this book.

David had joined the U.S. Air Force in 1969. During his high school years the draft had still been in effect, and after graduating on the honor roll, David decided to attend a small community college to get as much education as he could before his name was inevitably called by selective service.

As his induction date approached David realized he could obtain a deferral from the draft because of his high scholastic standing, but he decided instead to take a break from education and fulfill his military obligation as profitably as he could. Although he questioned America's reasons for fighting, he did feel that military service was his duty.

David had not been a part of the sixties' "revolution." He had never smoked marijuana nor taken LSD, nor had he demonstrated against the war in Vietnam like so many of his friends. He was a studious, intelligent young man who was not inclined to rebellion. He was described by friends and family as one possessed of unusual common sense. In keeping with his cautious and practical nature he negotiated a "contract" for medical corps service with his local air force recruiter and enlisted for a four-year tour of duty, thinking this would help him fulfill his ambition to become a doctor.

After an uneventful in-processing, David was sent to Lackland Air Force Base for the usual six weeks' basic training, and then on to a technical school for another six weeks of special training. But when the time came for his job assignment, to his great disappointment, he was assigned to the supply corps rather than the medical corps.

He felt betrayed by the air force, and immediately after receiving his AFSC job assignment number, he retired to his barracks to rehearse a protest to his commanding officer. Moments later, a nonuniformed man entered the empty barracks and asked him to step outside and take a walk. David was puzzled but went along without comment.

When the two had reached a quiet spot on the base, the man told David that he guessed he was disappointed about receiving the AFSC of a "box pusher" in a supply warehouse. David was surprised by the man's knowledge of his situation. Before he could reply, the man told David that the AFSC was just a cover, that he had actually been chosen to work in a sensitive area of intelligence.

The assignment sounded glamorous to David, and lifted his sagging spirits. He immediately decided to go along with the change of plans and accept the special assignment without protest. The unidentified man told David to be patient, and to learn well the special techniques of computer programming he would be trained in while waiting for his security investigation to be completed.

Within a few weeks David was issued a top-secret crypto security clearance and assigned to the air base at Minot, North Dakota. At Minot, he continued to feed supply numbers into a computer, developing his already excellent memory. He did his job well and soon he received a letter of commendation and was promoted to sergeant.

But for all his accomplishments, he had begun to grow restless. Although he knew his computer programming was just a cover for intelligence work, he was still not satisfied with air force life.

"I was beginning to not like the extreme regimentation and, I suppose, inside myself I was beginning to build up a resentment about being there.

"But after I woke up in the hospital I was not resentful. I was passive. I lay there thinking, trying to recall the last memories I had before I woke up in that bed. I didn't remember anything. It was like I'd been asleep for my entire life up to that point. Like I was Rip Van Winkle.

"The memories of what had happened I did recover over a period of time. But they were fuzzy at first. It seemed like somebody was violating me—raping my mind.

"I was strapped down in the bed. I was yelling and screaming about something. I'm not the type of person that cusses that much. I hardly ever use foul language, but I know that I said some pretty foul things to those men who were with me. They were officers, and in the service you can't call a superior officer an obscene name without getting punished. Yet I don't think I was ever reprimanded.

"One guy would ask me questions in an accusatory manner. Another guy would come over and say comforting things. Then the first guy would come back and accuse me again. Then the second guy would come and pat my arm and be friendly. I could remember their faces and their tone of voice, but I couldn't remember the content of what they were talking about."

David thought about his situation; suppose he *had* tried to commit suicide. He probably would be kicked out of the service. At best he might be given a medical discharge. So he began to prepare himself for that eventuality. He thought he wouldn't mind getting out of the service under any circumstances, even with a psychological discharge.

It didn't happen. Instead, David was visited by men in civilian clothes who told him that he'd been chosen for a special intelligence assignment. They said the details of his assignment could not be revealed until the proper time, and then he would not be allowed to talk to anyone about it. They said he would be receiving his orders soon.

"I had expected at least to have some stripes taken away for the suicide attempt," David said. "Instead, five different sets of orders came down. They were all typed military orders, regular orders, but they had me going to five different places at once. It was impossible.

"I took the orders to headquarters and told them that somebody had goofed. It was plain to see that somebody had screwed up. The way the military runs, it was not unusual. No one got excited about it. The guys in the office said that they would straighten it out.

"Then I was told that I had two weeks' leave coming. They ordered me home to wait while they got my orders straightened out."

Happy to get a break after eighteen continuous months of military life without leave, David went home.

"I was hoping they'd forget all about me, I was praying that this time the computer would completely lose me."

The first evening at home something compelled David to break security. Alone with his mother, he told her that he knew he had not really attempted suicide.

"I suppose that my first duty was to my family, and my second duty was to my country. After I'd discharged my moral duty to my mother, I was free to obey my government's wish and not remember anything about it. That's probably how it worked, in spite of their programming."

After David had been at home for the full two weeks, and was just beginning to think that maybe the computer had lost him after all, a telegram came. There were no written orders, no official seals, just a Western Union telegram ordering him to report to a base in northern California and from there to embark to the Far East on overseas duty. There were numbers on the face of the telegram, but at the time David gave them no special notice. These numbers may have been an assignment authorization, for seldom are servicemen sent overseas on the strength of a telegram alone.

"When I got to the base in California, I showed them the telegram and the air police hustled me to another airplane and flew me to Guam."

On the plane to Guam David ran into an airman he'd known at Minot. The airman's name was Max. Like David, Max had been attached to the supply wing at Minot, but he had been in a different type of supply operation.

In all the time they were together on Guam, David never learned the details of Max's assignment. Both of them were supposed to be supply men, but David thought Max had some pretty unusual qualifications for a supply man: for instance, he held a fifth-degree black belt in karate.

"Max and I had checked into the barracks when we got there, but after preliminaries we were put on a bus and taken to an isolated place eight miles outside the base. There were six L-shaped barracks set up inside a high electrified fence with barbed wire at the top. Inside the compound there was a movie theater, a store, a barbershop, a chow hall, and a recreation center. There were several hundred guys living in that compound.

"We could leave anytime we wanted. All we had to do was show the proper credentials to the air police at the gate. The compound seemed to be regular air force. The place was called 'Marbo,' and as far as I could tell, there were guys there who had all sorts of different functions in the air force, but nobody really discussed their jobs.

"Several of the guys at Marbo had been in the supply wing in North Dakota. But at Marbo they were working in other areas . . . In other words, guys who'd been in the supply wing in North Dakota were in the civil engineers or the air police. One air policeman on Guam, I remember, had been shoving around boxes just like other supply men when he was at Minot. Suddenly now he was an air policeman. I couldn't figure it out, and I wasn't about to ask questions.

"I guess we all assumed that we were all on special assignment, and I'm pretty sure that if I'd asked anyone about it, they would have avoided an answer. *I* certainly would have, if somebody had asked me."

David made rank fast in the air force. He was a good airman, a good supply man. Yet anybody he talked to about supply duties didn't know what he was talking about. His duties weren't like the others.

"My air force file shows that the first three digits of my AFSC are 647. A 647 is some kind of a box pusher. Yet, I never pushed a box all the time I was in the air force."

After their tour of duty, Max and David returned home together on the same plane. At the airport Max was called over the intercom and went off to answer the page. Two air police returned for his luggage and David did not see Max until after he was separated from the service for some months. Then it was a strange meeting.

David was walking down the streets of Disneyland and his eye fell on Max walking toward him in a crowd. David was delighted to see his old buddy again, but Max was strangely distant. "He didn't seem very interested in our reunion." David said, "He shook hands with me, and I began to talk, but he seemed kind of passive. I wanted to sit down and tell all the things that had happened to me since we last saw each other, but Max didn't want to talk. He cut me short, said good-bye, and left.

"That's something that's always puzzled me. How can a guy who was your constant companion for so many months, a guy who has fought for you and gotten to know you inside and out, not want to talk to you? How could he have just brushed me off like that?

"When I first got out of the service, all I could remember about my four years was that I'd had a lot of fun. I mean, all the pictures I have, and all the recollections I had, were of Max and Pat and I having fun, skin diving, laying on the beach, collecting shells, walking in the jungle. It never dawned on me until later that I must have *done* something while I was in the service."

Pat was a young woman from the Midwest who was assigned to serve as David's secretary. Almost instantly, when they met on Guam, they fell in love.

"Pat was something special. She was everything I would have ever dreamed of in a woman. I suppose she felt that I was everything that she wanted in a man. It didn't take long for us to go to bed after we met, and from then on, throughout my tour of duty Max, Pat, and I were inseparable."

David was not talking about a ménage à trois. Max was not attracted to Pat nor she to him. They all held each other to be good friends, but David and Pat's feelings for each other were strongest.

David now thinks it odd that the three of them got along so perfectly from the first moment they met. Max was David's kind of man, and Pat was David's kind of woman. In the years that have passed since he got out of the air force, David has come to believe that Max and Pat and he were matched up by a computer.

"We hit it off from the start. We had the same interests, we were nervous about the same things, and we would laugh at the same kind of jokes. We were three individuals who were very very close and where one lacked a quality another had something that filled that lack.

"The air force takes your psychological tests—your cumes—the cumulative progress reports which have been kept on just about every individual in the United States from the first grade through high school. These records have your IQ, your aptitude tests, and all the things they accumulate on you through your school years . . . they give them a complete examination to determine your psychological profile and everything about your likes and dislikes. They feed selected information, any information they are looking to match up, into a computer and run yours with other people's until they have a psychological match.

"In spy books I've read, undercover agents sent to foreign countries are usually teamed with a spy of the opposite sex. Even if two people are both married and have left families at home, the directors of intelligence usually send along someone who can take care of the natural human sexual needs of the other without risking a breach of security. That way, no horny agent is going to have to associate with a prostitute or someone who might turn out to be a double agent or counterspy.

"I'd talk with the other guys in the service and they'd talk about getting laid in Hong Kong or Japan or Korea. I didn't have to talk about anything. I didn't have to brag. I'd just smile at them, secure in my love for Pat."

David said that there were several other women in the barracks who, like Pat, were secretaries but had security clearance. And, as was the case with Pat, many of them also had close relationships with the men to whom they had been assigned.

Two months before their tour of duty was to expire David and Max were sent home. Pat stayed behind on Guam. But David and Pat arranged to meet once they were both out of the service. They exchanged home addresses, but somehow David lost hers and he is strangely unable to remember her last name, or even the town from which she'd come. David never saw Pat again.

"Looking back on it, it looks like it was awfully convenient. Pat was a liberated woman, she knew exactly who she was. And that's just the kind of woman I like to be around. She fulfilled every need that I ever had, to such a degree that it's a problem now. I can't meet a girl that's as good as she was. When you've been in paradise, it's hard to find paradise again. You always want to go back.

"I think of her all the time, but I just can't remember her last name. It's a total blank. I just can't remember."

During the entire thirteen-hour flight home David had to debrief himself into a tape recorder while sitting between two air policemen. He doesn't remember what he talked about. No one was "questioning" him; he just talked.

Upon his return, he was assigned to a base in California. Immediately upon reporting for duty, he found that he no longer had a security clearance. His job was to answer telephones on the base and to listen to complaints. He'd take calls from the wives of air force personnel and relay their complaints to the proper channels. That's *all* he did during his entire last year of service.

"When it came time to get processed out, I wanted to get the medals I earned when I was stationed in Guam. They were actually theater ribbons. I had so many ribbons when I left Guam that the officer I reported to told me not to wear them because I would attract attention to myself.

"During the out-processing they brought out my file. They do that regularly every year anyway. They show you your records and have you go over them and make sure that they're correct. Then you sign a paper that states the records have been approved by you. The last time I was shown my records, they'd been changed. Instead of all the typed dog-eared reports that were in my file before, there was this clean computer print-out.

"I asked the officer in charge what had happened to the notices of my being awarded those theater ribbons. He told me that since I had such a high security clearance some of the things that were in my files made it necessary to expunge a lot of the information from the record. He said that there was a top-secret file on me which was available to people who had the right clearances. The file he had me approve was the one which would be shown anyone who did not have the highest clearance. He said that because this was more or less a public record, it could not have anything on it of a sensitive nature. It was very misleading, that report. It looked like I had been a supply man, a box pusher, and I'd done nothing else, except try to attempt suicide. The phony hospital story was in the report—so deniability was built in.

"Then I went through the normal out-processing and went home. All I can say is that everybody, my folks, my friends, everyone who'd known me before noticed how changed I was. I was fearful, and under tight control."

David decided that he would first reorient himself to the civilian pace of life and then look for a job. But when he began to look for employment, he suddenly realized that he had some deep psychological problems.

At his first job interview, he was routinely asked to fill out the company's job application form. He sat down at a desk and started writing. He wrote his name and noticed that his hands were sweating. As he began to enter his address his heart began pounding so loudly it was audible. He became short of breath and felt like the walls were closing in. He fought to remain calm, but within a few moments he snatched up the form and bolted out the door.

That evening he discussed the strange physical effects that had come over him with his parents. They assured him he was probably just very anxious about getting the job.

The next day he went on another interview. Again he

was asked to fill out a job application. This time he got further in filling out the form: he put down his name . . . address . . . date of birth . . . Social Security number . . . health information . . . but when he came to the place in the form which required work information about the past four years the pounding in his ears, the shortness of breath, and the terrifying feeling of being confined in a small space came over him again, and he left the building with the form wadded up in his hand.

Over the next few months David applied for many jobs. The results were always the same. He could not overcome the terror that gripped him whenever anyone asked him for information about how he had spent the past four years.

David's parents suggested that he try to get a job working with computers and take advantage of the training that the air force had given him. The mere mention of computers made him fly into a rage. "I still couldn't face whatever it was that was blocking me. To this day, I can't stand the thought of a computer. I'd like to smash them all up. I realize, of course, that is irrational."

David remained hopeful that whatever was causing his anxiety would pass with time. Meanwhile, he decided to go back to college. He had no trouble getting into a major university since his high school and community college grades were high, and no one asked him for details of his service years. But during his first semester he encountered the same blocks that had kept him from getting a job.

"In my psychology course you had to get up in front of a circle of people and talk. You had to bare your soul. I just couldn't do it. I couldn't stand up and be calm and let people question me. They were all harmless questions, but I'd get the pounding heart, the sweaty palms, the shortness of breath and the feeling of claustrophobia again. I'd just clam up and leave the room."

It was then that David understood that he could no longer face the problem himself. He sought out a psychiatrist who'd been recommended by a friend.

"The first psychiatrist I went to was male. He had used hypnotherapy with me, and he found me to be a very easy subject. I'd go into a trance at the drop of a hat. But whenever he tried to regress me—saying, 'I want you to go back'—I'd just bring myself out of the trance, even if it was a deep trance. My heart would be pounding, my palms would be sweating, and I'd feel the same claustrophobia I'd felt whenever I'd confronted those application forms."

David found that he was much more relaxed with his second psychiatrist, a woman named Alice. Alice was also more successful with hypnotherapy. David would go into a trance quickly and deeply, but whenever Alice tried to regress him to his air force period, he would bring himself out of the trance as he had done previously. But she found that by regressing David to his childhood and approaching the air force period from earlier years, remembering was less difficult for him.

"At first she tried to have me relax. She talked in a very soothing voice, telling me to close my eyes. I felt like I was surrendering to her. It was easy to get me into a light trance. I laid down my defenses and was going deeper and deeper, but just as soon as she said, 'Now we're going to go back,' I sat straight up and was wide awake.

"Alice couldn't get over how fast I went under. One time, she said, she was just talking to me and her voice put me completely under when she wasn't even trying. I was highly suggestible.

"But whenever she'd say, 'Let's go back,' all the muscles in my neck would strain, and I would grip the arms of the chair until my knuckles turned white. Once I was holding a piece of paper in my hand, and when I came out of hypnosis, the paper was completely soaked with sweat. Only a minute after she'd said, 'We're going to go back,' I was wide awake.

"Alice never did succeed completely with hypnosis, but something must have been released because of her attempts. As soon as we were able to go back to the usual talking technique of psychotherapy, I started talking about my childhood. I'd never thought that much about it, I guess, but I couldn't remember much of my childhood. For instance, my grandfather had died when I was fourteen, and he had lived with us. Everyone says he and I were very close, but I had no mental picture of him at all. That's when Alice started trying to get me to remember my childhood. I don't know if I remembered my childhood before I went into the service or not. It seems like I did, because it wasn't a problem, but to this day, still, I can't remember much, and everything before the age of ten is completely blank.

"Alice and I kept working. At first, the memories we recovered were all painful memories. Alice thought that this was most unusual. Usually people remember the pleasurable things first. Then she tried to get me to remember only painful experiences. And once I'd remembered a lot she started trying to get me to remember the pleasurable ones."

David and Alice continued to work with standard psychiatric techniques and with hypnosis. Finally, after sixteen months of three sessions a week, Alice asked David to make a choice.

"We probably can penetrate the blocks around your air force years and find out how they were planted and why, but it may take a long time. On the other hand, we can work on every other area and get you to function normally without anxiety reactions whenever anyone asks you about those years," Alice said. "Now you have to decide if you just want to function normally, or if you want to unravel the whole mystery and find out who did it, why it was done, and what they have hidden from your own mind."

Since the therapy had nearly depleted his family's savings, David knew what the answer must be. He told Alice he would be content to just function normally. After two more months of treatment, Alice and David had their last session.

"After two hundred and six therapy sessions, Alice and I had one eight-hour session which more or less recapped all the information we had collected. She told me that when I first came in I'd talked in a monotone. I was very, very, controlled. I showed no emotions and had no inflection in my speech. I'd talked to her for the first three months that way. She said that there was a wall that she couldn't break down . . . Alice recommended that I continue working on my own by going to group therapy.

"I went to a couple of sessions, but when I got in front of a group I became fearful again. It was more than just stage fright, it was a horrible feeling. I still have it when I get up in front of a group to be asked questions.

"Alice did not figure out what this was about. I am now beginning to, but figuring something out is one thing, and actually overcoming it is another."

Alice's expert guidance and her deft use of hypnotherapy were helpful. While he did not recover his memory at once, in time David began to remember isolated events. He is now able to reconstruct a picture of at least some of the things he did while in hypno-service to his country.

"One day I had a vivid dream. Then it was like, little by little, memory cells exploding in my brain. I began to remember certain incidents. At first I didn't know if these were real memories or just dreams. Today, I still don't know if they are accurate or not, but they are so real in all their details that I believe they are the truth. Naturally when you've had amnesia you're not really going to trust your memories at first, but if the memories settle in—if you can recall more and more detail about an event—you know that you are recalling a true event.

"The most vivid memory I have is about Vietnam. I was standing at a long table on a beach. There were North Vietnamese soldiers sitting on one side and American officers sitting on the other. Everyone was in uniform. Our men were from the air force, navy, and marines. The marines had sidearms, and no one else had a weapon.

"What horrified me was that out in the harbor, off shore at some distance from the beach, was one of our battleships, and another battleship or gunboat. I guess that it was Vietnamese or Russian, but I'm not expert at naval craft identification. All I know is I was terrified because the big guns on the ships were trained, not on each other, but on us . . . I guess they were prepared to blow us all up should anything go wrong on the beach, or should there be a double cross.

"We had our interpreters, who were air force men. They did the translating and our officers waited for the translations. The discussion was very heated, but for some reason I remember vividly, nothing was being written down. That may have been the reason that I was standing there at one end of the table. I remember that they had been trying, somewhere along the line, to get me to have total recall. I can't remember the details, or the progression of events.

"I know that I had memory training. At Marbo, for some reason, I'd get up three hours earlier than anyone else and report to somewhere I can't remember and then go to work at eight-thirty. I remember riding the bus from Marbo to the base on Guam, and I was the only one on the bus. But I can't remember where I went before I reported for regular duty.

"I suspect that the computer work was part of the memory training, but I can't say that's exactly what it was. There must have been more to it. I just don't remember the details. But I have the impression that I was used as a human tape recorder.

"I do know one thing about that beach scene. When I came back from overseas, only three days after I came back it was announced that the North Vietnamese were going to give our prisoners of war back in an exchange. The meeting on the beach might have been an early parley about ending the war and exchanging prisoners. At least that's what strikes me as the best answer to the question of what that meeting was about.

"I might have been a witness. I really don't understand why—or why the gunboats were pointing their guns at us. I can't remember the date, or anything that places that memory in time.

"The thing that really bothers me about this whole thing is that I can sit here and talk to you, but I still can't sit down and say, 'Okay, I joined the service on such and such a day and this is what happened to me during a four-year period in chronological order.' Ever since I got out of the service I haven't been able to give a day-by-day account of what happened to me during those four years.

"Some people might call what happened to me *brainwashing*. I've called it that, but it's not really brainwashing. I think of brainwashing as something brutal. I don't think I was treated brutally. Also, what happened to me was something that was much more sophisticated than what I have read about brainwashing.

"I believe I'm telling the truth, and I'd like to see someone disprove it. I only have these fragments of memory, so if I went to the Air Force they'd pull out my folder and throw it on the desk and say, 'See, there it is in black and white . . . He's a nut. He tried to commit suicide by taking a patent medicine.'

"I feel I was used. Why would they use an enlisted man who is supposed to be a supply man? Every squadron has supply personnel, so I guess it's a perfect cover. A supply man is so common he wouldn't be noticed. How well it worked out, from their point of view, I just don't know. But from mine, well, it didn't work out too well. All the doubts and fears I have now, years later, and after a lot of psychiatric help, which I paid for myself, made the experiment, if it was one, a failure to me.

"I never thought about laying down my life, but maybe I laid down a lot more than my life in service to my country. My soul?"

Chapter Three
THE MIND LAUNDRY MYTH

David's own assessment of his mental confusion after his air force experience was that he had not been "brainwashed." By the time David had his mind controlled, "brainwashing" had become a catchall phrase, but what David had suffered was a much more subtle and hideous form of tyranny.

George E. Smith was a POW during the early days of the Vietnam War. Unlike David, George did not have a good education. It can even be said that he was a little naive, and therefore a good candidate for brainwashing of both the American and the NLF (Viet Cong) varieties. He was one of the first of the Green Berets captured in the Vietnam conflict in 1963.

It was the practice of the U.S. Army in those days to indoctrinate its men with poorly constructed lies, which, it was hoped, would motivate them to fight a war in which the U.S. had only dubious legal business and little moral argument. The "credibility gap" existed not only within the confines of the U.S. borders, but also in the far-flung fields of battle, all the way to Southeast Asia.

If brainwashing is making a person believe in lies, then our troops were already brainwashed by their own government. It was a simple job for the Viet Cong to gain the POWs' cooperation by telling them the truth—truth which was easily documented.

Smith described the attitude which was instilled in the American soldiers by their military indoctrination: "We were arrogant . . . the army is a separate society; it has its own hierarchy, and I could rise to a stratum in the army that I couldn't attain in the outside world. They'd driven arrogance into us in the Airborne, which is a high level in the army, but Special Forces was the highest level you could reach, the elite of the elite. Elitism was the philosophy they taught at Bragg: 'You are professors of warfare, you shouldn't fight unless attacked. It costs thousands of dollars to train one of you and you're too valuable to send into battle.'

"I believed it. I believed everything the army said. I never questioned anything they told me until I got to Vietnam, and then things didn't quite fit anymore."

Smith and three other men were captured in a midnight raid which followed a heavy mortar bombardment of their location. The Viet Cong took them deep into the jungles. When they reached the VC compound they were forced to build their own prison out of bamboo. Then, after the primitive compound was completed and the POWs had settled in, the interrogations began. These were nothing like Smith had been led to expect. They were "friendly chats" with an interpreter Smith called the "Man with Glasses." Every day he would tell his prisoners about the history of Vietnam and the U.S. role in that country. "It was right out of the movies," Smith said. "The prisoner was confronted by his interrogators, who were sitting on a higher level and making him look up to them.

"Look at you," Man with Glasses began. "You are pitiful." It was a typical brainwashing tactic, designed to make the prisoner think poorly of himself, to undermine his self-image. Sergeant Smith, like many others, already had a poor self-image long before he was captured, even before he enlisted in the army. That image wasn't enhanced any by finding that the authorities to whom he had been so obedient had misinformed him.

"We had known interrogation was inevitable and had feared it for so long, but it didn't go the way it was supposed to," Smith said. "The guards were off somewhere out of sight. No one shone lights in our eyes. In fact, I sat in the shade while Prevaricator (one of the interrogators) served me tea and candy and cigarettes.

"Man with Glasses did most of the talking, though he encouraged me to say anything I wanted to. He insisted on giving me their side of the story—why they were there in the jungle and why the NLF had gotten together and was fighting the U.S. and the Saigon regime. 'We are fighting for Vietnam. We do not try to take over your country. This is not in our plans. We are worried abour our country. We love it very much. We are proud people, and we want to keep our country.' Didn't I know I was wrong to be part of the United States effort in Vietnam? And if I did, would I write a statement saying so? He talked to me for about an hour, and at the end of the session he gave me a pack of the Cambodian cigarettes. 'For your enjoyment. Take them with you. When you are resting and smoking, I would like you to think deeply of what we have discussed.'

"If sitting in the shade drinking tea while I listened to this old guy talk was brainwashing, then it didn't fit any description I had ever heard. I recalled the stories I'd heard about Korea—the scene where they hypnotize you, or drop water on your head, or put you in complete stillness—something that will drive you out of your mind. Then once they've taken everything from your mind they start over again. When somebody says 'brainwashing,' this is what I consider they're talking about—the classic Korean example. Or the stories that came out of there, anyway."[1]

The word "brainwashing" summoned a terrifying image, but like so many other words it became corrupt in usage. It was applied to describe situations in which mere propaganda or influence were used. Indeed, the word may have been corrupt from the very beginning when it was coined by a CIA propaganda specialist, Edward Hunter. In his book *Brainwashing in Red China* he claimed that "Brainwashing, with the even more sinister brain changing in reverse, is the terrifying new Communist strategy to conquer the free world by destroying its mind."[2]

In the words of the noted Yale psychiatry professor Robert J. Lifton, brainwashing was popularly held to be an "all-powerful, irresistible, unfathomable, and magical method of achieving total control over the human mind."[3] It was in fact none of these things. Techniques which seemed to change the beliefs of American POWs and others behind the Iron Curtain employed no hypnosis, no drugs, no new methods for the control of the mind and certainly nothing magical.

Hunter revised *Brainwashing in Red China* and reissued it in 1971. In the introduction of the updated edition he continued his attack on the Communists, much as he does in his psychological-warfare journal *Tactics.*

"Change the word China to Cuba, and this book is a description of Communist warfare against the mind—brainwashing—in Cuba, as well as in China. This is the world pattern the Communists employ; what might, in military parlance, be called mind attack. It is the new dimension in warfare, added to artillery attack, naval attack, rear and frontal attack, air attack. Brainwashing's dual processes of softening up and indoctrination have been added to the arsenal of warfare, girding the Trojan Horse in twentieth century accoutrements." Though Hunter may have been correct about the Communist use of coercive psychological techniques on its own populations, he never once hinted that the U.S. government might just be establishing similar techniques of its own.

In 1958, in his testimony before the House Committee on Un-American Activities (HUAC) he continued to present brainwashing as a Communist weapon: "Since man began, he has tried to influence other men or women to his way of thinking. There have always been these forms of pressure to change attitudes. We discovered in the past thirty years, a technique to influence, by clinical, hospital procedures, the thinking processes of human beings. . . . Brainwashing is formed out of a set of different elements . . . hunger, fatigue, tenseness, threats, violence, and in more intense cases where the Reds have specialists available on their brainwashing panels, drugs and hypnotism. No one of these elements alone can be regarded as brainwashing, any more than an apple can be called apple pie. Other ingredients have to be added, and a cooking process gone through. So it is in brainwashing with indoctrination or atrocities, or any other single ingredient.

"The Communists have been operating for a full generation taking strategic advantage of the American principles, exploiting the best sides in our characters as vulnerabilities, and succeeding for a generation in changing the characteristics of Americans."

Given the anti-Communist climate of the Cold War years, Hunter's zeal did not seem excessive, even though few of his conclusions were supported by the eyewitness accounts given by the repatriated POWs. According to them, no drugs or hypnosis were used overseas; they told only of persuasion techniques.

Was Hunter's then an exercise in projection—an unconscious defense mechanism, in which he was shifting the blame from the U.S. onto another?

Hunter's *Brainwashing in Red China* was widely quoted. Through front page news stories, the American public became aware, for the first time, that governments (though only Communist ones were mentioned) could control people's thoughts and motivate them against their will and without their knowledge.

Two years later, in May of 1960, Francis Gary Powers was shot down over the Soviet Union and cries of brainwashing again made U.S. headlines. At his public trial in Moscow, Powers apologized to the Russian people for doing them wrong. Even though the CIA had told him that if caught, he could admit everything, the voices of the "soldiers" within the U.S. were quick to brand him a traitor, and those who were inclined to be more sympathetic said that he had simply been "brainwashed."

One psychiatrist, William Jennings Bryan, who had been the head of an air force medical survival training program which employed hypnosis to prepare pilots for resistance to brainwashing, went so far as to coin a term for the subtle new technique which he thought the Soviets had developed since the Korean conflict and had used on Powers. The U-2 pilot, Bryan said, had been "Powerized."

Bryan said that Powers' apologetic manner during the Moscow trial, his submissive, almost crippled words of testimony, his trancelike acceptance, all showed an amazing personality change since his capture.

"The pilot's apparent lack of real emotion during the trial was the most startling evidence that the Russian brainwashing through hypnosis has destroyed the normal, aggressive confidence and the cockiness characteristic of the air force fliers . . . The big tipoff came," Dr. Bryan said, "when Powers apologized for his American assignment, testified he knew he was wrong and said he felt no ill will toward his country's Cold War enemy.

"It is no longer a secret that Russia uses hypnosis as a powerful instrument to destroy the resistance of individuals she wishes to conquer," he said. "Brainwashing hypnosis as apparently used on Powers is vastly different from the permissive type of medical hypnosis . . . and the self-hypnosis used by air force fliers in caring for themselves after a crash . . . Powers exhibited no telltale marks of physical abuse or torture during the Moscow trial, and indeed, he may have even thought himself that he was being treated rather well, but his manner and personality were obviously so unlike the typical American pilot that only a brand new type of other powerful technique could have changed his personality in so short a time."[4]

Francis Gary Powers was returned to the U.S. in 1962 in a trade for Russian spy Rudolf Abel. He wrote in his book *Operation Overflight* (which was withheld from publication by the CIA until 1970) that the tactic he decided upon when captured was in accordance with his CIA instructions. He said, "When questioned, I would tell the truth."

Powers insisted that he did not tell the Russians anything which he thought they did not already know. In fact he often agreed to things they suggested simply to mislead them.

As for sophisticated, "Powerizing" techniques, Powers denied their existence. He even went so far as to suggest that the Russians were actually highly overrated in their intelligence-gathering methods.

"From what I had been taught about brainwashing, I had anticipated certain things: I would be lectured about communism, given only propaganda to read. Food would be doled out on a reward-punishment basis; if I cooperated, I would be fed; if I didn't, I wouldn't. Interrogation would be at odd hours, under bright lights. No sooner would I fall asleep than I would be awakened, and it would start all over again, until eventually I lost all track of time, place, identity. And I would be tortured and beaten until, finally, I would beg for the privilege of being allowed to confess to any crime they desired. None of this happened."

Immediately after Powers crossed the bridge from East Berlin he was examined by a West German flight surgeon under orders from the CIA. The surgeon took blood from his arm. Powers says the doctor told him "the blood samples were necessary to determine whether I had been drugged. This seemed to be the first question of almost everyone to whom I talked: Had I been drugged? They seemed almost disappointed when I told them I hadn't."

Powers was then flown to the U.S. "I still couldn't comprehend that after twenty-one months of captivity I was once again a free man," he said, "which was perhaps best, for though I was yet to realize it, I wasn't quite free, not yet. In a sense, I had been released by the Russians to become a de facto prisoner of the CIA."

The CIA men told Powers they would like to talk to him for a couple of days. The "couple of days" turned out to be over three weeks, in which Powers was thoroughly debriefed by a team of intelligence analysts and psychiatrists. The first question the psychiatrists asked was, again, had he been drugged by the Soviets? The second question they asked was, had he been brainwashed? When Powers answered "no" to both questions he was given tranquilizers, which were the first drugs he had received since his U-2 left Turkey for the overflight of the USSR. Powers noted, with some irony, that Americans are much more disposed to the use of drugs than are the Soviets.[5]

Perhaps even more ironic was the public disclaimer issued by CIA Director Allen Dulles, which said the U.S. had no use for brainwashing: "What had popularly become known as 'brainwashing,' while of great psychological interest to the West, as it is important to study defensive techniques, is never practiced by us . . . for the simple reason that we are not interested in converting people to our way of thinking either forcibly or by trickery, which is its main intent. We have never felt, as obviously the Soviets and the Red Chinese and the North Koreans have, that there is much to gain in putting a 'brainwashed' person on the air to denounce his own countrymen. We have enough people who come over to us voluntarily from communism and who need no prompting."[6] Dulles, it seemed, was either a reader of Hunter's or they both had been briefed by the same propaganda section of the CIA.

Brainwashing was the term the psychological warfare unit of the CIA thought up to explain why American POWs cooperated with the enemy in Korea. Brainwashing was explained as severe deprivation of food, clothing, and shelter, during which time a series of punishments and rewards were applied so effectively that a person's fundamental beliefs could be made to change 180 degrees from their original position. This brutal technique was not called torture; there was no propaganda value in something as old as torture. The CIA thought up the term "brainwashing" to lead people in the Western world to believe that the inscrutable Orientals had again, like Fu Manchu, invented a revolutionary technique controlling the human mind. The word "brainwashing" and the official government explanation of what happened to the Korean POWs was propaganda. It was aimed at fueling a home-grown fear of the Communists upon which the Cold War so greatly depended. Propaganda, of course, was nothing more than artful deception; the careful planting of "misinformation" and "disinformation," Cold War euphemisms for what had been called "the big lie" in World War II.

Modern propaganda began when Nazi Germany perfected the art of "the big lie." The Soviet Union and other Communist countries took the methods of the Nazis and improved upon them. The United States did not actively engage in wide-scale propaganda until World War II, when the OSS and the Office of War Information started. But then it was well understood that the guiding principles of propaganda were: "When there is no compelling reason to suppress a fact, tell it . . . Aside from considerations of military security, the only reason to suppress a piece of news is if it is unbelievable . . . When the listener catches you in a lie, your power diminishes . . . For this reason, never tell a lie which can be discovered." As far back as 1940, American propaganda services had orders to tell the truth. It was a sound premise for effective propaganda, but it was a premise which was ignored by the succeeding generations of Cold Warriors.

Somewhere along the line the CIA's Covert Action Staff lost sight of the value of using the truth as the main weapon. Taking over from OSS, they soon became experts in "the big lie."

This policy surfaced to the attention of the American people during isolated events such as the U-2 incident and the Bay of Pigs invasion of Cuba when Presidents Eisenhower and Kennedy took the blame for what were obviously CIA lies. In the light of recent history it would appear that these chiefs of state were somehow convinced that it was better to issue a false confession that they had lied to the nation than to admit that they had been lied to by their own intelligence agency.

In the years since the founding of the CIA in 1947 there were hundreds of such lies and false denials and domestic propaganda campaigns which did not immediately gain public attention.

Brainwashing, as planted in the press, is one little propaganda weapon in a vast arsenal. But it is a weapon that has remained effective against communism, cropping up in news accounts whenever it is needed—whenever the Cold Warriors' domestic covert action arm thinks that the public is going "soft on communism."

Albert D. Biderman, a senior research associate of the Rand Corporation's subcontractor, the Bureau of Social Science Research, conducted a study of news items published about our POWs in Korea. Biderman's analysis confirmed that this kind of propaganda was "successively dominant in the press during and after the Korean War. During the war, Propaganda focused on prisoner atrocities; when the war had ended, the focus shifted to stories involving the brainwashing of POWs.

"Beginning with exchanges of prisoners," he wrote, "prisoner misconduct received gradually increased attention until, several months after the war, it came to overshadow the other themes."

Throughout the Korean conflict, propaganda and counterpropaganda campaigns on both sides grew in intensity until eventually POWs became the most critical issue of the war, the "stumbling block" in the drawn-out truce talks that delayed the war's termination.

In 1953, some 4,000 surviving American POWs became the subjects of another type of propaganda—propaganda by Americans, about Americans, directed at Americans. According to Biderman, "The theme of this propaganda was that there had been wholesale collaboration by the American prisoners with their Communist captors and that this unprecedented misbehavior revealed alarming new weaknesses in our national character. This post-truce propaganda . . . was an outgrowth of propaganda activities during the war."

Desperately trying to believe that U.S. propaganda was motivated by good intentions, Biderman suggested that the "brainwashing theme" was pushed at home because the Cold Warriors were "apparently worried that a number of American prisoners would return espousing the Communist view." Biderman noted that "the Defense and State Departments and the Central Intelligence Agency issued a stream of press releases during the days prior to the first prisoner exchanges in Korea to prepare the public for the shock of finding that many of the POWs had been brainwashed. The theme of these releases was that evidence of Communist indoctrination or 'pro-Communist' statements by Americans when they were released would be discounted because the prisoners would have been subjected to the well-known tortures that Communists used to brainwash their opponents."[7]

And just what were these "well-known tortures"? The general principles of the Chinese brainwashing techniques were repetition, pacing of demands, the forced participation in classes of prisoners, propaganda which would insert Communist ideas into familiar and meaningful contexts, punishment, threats, rewards, suggestion, pleas for peace, manipulative tricks, and deprivation of all but the minimum necessities of life. There was little that was new or innovative about the techniques used by the Chinese. They did not use drugs or hypnosis, nor did they invent any mysterious new devices for breaking the mind and will of a man.

Actually the Chinese controlled information in their POW camps just as they controlled the mass media in their own country. The system they used in the camps of propagandizing through lectures, movies, reading, and testimonials was based on the same system used on the Chinese population, and is not without parallel in Western education and advertising practices.

Nor are the punishment-and-reward techniques used by the Chinese in their interrogations exclusively Oriental. These same practices are employed by Western intelligence agents, police, and, more subtly by reporters trying to elicit information from a hostile subject. Confession and self-criticism have been used in religious movements as a basis of conversion, or as a way of perpetuating the faith, from time immemorial.

Dr. Edgar H. Schein of the Massachusetts Institute of Technology was one of many persons who contributed to the army study of the returned POWs. Of the central reason behind the brainwashing propaganda which the army study disclosed, he wrote "When things go wrong, it is far less ego-deflating to say that we have been brainwashed than to recognize our own inadequacy in coping with our problems. A crucial question, however, is whether such changes in our society and such preoccupations represent weaknesses and signal the deterioration of some of our highly valued institutions, or whether they are merely the symptoms of the changing world. Are we becoming mentally apathetic and hence more prone to totalitarian solutions, or are we finding new ways in which to relate ourselves to our international and internal problems? Many observers of the contemporary scene, among them the novelist and philosopher Aldous Huxley, and Joost Meerloo, a psychoanalyst, feel strongly that we are headed squarely in the *wrong* direction—that the combination of certain social forces and the weapons against the mind now available will inevitably lead to the destruction of the democratic way of life and the freedom of mind which goes with it, unless we recognize clearly what is happening and put counter-forces into operation."[8]

In succeeding years, talk of "brainwashing" continued. Usually it was heard that the Communists had "brainwashed" somebody, but on April 7, 1967, presidential hopeful Governor George Romney turned that around. Romney, who had gone to Vietnam believing in the rightness of the U.S. involvement there, came home saying that he had suffered "the greatest brainwashing that anyone can get when you go over to Vietnam, not only by the generals, but also by the diplomatic corps over there, and they do a very thorough job."

Nine governors who had accompanied Romney on the tour disagreed with him. Governor Philip H. Hoff said that Romney's brainwashing statement "tends to be almost incredible." Finding he had no support among his colleagues Romney quickly told reporters that he had not been talking about "Russian type brainwashing, but LBJ type brainwashing." He said he meant the same thing the press meant "when you write about the credibility gap, snow job, and manipulation of the news."

Webster's Third New International Dictionary gives the second meaning of brainwashing as "persuasion by propaganda or salesmanship," but the press and public thought that Romney had meant the word in its first sense: "A forcible indoctrination to induce someone to give up basic political, social, or religious beliefs and attitudes and to accept contrasting regimented ideas."

And the public let it be known that it would not vote for

a brainwashed presidential candidate. Romney's popularity fell so dramatically in the polls that he eventually dropped out of the race for the presidency. The word "brainwashing" proved to be more charged with emotions than anyone had supposed.

In one of the first mass market books published on the subject following the army's release of the study of the Korean POWs, Eugene Kinkead wrote, "Unfortunately, the distinction between brainwashing and indoctrination is far from clear to the average American. The army defines indoctrination as an effort to change a man's viewpoint while he is still a thinking individual by regulating his thoughts and actions. This falls far short of the effect produced upon some defendants seen in Communist courts, defendants who had obviously been completely broken, and had ceased to be thinking individuals. I am afraid that the general conception has been that Communist techniques of manipulating human beings are so persuasive, so completely irresistible that no prisoner can keep his integrity in the face of them—and, by analogy, that no people, including ours, can stand against such an enemy. This is what distresses me so much about the popular and improper use of a word like 'brainwashing . . .' "[9]

Perhaps. But by 1967, when George Romney claimed he had been brainwashed, our own government was already far beyond what Kinkead referred to as "brainwashing." The United States government did not have to stoop to the slow and exhausting process the Chinese and Russians used. In the age of electronic brain stimulation, neuro-psychopharmacology, and advanced methods of behavior modification and hypnosis, the government certainly didn't have to resort to methods as unsophisticated as brainwashing.

The techniques of mind control developed, even by 1967, were making brainwashing seem like the metaphor it was: a washboard and scrub-bucket technique which had little use in a world where the sonic cleaner, with high-frequency sound, higher than the human ear can hear, vibrates the dirt from the very molecules of matter—or the mind.

Brainwashing was largely a campaign waged in the United States home press. It served as a sharp-edged propaganda weapon and was aimed at the American people to add to the already considerable fear of the Communists. It also covered official United States embarrassment over a seeming rash of defections and collaborations with the enemy, and perhaps most important, offered moral justification for immoral and illegal experiments to scientists working under government contract. They were urged as a matter of patriotism to "beat the Communists in the mind-control race."

It is doubtful that all of the "collaborators" in the Korean conflict succumbed to brainwashing. The eyewitness testimony of air force Col. Laird Guttersen, one of the few heroes of the Vietnam conflict, and a real hero of the mind-control war, would suggest that they didn't.

Guttersen had been in charge of the air force seminar on Korean brainwashing at Maxwell Air Force Base. An expert hypnotist, he later used self-hypnosis to block pain and keep himself alive in a North Vietnamese POW camp where he spent more than twenty-seven months in solitary confinement.

He took the time during his campaign for the U.S. Congress to offer me his views on brainwashing and mind control.

As early as 1956 Colonel Gutterson realized that what was called brainwashing was nothing more than psychological indoctrination. "Controlling the mind is one thing," he told me, "but remember, this does not occur with psychological indoctrination. Nor does it occur, normally, with hypnosis. The concept of complete and total mind control was projected by the 'brainwashing' myth, and it was the theme of the book *The Manchurian Candidate;* but mind control is not what happened to the Korean or Vietnamese POWs. What the Chinese, the Russians, the Vietnamese did was mind influence, *not* mind control."

Guttersen said that while it was generally believed that brainwashing was the result of drugs and hypnosis, to his firsthand knowledge, from the Korean conflict to Vietnam, "there are no documented cases of drug- or hypnosis-induced mind control. Reading the examples of what the POWs stated in both Korea and Vietnam, and what I saw in Hanoi, there are only men saying, 'I couldn't have done or said those things unless I had been drugged.' There are no specific reports of anyone saying, 'They stuck a needle into me and I did so and so,' or 'They gave me something to eat, and then I did so and so.' There were men who said, 'I acted in a very strange way, just like I was in a dream or something. I must have been drugged.'"

There was a cover-up for a snafu in some of the original Korean briefings of our combatants who, Guttersen said, were told to cooperate if captured.

"I remember a specific briefing, though later it was denied, where a group of us were told that we would be well advised, if we got shot down, to whip out a bottle of vodka and a red flag and start waving it. We were advised to cooperate in any possible way with the enemy because anybody back home would know that we were cooperating under duress. We were told that if we cooperated with our captors, it would not give them an excuse to torture us. That was a specific briefing given to us. Of course, now we know that a good number of our captive men followed that advice and did collaborate on the basis that 'What the hell, nobody would believe me anyway. I'll just play the game.'

"But after they collaborated, it was denied that they had ever been told to do it. When it was brought up by the returned POWs who had received the briefing, it was denied by the military. But many of us who sat in on those briefings knew about them. This could be one of the reasons why they later came up with the Code of Conduct, in order to provide specific guidance to all military personnel, so that nobody would ever be told to collaborate with the enemy again."

The word "brainwashing" became commonplace after the Soviet Union presented evidence before the United Nations that charged the United States with the use of germ warfare in Korea—a major violation of the Geneva Convention. The Soviet evidence contained the confessions of several captured United States pilots stating both in documents and on film that they had dropped germ bombs on North Korea. By the time these men were repatriated, their stories had changed.

Marine Corps Colonel Frank H. Schwable was the first American to sign a germ warfare confession. His confession named names, cited missions, described meetings and strategy conferences. Before a military court of inquiry Schwable said: "I was never convinced in my own mind that we in the First Marine Air Wing had used bug warfare. I knew we hadn't, but the rest of it was so real to me—the conferences, the planes, and how they would go about their missions. . . .

"The words were mine," the Colonel continued, "but the thoughts were theirs. That is the hardest thing I have to explain: how a man can sit down and write something he knows is false, and yet, to sense it, to feel it, to make it seem real."

A CIA memo dated April 11, 1953 addressed to the Chief of CIA's Plans and Preparations, contained a report of an exchange that took place between then United Nations Ambassador Henry Cabot Lodge and an unidentified CIA agent. The CIA agent began to brief Lodge on the germ warfare confessions of Schwable and others when, according to the memo, Lodge interrupted expressing ". . . a profound distaste for the entire matter," adding that "he hoped he would never hear of it again—it had been a nasty and difficult issue, principally because of the difficulty of *explaining away* the film and the statements of the American fliers. . . ." (Emphasis added.)

The CIA memo continued with the agent reporting. "I said that we fully shared his view that 'the issue was finished in the United Nations,' but that it had been our experience that *'the bug' comes from a very hardy strain and had exhibited apalling vitality*. For this reason, I said that I thought it would be a mistake to be too complacent about the matter. To the last statement Senator Lodge replied with a question as to just what explanation we could give of the statements of the American fliers—how did we account for this and what could be done about it? I said that our best guess was that the statements had been in one way or another forced out of the captive airmen and that one of the techniques which we thought had possibly been used was the Soviet (and now Chinese) techniques of 'brainwashing.' Senator Lodge said that he thought the public was very inadequately informed about 'brainwashing' and that in the absence of a much larger quantity of public information than now exists on the subject, the impact of the fliers' statements is terrific. I replied by stating that we shared his view and pointed out that the Department of Defense is expected to issue a lengthy statement. . . ." (Emphasis added.)

Shortly thereafter, the word "brainwashing" was on the front page of every paper in America. We had not used germ warfare, CIA propaganda claimed, the Communists had used brainwashing.

Chapter Four
WITHOUT KNOWLEDGE OR CONSENT

"I can hypnotize a man—*without his knowledge or consent*—into committing treason against the United States," boasted Dr. George Estabrooks in the early 1940s.

Estabrooks, chairman of the Department of Psychology at Colgate University, was called to Washington by the War Department shortly after Pearl Harbor. Since he was the ranking authority on hypnosis at the time, they wanted his opinion on how the enemy might be planning to use hypnotism. "Two hundred trained foreign operators, working in the United States," Estabrooks told the military leaders, "could develop a uniquely dangerous army of hypnotically controlled Sixth Columnists."[1]

At that time, only a handful of men knew of the government's experiments with hypnosis for the purpose of controlling minds in the interest of "national security." In that decade there had been no concentrated assassinations of presidents, candidates, or civil rights leaders. There had not yet been Watergate, nor any disclosures of government agencies invading the privacy of United States citizens. The CIA had not yet been conceived, and even its parent, the Office of Strategic Services (OSS), did not exist.

It was unthinkable at the time that an agency of the U.S. government would employ mind-control techniques on its own people. Therefore it was natural for George Estabrooks to believe that if America were threatened by hypnotic mind control, the threat would be posed by a foreign enemy working within the United States.

So in 1943 Estabrooks sounded his public alarm, and

planted the seed for what would become priority top-secret research for the next twenty-five years. Couching his disclosure in hypothetical terms and saying that the hypnotized mind "could be" put to military use, he then portrayed a scene which he said could "very easily take place."

It would be possible, he said, for "the enemy" to plant a foreign agent as a doctor in a hospital or his own office. This "doctor" could, by means of fake physical examinations, place thousands of people under his power over a period of time. Estabrooks projected how, by hypnotizing key officers and programming them to follow suggestions, this "masked maneuver" could enable a lowly first lieutenant to take over the reins of the entire U.S. Army.

His alternate scenario depicted the General Staff summoning a colonel from Intelligence to an emergency meeting in the Pentagon two days after an outbreak of war. Shortly after entering the room where Pentagon "brain trusters" were gathered, the colonel is put into hypnotic trance by an army psychologist and told there has been a change of plans for the defense of major territory. The details of the plan have to be conveyed in absolute secrecy to the Pacific Command. Since the enemy has been very successful in monitoring U.S. communications, a new, highly reliable procedure is needed to slip the message past the enemy. The colonel, under the influence of hypnosis, will carry the top-secret message.

"When you wake up," the hypnotized colonel is told, "you will no longer have the slightest knowledge of the secret information carried in the lower layers of your mind." The colonel is then given instructions to proceed by airplane to Honolulu. He is told that in his normal waking state he will hold the impression that he is on a routine mission and must report after his arrival to General Y.

"He is the only man in the world who can hypnotize you again. Put to sleep by General Y—and only him—you will correctly recall all the details of this conversation and disclose the secret instructions we have just given you."

Estabrooks said later he had given the Pentagon episode *only* as a practical example of how the new science of hypnotism *could* be used for military purposes.

Going even further with his alarming predictions, Estabrooks told how disguised techniques of hypnosis could be employed to create an entire army of saboteurs within our own country. "Let us suppose that in a certain city there lives a group of a given foreign extraction. They are loyal Americans but still have cultural and sentimental ties to the old country. A neighborhood doctor, working secretly for a foreign power, hypnotizes those of his patients who have ties favorable to his plans. Having done this he would, of course, remove from them all knowledge of their ever having been hypnotized.

"Next comes a one-month period of indoctrination under hypnosis. By various means, including the offer of substantial rewards and educational processes designed to strengthen their ancestral loyalties, their cooperation is obtained."

Estabrooks explained how individuals so controlled would have no conscious aversion to Americans and would continue to behave as good citizens. Subconsciously, however, they would be saboteurs and agents of the enemy.

"All right, you say. This sounds beautiful on paper. But what about the well-known 'psychological principle' that no one will do anything under hypnosis that he wouldn't do when he's awake?" Estabrooks asked.

"My experiments have shown this assumption is poppycock. It depends not so much on the attitude of the subject as on that of the operator himself . . . In wartime, the motivation for murder under hypnosis doesn't have to be very strong," Estabrooks warned.

"During World War I, a leading psychologist made a startling proposal to the navy. He offered to take a submarine steered by a captured U-boat captain, placed under his hypnotic control, through enemy mine fields to attack the German fleet. Washington nixed the strategem as too risky. First, because there was no disguised method by which the captain's mind could be outflanked. Second, because today's technique of day-by-day breaking down of ethical conflicts brainwashing was still unknown.

"The indirect approach to hypnotism would, I believe, change the navy's answer today. Personally," Estabrooks concluded, "I am convinced that hypnosis is a bristling, dangerous armament which makes it doubly imperative to avoid the war of tomorrow."[3]

George Estabrooks may have greatly contributed to the U.S. government's interest in hypnosis. For during the years that followed, seeking ways both to improve the mind *and* to control it, various government agencies, many of them with intelligence functions, secretly pursued research in hypnotic techniques.

A number of related events during the 1940s demonstrated the extent of the government's interest in hypnosis. Beyond changing beliefs, they sought ways to motivate people to commit acts which they would not commit in a normal state.

Dr. Bernard C. Gindes wrote of an amnesia experiment he undertook for the U.S. Army in the late forties. "A soldier with only grade school education was able to memorize an entire page of Shakespeare's *Hamlet* after listening to the passages seven times. Upon awakening, he could not recall any of the lines, and even more startling was the fact that he had no remembrance of the hypnotic experience. A week later he was hypnotized again. In this state, he was able to repeat the entire page without a single error. In another experiment to test the validity of increased memory retention, five soldiers were hypnotized en masse and given a jumbled 'code' consisting of twenty-five words without phonetic consistency. They were allowed sixty seconds to commit the list to memory. In the waking state, each man was asked to repeat the code; none of them could. One man hazily remembered having had some association with a code, but could not remember more than that. The other four soldiers were allowed to study the code consciously for another sixty seconds, but all denied previous acquaintance with it. During rehypnotization, they were individually able to recall the exact content of the coded message."[3]

In 1947, J. G. Watkins induced criminal behavior in deeply hypnotized subjects during an army experiment. Watkins suggested a distorted view of reality to his subjects by inducing hallucinations which allowed them to avoid direct conflict with their own moral concepts. He carefully chose his suggestions to be in line with his subjects' preexisting motivational structures, and so was able to induce so-called antisocial behavior.

Watkins took a normal, healthy army private, a young man whose tests indicated a most stable personality, and put him in a deep trance. Though merely striking a superior officer is a court-martial offense in the army, Watkins wanted to see if he could get his subject to *strangle* a high-ranking officer.

After the subject was deep into trance, Watkins told him that the officer sitting across from him was a Japanese soldier who was trying to kill him. He must kill or be killed, Watkins suggested, and immediately the private leapt ferociously at the officer and grabbed him by the throat. In his waking state, the private would have been aghast at the thought of trying to strangle a superior officer. But under hypnosis, believing the officer was a dangerous Japanese soldier, the young private had to be pulled off his superior by three husky assistants. The officer came within a hairsbreadth of being strangled, as the young man was most persistent in his attempt to kill what he regarded as the enemy.

Watkins repeated this experiment with other subjects. The second time he used two officers who were good friends. One of them was given the hypnotic suggestion that the other was a Japanese soldier and that he must "kill or be killed." The man who had received the command not only made a powerful lunge at his friend, but as he did, he whipped out and opened a concealed jack knife, which neither the doctor, his assistants, nor his friend knew he had. Only the quick action of one of the assistants, who was a judo expert, prevented a potentially fatal stabbing.

In both cases, reality was so distorted that the subjects took murderous and antisocial action. If they had accomplished their "defensive" acts, both men could have been convicted of murder, since the law did not recognize motivation through hypnosis as a fact. The courts, in all but a few cases, had adopted the traditional scientific view that criminal behavior cannot be induced under hypnosis. That view still stands today.

To test the premise, which was then widely held, that a normal person under hypnotic trance could not be made to divulge information which would be self-incriminating, Watkins conducted a number of experiments where a monetary bribe was offered to withhold information. Watkins discovered that "when placed in a trance they 'spilled' every time, either verbally or in writing."

The subject of one of these experiments was an enlisted WAC in military intelligence. Her commanding officer ordered her not to reveal a list of what were made to appear to be real military secrets. Under hypnosis she "spilled" everything.

Another experiment was discontinued when it was discovered that a research worker in the government arsenal was spilling vital and top-secret war information to the friendly army hypnotist, who did not have a "need to know." He did this loud and clear while in a trance before an audience of 200 military professionals. If the subject had been allowed to continue, the disclosures of information would have resulted in a general court martial, no matter how the doctor might have tried to persuade intelligence headquarters that this was "just a test."

Much of the army's experimentation with manipulation by hypnosis was inspired by the reports of Wesley Raymond Wells, a doctor at Syracuse University. Wells's research, in turn, had been inspired by the fiction of the 1880s and 1890s, which described criminal acts as being induced by hypnosis. Wells was taken by the idea that "the most striking feature in a hypnotized subject is his automatism." Although earlier experiments had elicited no immoral or criminal behavior from subjects under hypnosis, the results of experiments which asked subjects to resist various suggestions indicated to Wells that people might be more suggestible than was generally believed.

In the late 1930s, Wells conducted a simple experiment with a student volunteer. He chose a subject who had stated that he expected he would be below average in hypnotizability and claimed he could not be put into a trance. Before inducing trance, Wells urged him to do his utmost to resist, in every possible way, first going into the trance, and then doing anything against his own moral code.

When the student told Wells that he was ready to begin the contest, the doctor put his hand on the subject's chest, counted to seven, and found that the subject had already fallen into a deep trance! After testing the subject's muscle control and ability to obtain amnesia and hallucinations, Wells proceeded to suggest that the subject get up from his chair, go over to Wells's overcoat which was on a coatrack across the room, and take a dollar from the right-hand pocket. Wells suggested that the subject see the coat as his own, and take the dollar thinking that he had left it in the pocket. When the subject followed all of Wells's suggestions, he then told him to put the dollar in his own breast pocket and return to his chair. As he was about to sit, Wells said to him that when he sat in the chair he would remember only that he had had this extra dollar when he came into the office, and that later he would spend the dollar, just as if it were his own.

Afterwards, during the student's recall of his experiences, Wells found that everything had worked according to the hypnotic program he had implanted. This was, of course, a clinical sort of test for amnesia.

"Whether his amnesia would have withstood 'third-degree' methods of the police or the lie detector methods of the psychological laboratory is another question," Wells said. "On the basis of my previous experimental study of posthypnotic amnesia, I would state it as my opinion that hypnotically induced amnesia in the case of so good a subject . . . would have withstood any possible tests, or at least it might have been made to withstand any possible tests if added precautions had been taken in the hypnotic production of the amnesia."[4]

Wells' report of this experiment, published in a psychology journal in 1941, brought a negative reaction from the scientific community. Milton Erickson was among the first to say that Wells's experiments were at best inconclusive. Erickson reported that after attempting to duplicate similar hypnotic inducements of crime with fifty subjects, he had failed. He concluded from his own investigations that "hypnosis cannot be misused to induce hypnotized persons to commit actual wrongful acts either against themselves or others . . ." The so-called antisocial acts induced by Wells and others, Erickson maintained, were most likely motivated by factors other than hypnosis or suggestion.

"We know that it is possible, without recourse to hypnosis, for one person to induce another to commit a wrong, a fact we may explain loosely as the influence of one personality upon another," Erickson explained. "To settle this question is difficult, since it involves three inseparable factors of unknown potentialities—specifically, the hypnotist as a person, the subject as a person, and hypnosis as such, to say nothing of the significant influence upon these three, both individually and collectively, of the suggestion and the performance of a questionable act."[5]

But even Erickson conceded that the primitive being, the libido, which dwells in everyone, makes almost any crime possible. When a hallucinatory state has been induced and the subject thinks he or she is acting out of self-preservation, the primitive mind takes over and the killer instinct is unleashed.

In the late 1930s psychologists began grappling with the problem of human will, as the theologians before them had done for centuries. Some maintained that "will" meant conscious volition; others, that it meant nothing but the manifestation of the belief system, that is to say, the result of the earliest conditioned responses. The area of will still lies outside the limits of modern psychology. Many experts are loath even to use the word "will" since it represents a most ill-defined dimension of human nature.

Summing up a carefully constructed semantic argument, psychologists often say, "A person cannot be made to do anything against his will or basic moral precepts." That statement, taken at face value, is certainly true. A normal person would not wittingly kill a friend. But if he was made to hallucinate that his friend was an enemy, and it was a "kill or be killed" situation, he would initiate a natural response to preserve his own life. In the process he might even take the imagined enemy's life. After the hallucination passed, he would realize he had killed his friend. This criminal act would be considered, in one sense, an act of will; but the real cause of the action would not be understood outside the hallucinated state. Only the killer's grief would remain, to attest to his knowledge of what he did, and that *he really* did not *want* to do it.

Whether or not hypnosis can be used to deeply motivate people to commit antisocial acts despite the call of their own conscience is still an open question in academic circles.

George Estabrooks had evidence which made him conclude that "one in every five of the human race are highly suggestible, at least half are suggestible to a very considerable degree." And he warned, ". . . mere figures do not tell the story. That one fifth has a power far beyond its numbers; for this type of man, acting under direct suggestion, is no mere average person. He is a fanatic, with all that fanaticism may imply for good or evil . . . Can this prospective subject—this one in five individual—be hypnotized against his will?"

"The answer to this very vital question," Estabrooks concluded, "is 'yes,' though we prefer to say 'without his consent' instead of 'against his will.' We do not need the subject's consent when we wish to hypnotize him for we use 'disguised' technique . . ."[6]

Believing in Estabrooks' logic, pragmatists in the government began to explore the possibilities of ways to change belief and motivate behavior. They let scores of contracts for research into hypnosis, behavior modification, conditioning, and virtually anything that held even a slim chance of being able to give them control over the individual human mind and will.

Meanwhile foreign governments unfriendly to the United States were involved in similar psychological research. But the U.S. government's fear of losing superiority in this new and untested field ran away with them. Intelligence analysts believed a "mind-control gap" existed, and to close it they mobilized "think tanks" to develop a usable program of experimental research, *at once.*

From one such think tank, the Rand Corporation, came a report entitled *Are the Cominform Countries Using Hypnosis Techniques to Elicit Confession In Public Trials?* Dated April 25, 1949, it helped set the stage for using national security as the rationale for resorting to mind control to motivate criminal acts, both at home and abroad.

"The successful use of hypnosis," the report said, "would represent a serious threat to democratic values in times of peace and war. In addition, it might contribute to the development of unconventional methods of warfare, which will be widely regarded as immoral. The results of scientific research in the field under discussion would obviously lend themselves to offensive as well as defensive applications and to abuse no less than to use. It must be assumed that almost all of the scientific personnel in the field of hypnosis are keenly aware of these social implications of their work and that they are interested in limiting the practice of hypnosis to therapeutic applications." That assumption proved to be untrue.

The Rand report recommended "that these moral and political implications of experimental research on hypnosis be explored as fully as possible prior to official encouragement or sponsorship of such research, so as to establish the most effective safeguards against its unintended consequences."

The Rand study dwelt at length upon Soviet experiments in hypnosis dating back to 1923. "At the State Institute of Experimental Psychology in Moscow," the report stated, "it was demonstrated that hypnosis could be used in inducing an innocent person to develop intense guilt feelings and to confess to a criminal or immoral act which he did not commit. In 1932 the experiments on hypnotically implanted 'crimes' were reported (in English translation) by A. R. Luria, who at that time was a professor in the Academy of Communist Education."

Quoting Luria, the report described how hypnosis was used as a device for producing emotional disturbances in order to control behavior. "We suggested to the person under test, while in a sufficiently deep hypnotic state, a certain situation, more often a disagreeable one, in which he was playing a role irreconcilable with his habits and contrary to his usual behavior—we thus obtained an actual and rather sharply expressed acute effect. After awakening the person under test . . . we had a subject who was 'loaded' with certain definite affective complexes, which mostly remained unknown to himself . . ."

Luria described an experiment with a twenty-year-old female college student who was told under deep hypnosis that she was sitting in her room studying when a neighbor child, a boy of six, came into the room. She was told that the child shouted when he came into the room and disturbed her studies. She asked him to stop, but he did not listen. The young woman was then told that she would get angry and forget herself. She would take a stick and beat the boy, first on the back and then on the head. The boy would cry out from the wounds on his head, but she would keep on beating him. She would then feel very ashamed and would be unable to understand how such a thing could happen, how she could beat up a child. Finally, she was told that she must try to forget the incident altogether.

Luria explained that he had chosen this situation with a definite purpose. Since the hallucinated event was entirely unacceptable by the moral standards of the young woman's personality, it was natural that she would feel repentant. He reinforced her natural desire to forget by suggesting to her that she remove the memory of the event from her mind.

In subsequent trances the subject was questioned about

the "beating." With great difficulty she reconstructed the event, but shifted the emphasis on several points so that the imagined event would conform more to her basic moral code. At first she refused to remember that she had "beaten" the child. She then conceded that she had "pulled his ears." Then, finally, she admitted she had "beaten him," but she maintained she had not beaten him with a stick. Luria said that this showed how unacceptable the situation was to her personality. The student said twice, "my conscience has tortured me." Luria said this showed the effectiveness of the hypnotic suggestion.

Of the experiment, Irving Janis, author of the Rand report, observed, "in this particular case, the implanted memory was initially referred to by the examiner as a 'dream' rather than as a real event. But from the detailed reports of other investigators, this procedure does not appear to be necessary for eliciting a false confession: a hypnotized subject will often accept and confess to an implanted memory as a real event in his own past life."

The Rand report itself suggested that this trick of hypnotic suggestion might be used on a defendant awaiting trial. The defendant could be "prepared" in a series of hypnotic sessions to accept guilt about a criminal act he did not commit, and then, if placed in a hypnotic trance while in the courtroom, the prosecutor's interrogation would elicit a false confession.

Fearing the Communists' use of hypnosis, the Rand report warned that hypnosis, once accomplished, is hard to detect. Contrary to reports in the nineteenth century, "a hypnotized subject is not blindly obedient, nor does he act like an automaton when in trance. Hypnotic suggestions are acted out and elaborated in a way that is consonant with the individual's habitual social behavior and his basic personality traits." The report stated that while often "the hypnotized subject seems literal and humorless . . . he appears entirely unselfconscious, and very often he acts abstracted, inattentive, almost as if he were insulated against his surroundings," this is not always the case. A number of experienced hypnotists had been able to train their subjects to perform "in such a way that observers could not tell that the subject was in a trance or that he was acting under hypnotic suggestions."

The Rand report outlined the following procedure that

would elicit a false confession. "First, make the subject feel guilty about some acts he had thought about or had actually carried out in the past. Second, make him feel guilty about having committed some crime of which he was actually innocent. The implanted guilt would compel the subject to confess when examined by a hypnotist or anyone else designated by the hypnotist. Third, train the subject, by means of posthypnotic suggestion, to go into the trance whenever a simple signal was encountered." The subject would be trained to give his false confession in a normal, convincing manner, so that observers would not be able to detect the trance state.

To induce hypnosis in an unwilling subject, the report suggested any of three possibilities which were then well supported by research findings:

1. As part of a medical examination, talk relaxation to the subject, thus disguising the hypnotic induction. For example, the person could be given a blood pressure test, told that he must relax completely in order to give an adequate test record, and then be given suggestions to go to sleep which would result in a hypnotic trance.

2. Induce hypnosis while the person is actually asleep from normal fatigue. This could be done by simply talking softly into the sleeper's ear.

3. Use injections of drugs to induce hypnosis. The hypnotic drugs would relax the subject and put him in a "twilight state" where the subconscious mind is very susceptible to suggestion.

Subjects who refuse or resist the simple "talking" methods of hypnotic induction could be given a few grams of paraldehyde or an intravenous injection of sodium pentothal or sodium amytal. The appropriate dosage of these drugs invariably induces a state of light hypnotic sleep. During sleep, the subject could then be given suggestions which would produce the characteristic deep hypnotic trance. While in the first drug-induced trance, the patient could be given posthypnotic suggestions to the effect that he would be susceptible to hypnosis thereafter without the use of drugs. Subsequently the subject could be allowed to practice carrying out posthypnotic suggestions. He could then be rehypnotized, still without his conscious cooperation, but this time without the use of drugs.

The report admitted that at the time of its writing there

was no certain knowledge of just how successful each of the three methods described might prove to be with individuals "who are on their guard against being victimized by hostile authorities."

"The drug technique," suggested the report, "would probably turn out to be the simplest and most efficient of the three and so it would be the most likely candidate for . . . hypnotizing defendants against their will."

Another important use of hypnosis for the government, the report said, would be the induction of amnesia: "Once a deep hypnotic trance is achieved, it is possible to introduce posthypnotic amnesia so that [a subject] . . . would not know . . . that he had been subjected to hypnosis, to drugs, or to any other treatment."

The report then turned to the problem of producing the deep hypnotic trance essential to posthypnotic amnesia. It stated that, based on research reports of that time, "in about 90 percent of any unselected population it should be possible to produce the deepest (somnambulistic) type of trance. According to numerous authorities, a light trance is sufficient to elicit a 'confession' of actual misbehavior which might otherwise be withheld; but, for carrying out complete posthypnotic amnesia, it is a somnambulistic trance that is required."

The Rand document expressed fear that Soviet investigators had found other techniques which could produce deep hypnosis in perhaps 90 percent or more of all individuals. Anticipating future advances, the report speculated on more efficient ways to develop greater depth in hypnotic trance. It suggested that a subject could be placed in a trance many times each day until a sufficient depth of trance was achieved. It was thought that hypnotizing the subject and then awakening him several times in the same session might speed up the process. This technique of successive and rapid trance induction would, it was hoped, make the subject easily susceptible to deep trance in a few days.

To increase speed and depth of hypnosis, special uses of hypnotic drugs were also suggested. "For example, a series of drug-induced trances, as against only one such treatment, might serve to develop the majority of cases into somnambules. Moreover, certain unique drug compounds may be especially effective in inducing very deep states of hypnosis."

The report then said, "Conceivably, electroshock convulsions might be used as an adjunctive device to achieve somnambulism in a very high percentage of the cases. Many studies have shown that there is a temporary intellectual impairment, diffuse amnesias, and general 'weakening of the ego' produced during the period when a series of electroshock convulsions is being administered. From my own and others' investigations of the psychological effects of such treatments, I would suspect that they might tend to reduce resistance to hypnotic suggestions. It is conceivable, therefore, that electroshock treatments might be used to weaken difficult cases in order to produce a hypnotic trance of great depth."

In 1958 the Bureau of Social Science Research (BSSR), a subcontractor to the Rand Corporation, issued a "technical report" on hypnosis to the air force that took up where the earlier Rand report had left off. Once again a "think tank" was calling for action in the mind-control race against the Communists.

"To both the lay person and the behavior scientist," the author, Seymour Fisher, wrote in the introduction, "hypnosis has long been regarded as a potentially powerful instrument for controlling human behavior. Undoubtedly, the intelligence divisions of many countries have given serious thought to this potential and have done classified research in various areas of hypnosis . . . it is conceivable . . . that these techniques could have been used and covered up so successfully that they might be *impossible* to recognize . . ."

Fisher outlined areas of future research where Americans could advance in the mind-control race. He urged the government to develop tests to determine who was and who was not a good hypnotic subject. He urged further research in pharmacology, suggesting that a number of drugs little known at the time might be effective in inducing hypnosis.

He predicted that some drugs would prove useful in reducing the amount of time required to induce complex hypnotic behavior and that others would be useful in reinforcing the lasting effects of hypnotically induced behavior control. He predicted that drugs would be developed which would permit far greater control over autonomic processes. Some drugs, he suggested, would be found to permit control over learning and perception as well. He also predicted that new drugs would be discovered which would be capable of inducing deep hypnosis in virtually *any* individual regardless of his degree of cooperativeness.[7]

All of these techniques, involving drug-induced hypnosis and electroshock convulsions, were eventually developed and used to reduce some of our own citizens to a zombie state in which they would blindly serve the government. Regardless of the Constitution and the laws which supposedly protect the individual against government coercion, "zombies" were covertly created to do the government's more unsavory bidding. Such "zombies" asked no questions about the legality of their assignments. Often their assignments were never consciously known. And if they were ever questioned about their own actions, amnesia protected them from self-incrimination.

What had started out a race against the Communists slowly turned into a private war from within.

Chapter Five
PAIN-DRUG HYPNOSIS

In 1951, a former naval officer described "a secret" of certain military and intelligence organizations. He called it "Pain-Drug-Hypnosis" and said it "is a vicious war weapon and may be of considerably more use in conquering a society than the atom bomb. This is no exaggeration. The extensiveness of the use of this form of hypnotism in espionage work is now so widespread that it is long past the time when people should have become alarmed about it . . . Pain-Drug-Hypnosis is a wicked extension of narcosynthesis, the drug hypnosis used in America only during and since the last war . . ."[1]

That statement was the tip of a vast iceberg of mind-control research using drugs as an aid to hypnotic induction. In the 1950s, under air force (and ultimately CIA) guidance, a series of papers was written defining the limits to which a government (ours or an enemy's) could go "to make persons behave against their will." In the introduction to one of these, the authors stated that the purpose of their study was "to review available scientific knowledge on the use of pharmacologic agents to influence the communication of information which, for one reason or another, an informant does not wish to reveal."

They went on to say that, contrary to the alleged necessity for conducting such drug experiments, "no published reports have come to our attention . . . detailing the scientific application of drugs by intelligence agencies of any nation as a means of obtaining information. The methods of Russian interrogation and indoctrination are derived from age-old police methods that have been systematized, and are not dependent on drugs, hypnotism, or any other special procedure designed by scientists."

The report, expressing concern over "proper" drug experimentation, urged that control placebos be administered "silently" so that no one would know who was getting what or when. Also discussed were the effects of drugs on different individuals in various settings, the relation between dosage levels, the effects of food, drink, and other physiological needs, and the effects of individual variables, such as sex, intelligence, medical and psychiatric status, life situation, and so forth upon drug reactions.

The top priority for testing in mind control were those drugs which were found to induce hypnosis. The administration and effects of barbiturates, amobarbital, secobarbital, pentothal, and sodium amytal were studied. Nonbarbiturate sedatives and calmatives such as ethchlorvynol, glutethimide, methyprylon, methylparafynol, captodramin, and oxanamide were also tested. A whole range of amphetamines and their derivatives were discussed as good tools to "produce a 'push'—an outpouring of ideas, emotions, memories, and so forth." New drugs such as ritalin, marsilid, and mescaline were thought to hold great promise for mind-control applications. Perhaps the most promising of this last group was a "consciousness-expanding" drug called LSD-25.[2]

Four months after the first nuclear reaction was created in a pile of uranium ore in Chicago, the psychotropic effects of LSD-25 were discovered by a thirty-seven-year-old Swiss chemist working at the Sandoz research laboratory in Basel, Switzerland. On April 16, 1943, Dr. Albert Hofmann accidentally absorbed a minute quantity of the rye fungus byproduct with which he was experimenting. He later filed a report which described history's first LSD "trip."

"I was forced to stop my work in the laboratory in the middle of the afternoon and to go home, as I was seized by a peculiar restlessness associated with a sensation of mild dizziness . . . a kind of drunkenness which was not unpleasant and which was characterized by extreme activity of imagination . . . there surged upon me an uninterrupted stream of fantastic images of extraordinary plasticity and vividness and accompanied by an intense kaleidoscope-like play of colors . . ."[3]

Sandoz Laboratories had actually been manufacturing LSD since 1938, when it was first used in an experiment with monkeys. Their scientists observed then that the substance caused a marked excitation of the animals, but these results did not motivate scientists to follow up with further research. Work with LSD fell into abeyance until the spring of 1943 when Hofmann prepared a new batch for the storeroom, and accidentally ingested some himself.

Dr. Hofmann described that LSD experience: " . . . I did not know what was going to happen, if I'd ever come back. I thought I was dying or going crazy. . . . My first . . . experiment with LSD was a 'bum trip' as one would say nowadays."

Dr. Hofmann's new discovery was investigated by the European psychiatrists as a possible key to the chemical nature of mental illness. In 1950 LSD was introduced to American psychiatrists, and interest spread rapidly in the scientific community here.

In 1953, the CIA made plans to purchase ten kilograms of LSD for use in "drug experiments with animals and human beings." Since there are more than 10,000 doses in a gram, that meant the CIA wanted 100 million doses. The CIA obviously intended to "corner the market" on LSD so that other countries would not be ahead of the U.S. in their potential for "LSD warfare."

That year Sandoz Laboratories filled many orders for LSD from both the CIA and the Department of Defense. According to Hofmann, they continued to do so up until the mid-sixties. The army would visit the labs every two years or so, to see if any technological progress had been made towards the manufacture of LSD in large quantities. Dr. Hofmann said that he had never been told the reason for the army's interest in the drug, but he assumed, from the large quantities being discussed, that it was to be used for weapons research.

As an employee of the pharmaceutical house Dr. Hofmann was in no position to warn the army researchers away from the drug despite his belief that it would be extremely dangerous if used improperly and despite his personal distaste for their work.

"I had perfected LSD for medical use, not as a weapon," he said. "It can make you insane or even kill you if it is not properly used under medical supervision. In any case, the research should be done by medical people and not by soldiers or intelligence agencies."

In 1963 Hofmann received a letter from a scholar at Harvard requesting twenty-five kilograms of psilocybin for research purposes. Psilocybin was a psychedelic substance similar in effect to LSD but more subtle and much less powerful. Before the sales department at Sandoz would act on this order for "the extraordinarily large quantity of psychedelic compounds," they asked the scholar to provide them with the necessary import license from U.S. health authorities. He failed to provide it. Later Hofmann commented on "the unrealistic manner with which he handled this transaction [which] left the impression of a person unconcerned with the regulations of society."[4] The scholar's name was Timothy Leary.

Leary had been experimenting with psychedelic substances for several years by the time he wrote to Hofmann. In 1961 he had conducted experiments with LSD at the Concord Correctional Facility in Concord, Massachusetts. That research was funded by the Uris Brothers Foundation in New York City, under the auspices of Harvard University. What Leary learned from the Concord prisoners was published in 1962 in his paper entitled "How to Change Behavior." In it, Leary explained what a powerful tool LSD was for changing ways of thinking and living.

While Leary did receive NIMH grants while at the University of California at Berkeley from 1953–56 and while working for the U.S. Public Health Service from 1954–58, he denies that any of his psychedelic research projects at Harvard were funded by the government. However, they may have been indirectly supported by it. In response to my query, National Institute of Mental Health Director Bertram Brown said that, although such research at Harvard University was funded by HEW and NIMH grants from the period of 1956–63, "records available for projects supported during that period generally do not go below the major institution level; e.g., awards are identified as being made to Harvard University, but not to departments or centers within that institution . . ." Here we encounter another example of the government's built-in deniability.

Harvard claimed that its records on Leary's research could not be located.

Tim Leary and Richard Alpert were fired from Harvard

in 1963, ostensibly for giving LSD to an undergraduate, but basically because of increasing controversy over the nature of their research. Leary and Co. retreated to Mexico, where they attempted to carry on LSD experiments outside the U.S. government's purview. In June of 1963 they ran afoul of even the notoriously corrupt Mexican government and were expelled from that country for "engaging in activities not permitted to a tourist."

From Mexico they moved to Millbrook, New York, and established the International Federation for Internal Freedom (later the Castalia Foundation), which served as a platform for Leary to propagandize for LSD which, he now believed, could save the world from nuclear perdition by "blowing the mind."

Leary frequently took LSD himself. His speeches, which were addressed to overflow audiences, were tailor-made for true believers in the new drug cult. Leary issued many public statements on the benefits to the individual and society of LSD. Always politically naive, he predicted that there would come a day when "a new profession of psychedelic guides will inevitably develop to supervise these experiences."

Finally, in the mid-sixties, Leary coined his famous slogan, "Turn on, tune in, drop out," and spoke at college lectures to the legions of young people who had illegally experimented with LSD and other psychedelic substances. Through magazine interviews, television appearances, movies, records, and books Leary projected himself as the culture hero of a new generation which was fighting for an individual's right to alter his own consciousness—a right which Leary maintained was guaranteed by the Constitution of the United States.

A CIA memo dated November 1, 1963 and obtained by John Marks under a Freedom of Information suit in August, 1977, featured Dr. Leary, Dr. Richard Alpert and their organization which advocated the expansion of consciousness through psychedelic chemicals, the International Federation for Internal Freedom (IFIF). In alarming tones the memo ordered all CIA groups involved in mind control operations to report if any agency personnel were involved with either Leary or Alpert or IFIF. The response to this in-house memo, if there was one, was not released by the CIA.

By 1968, society seemed to become divided into those who had taken illegal drugs and those who hadn't. Eventually LSD, marijuana, and cocaine were available on street-corners and schoolyards throughout the land. If the government *had* covertly supported the unwitting Leary and associates, the snowballing effects of their LSD propaganda now caused a reversal of policy. It became obvious to them that LSD and the other psychoactive drugs were politically dangerous. They allowed people to see through the indoctrination of the government, the credibility gap, and the government propaganda for the Vietnam War. The "acid heads" adopted a visionary fervor and began actively criticizing the war in Vietnam and calling for many social reforms. The "psychedelic revolution" embarrassed the government at every turn.

If the government didn't actually "begin" the psychedelic revolution, it was certainly responsible for shutting it down. It did this by controlling the availability and quality of drugs. Underground LSD labs were raided, and it wasn't long before its quality degenerated and the supply dried up. Several studies have shown that when LSD became illegal (October 6, 1966) *real* LSD ceased to be available on the street. What was sold as LSD was every other kind of chemical, including several forms of veterinary tranquilizers! Often methedrine was sold as LSD, as well as heroin mixed with amphetamines.

Simultaneously, as the LSD supply dried up, large supplies of heroin mysteriously became available. It was strong heroin, imported from the Golden Triangle in Southeast Asia (largely under CIA control). Many young people who had had their "consciousness expanded" too far to distinguish between one drug and another turned to heroin. The government-inspired hysteria over drugs had led many to think, "Well, they lied to us about pot, they must be lying about heroin." And so when psychedelics were no longer easily obtained, and heroin was, many young people became addicts.

The political visions of the psychedelic generation faded, as many who had "turned on" dropped out of city life and fled to the country. Those who stayed in the cities followed Leary's advice and dropped out from participation in the main stream of the society. Many of them followed an alternate route in the American tradition by living as pushers and bootleggers, making large sums of money from the newly created demand for illegal drugs.

In 1958, Dr. Louis Gottschalk, the CIA's "independent contractor," had prepared a think tank report which suggested that the intelligence agencies might control people through addiction.

The report put it this way: "The addiction of a source to a drug which the interrogator could supply, obviously would foster the dependence of the source on the interrogator. Where the source was addicted previous to the situation, the interrogator might find already established a pattern of evasion of laws and responsibilities which the addict had developed to meet his need for the drug in a society which proscribes its use."

The report went so far as to recommend that wounded GIs who had become addicts to pain-killing drugs be recruited from hospitals. It stated: "Where the source had become addicted in the setting as a sequel to the treatment of injuries, the ability of the interrogator to give or withhold the drug would give him a powerful weapon against the source . . ."[5]

In the late sixties, when it became known that thousands of GIs serving in Vietnam had become addicted to Laotian heroin, the U.S. Bureau of Narcotics tried sending a team of agents to Laos, but its investigations were blocked by the Laotian government, the State Department, and the CIA. While the Laotian government's hostility toward the bureau is understandable, the reticence shown by the American government and the CIA requires some explanation. According to U.S. narcotics agents serving in Southeast Asia, "the Bureau encountered a good deal of resistance from the CIA and the Embassy when it first decided to open an office in Vietnam . . ." Did this policy bear some relation to Gottschalk's think-tank statement, made some thirty years earlier—to create an army of drug dependent people who could be controlled by their suppliers—in this case the CIA?

The CIA also contributed indirectly to the heroin traffic by training men who then turned to smuggling. In the 1974 Pulitzer Prize-winning study of the heroin trade by the staff and editors of *Newsday*, it was revealed that U.S. Bureau of Narcotics and Dangerous Drugs (BNDD) agents in Miami cross-checked a list of men who landed at the Bay of

Pigs against police records. They found that at least 8 percent of the 1,500-man CIA-trained force had subsequently been investigated or arrested for drug dealing.

"If it hadn't been for their CIA training," one BNDD agent was quoted as saying, "some of these might never have gone into the [smuggling] business." He added that their training in paramilitary operations, weapons use, and smuggling of equipment and men from one place to another is well suited for illegal drug importing.

The head of the Office of Strategic Intelligence at BNDD, John Warner, said, "The key to heroin trafficking is the principle of compartmentability. It's the same way the CIA operates. Most people don't know what the whole project involves; most just know their particular job.'"[6]

Former CIA agent Victor Marchetti was reported as stating "The CIA is implicated in the drug traffic in several countries. The Mafia, thanks to the CIA, has a free hand in the vast opium traffic from Turkey through Italy to the United States."[7]

On July 19, 1975, Sen. Charles H. Percy, (R., Ill.) released a letter charging that the CIA had the Justice Department drop a drug case to protect its own involvement in drugs. Percy's letter said that the CIA refused to give federal prosecutors evidence in a case against Puttaporn Khramkhruan, a CIA employee, and one other person. Percy complained that "apparently CIA agents are untouchable—however serious their crime or however much harm is done to society."

The senator's letter said he had written the Justice Department to find out why charges were dropped against the two men, who were allegedly attempting to smuggle fifty-nine pounds of opium into the United States from Thailand. The reply he received, from Deputy Assistant Attorney General John C. Kenney, stated that CIA Associate General Counsel John Greany had "insisted that there were other considerations at stake and that the material sought by the prosecutors would not be turned over." Kenney said Greany had explained that if Khramkhruan and his associate went on trial, "the situation could prove embarrassing because of Mr. Khramkhruan's involvement with CIA activities in Thailand, Burma, and elsewhere."

The CIA knew that heroin causes no "consciousness expansion." It brings on a physical feeling, a warm, glowing "high," and then dullness and insulation. But the government was interested in behavior control, and heroin, like LSD, was an important tool in gaining such control.

While some clandestine agencies of government were busy distributing drugs to pleasure-seeking underground America, in the laboratories they were studying drugs for their capacities to provide access to the mind for purposes of behavior control. Seeking the perfect "incapaciting agent," army chemists at Edgewood Arsenal came up with a drug known as "BZ" whose effects were ten times more powerful than LSD. Described as a hallucinogenic "super-drug," BZ was said to be so powerful that a person who took it often experienced amnesia for long periods of time afterwards.

To test its effects BZ was given to 2,490 "volunteers." General Lloyd Fellenz, former commander of the Edgewood facility, said that the purpose of the BZ experiment was to produce an incapacitating gas or drug which could be placed in an enemy's water supply.

Dr. Solomon Snyder, professor of psychiatry and pharmacology at Johns Hopkins University Medical School, had formerly worked at Edgewood. "The army's testing of LSD was just a sideshow compared to its use of BZ," Dr. Snyder said. "Nobody can tell you for sure it won't cause a long-lasting effect. With an initial effect of eighty hours, compared to eight hours for LSD, you would have to worry more about its long-lasting or recurrent effects."[8]

Dr. George Aghajanian, who had also worked at Edgewood, confirmed Snyder's opinion. "With LSD," Aghajanian explained, "you tend to dwell on the experience and recall it and that can lead to flashbacks. But with BZ an amnesia occurs afterwards that blocks the experience out."[9]

Predicting the course of future events, Gottschalk's report stated: "The volume of effort devoted to studying the behavioral effects of drugs has expanded tremendously in recent years and will probably continue to grow. In part, this may be attributed to the ready financial support such activities have achieved. The interest of scientists in employing drugs in research, however, transcends an interest in drug effects, per se. Drugs constitute valuable tools for experimentation directed toward developing basic physiological and psychological knowledge. Work by scientists in several such areas, in particular, will increase knowledge of drugs which may be exploitable by interrogators."

Gottschalk's conclusion was that "drugs can operate as positive catalysts to productive interrogation. Combined with the many other stresses in captivity that an individual may be obliged to undergo, drugs can add to the factors aimed at weakening the resistance of the potential informant . . . But for many reasons, the use of drugs by an interrogator is not sure to produce valid results. The effects of drugs depend to a large extent on the personality makeup and physical status of the informant and the kind of rapport that the interrogator is able to establish with the informant. Knowing the predominating pharmacologic actions of a number of psychoactive drugs, an interrogating team might choose that chemical agent which is most likely to be effective in view of the informant's personality, physical status and the various stressful experiences he has already undergone . . ."[10]

This study and subsequent ones verified the fact that a number of drugs could conveniently be used to take over the human mind against the will of the individual. Through the use of drugs, the skilled mind controller could first induce a hypnotic trance. Then, one of several behavior modification techniques could be employed with amplified success. In themselves, without directed suggestions, drugs affect the mind in random ways. But when drugs are combined with hypnosis, an individual can be molded and manipulated beyond his own recognition.

The government's interest in controlling minds and motivating involuntary behavior was focused not only on individuals but also on large groups. Mass hypnosis and "crowd psychology" were well-known phenomena, and to that end propaganda techniques had already been developed. But mass "narcosis" was a new concept out of which grew the idea of "nonkill" warfare, where vast populations could simultaneously, or in one action, be drugged into submission.

In 1961, in an appearance before the Subcommittee on Science and Astronautics of the House of Representatives, Maj. Gen. Marshall Stubbs, head of the Army Chemical Corps, gave a speech cautioning that "we have not gone far enough in our research on these incapacitating compounds to be confident that they have real potential in warfare. We do not want to exaggerate claims for them to create the impression that we are on the verge of bloodless war."

General Stubbs admitted, "We are attempting to completely separate the incapacitating agents from the lethal agents so that any castigation normally given to toxic agents will not be associated with them, since they do not maim or kill. As a result we hope to have a weapon which will give the commander much freer rein in its use as compared to the toxic agents. It is my hope that through the use of incapacitating agents, the free world will have a relatively clear and rapid means of both fighting and deterring limited war, which has come to the forefront in the international political scene in the last several years. It is one means by which we can maintain some degree of equality in the face of overwhelming manpower superiority of the Communist-dominated nations."

One idea consistently expressed in the utterances of government employees was the idea that "we must beat the Commies to the punch." To that end the army launched a crash program investigating nerve gases, riot control gases, defoliants, herbicides, and biological agents such as anthrax, Rocky Mountain spotted fever, and bubonic plague. It also developed what it called "harassing agents"—chemicals that cause headaches, vomiting, and severe pain.

The idea was that one saboteur would be able to carry enough in his pocket to temporarily incapacitate the population of a city the size of New York. A two-suiter piece of luggage could hold enough drugs to disable every man, woman, and child in America. Most of the drugs the government experimented with were odorless, colorless, and tasteless and therefore undetectable They were easily soluble in water, and only slowly would they lose their potency in chlorinated water supplies. Food which came in contact with these chemicals remained contaminated for days unless thoroughly washed. The inhalation of particles of these drugs suspended in the air produced the same effects as ingestion. Dissolved, they could penetrate the skin and enter the bloodstream without having been ingested.

The army assumed that a city exposed to such chemical attack would cease to function, the inhabitants so confused by the "trip" that the army could march into the city and take over, facing only minimal resistance. And the next day, the populace would return to normal consciousness and be fit to work for the occupying army.

To test their assumption, the army gave a squad of soldiers LSD in coffee without their knowledge. After the drug effects began, the soldiers were ordered by their sergeant to perform normal and routine tasks while they were filmed by a hidden camera. They could not follow even the simplest command nor accomplish the most ordinary task with an acceptable degree of competency. Two of the men simply giggled helplessly throughout the entire afternoon. As the platoon sergeant was not a coffee drinker, he did not receive the drug. Neither had he been told about the test. Accordingly he grew more and more frustrated and perplexed as his men acted more and more erratically.

Further studies indicated, however, that in actual warfare things would not be that easy. Urban populations spend relatively little time out of doors. Since most of these drugs settled out of the atmosphere quickly and did not pass through air-conditioning systems, they would therefore not affect everyone. If the water supply were lightly laced with a psychedelic, an individual would have to drink a pint of tap water before being affected. The concentration could be made heavier, enough so that one would only have to brush his teeth or wash his face before getting "high," but with concentrations that large, even an infant's formula or a cup of tea would be a dangerous poison.

Further, those exposed to minute amounts of these "incapacitating agents" might be able to fight off the symptoms. Those heavily dosed would suffer enormous mental distortions and could become wildly irrational. Mildly intoxicated persons might go about as if in a normal state, unaware that their judgment and motor skills were impaired. The resulting number of accidents would be monumental. Thus, it became clear to the government that even the supposed "nonkill" type of warfare *could* take thousands of lives.

Eventually the army did shelve its plans for drug "nonkill" warfare. But the major obstacle, as they saw it, was not that it might kill the enemy, but that as of yet the army was unable to immunize its *own* troops against drug effects. Not until 1975 was a reliable LSD antidote developed.

Chapter Six
THE GUINEA PIG ARMY

In June, 1975, it was revealed publicly for the first time what many had suspected—that the CIA and a number of government agencies under its direction had actually been giving behavior-influencing drugs to citizens within the United States for more than twenty years.

I was in Washington at the time, searching the catalogue card files at the National Technical Information Service. A previous search by friends in military intelligence of the M.I. Classified Index had revealed nothing but peripheral references to the object of my study: government research in drugs, hypnosis, behavior modification, and related subjects.

The NTIS file is supposed to contain a complete numerical listing of all government contracts, by contract number, whether or not they are classified. The contract cards were indeed numbered in consecutive order, but the ones I was looking for were missing; the index simply skipped over them and continued on in numerical sequence. Other cards in the index were marked "classified," and I would not have been able to obtain the papers to which they referred. But the reports I was looking for were not even cited in the index, although references to them in scientific journals indicated that they had once existed. Classified or not, these documents had been removed from the record.

That afternoon press accounts of the *Rockefeller Report to the President on CIA Activities* said, "Beginning in the late 1940s, the CIA began to study the properties of certain behavior-influencing drugs (such as LSD) and how such drugs might be put to use in intelligence activities."

Further, according to the report, "The primary purpose of the drug program was to counter the use of behavior-influencing drugs clandestinely administered by an enemy, although several operational uses outside the United States were also considered."

"The drug program," the report went on to say, "was part of a much larger CIA program to study possible means for controlling human behavior. Other studies explored the effects of radiation, electric shock, psychology, psychiatry, sociology, and harassment substances."

As it would do two years later, the press played up the drug angle and ignored the other experiments. The CIA had been actually experimenting with all kinds of mind-control techniques for twenty-odd years.

It gave me little comfort, but it reaffirmed my sanity, to read in the report that "unfortunately only limited records of the testing conducted in these drug programs are now available. All the records concerning the program were ordered destroyed in 1973, including a total of 152 separate files."

As I left NTIS, George Orwell's prophecy in *1984* came to mind: "Who controls the past controls the future. Who controls the present controls the past." How long would it be before our society would perfectly mirror that state Orwell envisioned when he said: "All that was needed was an unending series of victories over your own memory. 'Reality control,' they called it . . . 'double-think.' "

In *1984*, the government continually changed its past by creating new historical fictions to justify its present. I wondered if we had already gone beyond 1984, where, as Orwell said, "truth is falsehood," and "ignorance is strength."

Five days after the Rockefeller Report was released, the public flap began. The children of Dr. Frank Olson were informed by the CIA that their father had been the individual the Report cited as the "employee of the Department of the Army who was given LSD without his knowledge while he was attending a meeting with CIA personnel working on the drug project." Olson had died when he fell, jumped, or somehow exited from a twelfth-floor hotel window in New York, while still under the influence of what was then billed as the most powerful mind-altering drug known to man.

For twenty-two years the cause of Olson's death had been concealed. His family had been led to believe that he had committed suicide because of a mysterious, unexplained "mental breakdown." At no time after Olson's death was his family offered a true explanation of the real circumstances which had caused it.

Eric, the eldest son of Dr. Olson, said, "I'm very angry at the CIA because they let us grow up thinking our father had inexplicably committed suicide." Young Olson said that his family had decided to sue the government, not only out of a desire to collect monetary damages but because "we think there's more information involved in this. It's also a way of holding the CIA publicly accountable for what they did."

The Olson family discovered that an individual damaged while in government employ cannot sue the government. But this didn't stop them. They asked the Senate to vote them a special bill of recompense for the death of the head of their household. On May 18, 1976, the full Senate approved S.B. 3035 by voice vote and sent it on to the House. Senate Bill 3035 specifically authorized appropriations totaling $1.25 million to be paid to the Olson family. The House of Representatives, being more conservative at the time, cut the Senate's generous award and the Olson family eventually received only $750,000. A similar case, tried in a civil court, might have brought the Olson family as much as three million dollars.

Months before Olson plunged to his death, Harold Blauer, a professional tennis player, died after being given repeated doses of experimental psychochemicals by the army at the New York State Psychiatric Institute in New York City. For years the Blauer family had been trying, to no avail, to find out the true cause of Harold Blauer's death. In the wake of the Olson scandal, the army relaxed its cover-up and finally surrendered Mr. Blauer's medical file to his daughter, Mrs. Elisabeth Barrett.

The chemical identities of the drugs he had received were not given; the drugs were listed only by number. The numbers were said to represent various hallucinogens, but because of "national security" it has never been revealed what the chemicals were that killed Harold Blauer.

The crucial part of the army's medical report stated: "Prenarcosis:—apprehensive—considerable persuasion required—injection administered at 9:53 A.M.; postnarcosis:—9:59, subject so restless has to be restrained by nurse—out of contact with reality—arms flailing—sweating profusely; 10:01, rapid oscillation of eyeballs; 10:11, body rigid all over, 10:15, stimulant administered; 10:20 to 11:45, deep coma; 11:50, artificial respiration administered; 12:15, doctor pronounces subject dead; 12:30, hospital authorities notified; 3:30, body transferred to city morgue."

Harold Blauer died without ever knowing what drug he'd received. And from the words in the report—"considerable persuasion required"—it looks as though he hadn't volunteered, either.

Frank Olson died without really knowing he'd been given a drug. It had been slipped into his drink and he was told it was LSD only after the mind-bending effects had begun.

Both Blauer's and Olson's deaths were covered up by the excuse of "national security." Their families were deliberately misled about the cause of death. No monetary compensation was offered except for the pensions or allotments due the families under normal circumstances.

In the wake of these personal tragedies, increasing public pressure led other government agencies to make their confessions. The army announced that since 1956 it had tested LSD on nearly 1,500 unwitting servicemen, and on several thousand more volunteers, a total of 6,940 in all. At the same time the army made this disclosure, it requested permission from the Defense Department to conduct further tests with at least two new drugs—drugs which were many times more powerful than LSD. Permission was granted with the stipulation that the "guinea pigs" be volunteers only.

Within days of the army's admission of drug testing, the Department of Health, Education and Welfare revealed that it had administered LSD to about 2,500 prisoners, mental patients, and paid volunteers between 1954 and 1968. HEW said further that it had given seven and a half million dollars in grants to more than thirty university researchers who independently ran LSD tests on human subjects.

What was not revealed until much later was that the CIA had used every possible military and civilian agency of government, as well as a number of universities and private research groups, to test LSD and other drugs, plus a whole array of psycho-technologies in an all-out search for reliable methods of controlling the human mind.

But the CIA's record was pretty good; for out of all the thousands of individuals who were given LSD or other drugs without their knowledge, only three are known to have died.

In 1955 a new drug-testing program was begun at the Edgewood Army Chemical Center. Volunteer soldiers were recruited but were not told what drugs they would be given, nor that men had died as a result of similar experiments. They were told they'd suffer only temporary discomfort. Seven thousand soldiers underwent the Edgewood Arsenal's tests. Five hundred eighty-five men were given LSD; the rest were administered other unspecified drugs.

Dr. Gerald Klee was one of the first psychiatrists to work on the drug-testing program for the army. When questioned by television crews as to how the volunteers had been recruited, he said that he didn't really know. They had come from all over the country, believing only that they were going to the Chemical Center to be used as subjects in chemical experiments.

"Most of them were not highly educated, and even if they had been told exactly what they were to be given, they wouldn't have understood it," Dr. Klee said. "The advantage to them was time off to get away from some place they didn't want to be, to be near their family, girlfriends, whatever, and they had a pretty good life while they were there, as a matter of fact. They spent very little of their time in the experiments and had a lot of free time . . ."

Wendell Queen was an army sergeant in 1964 when he volunteered for the drug experiments at Edgewood. Years later, when the Olson case was made public, Mr. Queen tried to find out what drugs he had been given. He ran into a wall of security. The army stated that it had no record that he was ever given drugs.

But Sergeant Queen remembers differently. He had been given a drug that penetrated his skin, not through injection but simply by being placed on his arm with an eye dropper. "They just took a small drop and put it on my arm, and my arm became inflamed and kinda itchy, something like a bad mosquito bite," he said. He was not told what drug it was. He was told only that the effects would be temporary.

Several hours afterwards, he began to float. "I began to feel kinda happy and the room started turning around," Sergeant Queen related. "I had lost all my senses. I had no sense of balance or sense of the environment around me. . . . Later on that night I really got paranoid and if anybody would come close to me I would think that they were going to kill me . . ."

Sergeant Queen had "flashbacks" for several months after that experiment when he would relive the states of mind he had experienced on that day.

"My roommate told me later that one night I woke up screaming and hollering 'don't kill me, don't kill me.' He said I became so violent that I began tearing my bed up," Sergeant Queen said.

Sergeant Queen remembers that at Edgewood he tried making a joke about being a human guinea pig. The medic administering the test didn't appreciate his sense of humor. "He said that the doctors were the only human guinea pigs around there because they took every new drug first. He said that they always got a bigger dose than anyone else ever did."

According to the army, their LSD testing program came to an end in 1967. An army spokesman promised a follow-up study on the 585 men who had been given LSD, but actually carried it out with only thirty-five officers—and superficially, at that. Still, the army maintained that there had certainly been no LSD deaths since Olson and Blauer. Once again it was not telling the whole truth.

George Danald, a colonel at the Army Chemical School in Fort McClellan, Alabama, agreed to become a guinea pig in 1959. He believed in progress, and he believed that without experimentation and research there could be no progress. Thus, when the opportunity presented itself to him, he readily submitted to an injection of what was said to be LSD.

Immediately after he took the drug, according to his wife, "his overall characteristics seemed to change, his attitude changed, mannerisms changed, and I'm sure a great deal more that I didn't notice at the time."

A year after Colonel Danald's psychedelic experience he

was transferred to Edgewood Chemical Center. Every day it was his habit to pick up his daughter Dawn promptly after school. One day he didn't meet her and Dawn walked to the Officers' Club looking for him. His car was in the parking lot, so assuming her father was inside, she went into the club and asked if anyone had seen him. When nobody seemed to remember that he'd been there that day, she went up to their apartment on the floor above and knocked on his door. There was no answer, so she went in.

The sitting room was littered with papers. She walked into the bedroom and noticed that the twin beds were apart. When she turned on the lights, she saw her father's body slumped at the foot of the bed.

In shock, she went to her room next door and telephoned her mother, who was at work. "Mommy, I found Daddy," she said. "He's on the floor and he looks awful white."

Colonel Danald had been dead for five hours when Dawn found him. He had taken his own life by putting a .25 caliber bullet through his temple. The pistol was still in his hand.

Colonel Danald did not have a history of mental instability. Until the time of his experience at Fort McClellan, he had never had a depressed moment. The only clue his family had to his apparent mental anguish was that, a few months before he died, he had once threatened to kill himself in a family argument. No one had paid any attention to that since he had been such a stable person in the past.

Mrs. Danald believes that her husband's death was caused by the mind-bending effects of the experiment, but she has so far been unable to prove her case. She and her family have received no compensation except the benefits which would normally accrue to a lifetime army officer.

Mary Ray was a research assistant at a psychiatric hospital which held military contracts to test LSD from 1958 to 1969. She helped doctors conduct experiments on more than 900 people. Some of them were mental patients. In 1966 she offered herself for LSD testing. Her description is typical of a "bum trip."

"I was in a state of becoming the universe. I became objects," she said. "I was no longer a person. Then, I got to a state of absolute terror. The closest thing I can remember being like that was as a child, when I was given ether . . . it was the feeling like just before losing consciousness."

But Mary was able to bring herself back from the LSD void: "I realized that I was a person, out of this billowing black seething weirdness, this horror . . .

"I looked down and I saw my arms which were two white rivers with black threads and they were my veins. I realized that, and I felt that if I tried really hard, somehow I could sever the veins. I realized even though I was not really a person that I could end all this living nightmare, this hell, by cutting my veins.

"Then I concentrated on this problem for what seemed centuries, because time did not exist. It was a strange time distortion. I tried desperately to try to kill myself. There is no question in my mind, that if I had had some sort of sharp instrument, and if I were alone, I would have killed myself . . ."

The doctors and medics in attendance were helpless. "No one seemed to know how to handle the situation. No one knew what to do. It seemed like they were kids *playing* scientists."[1]

Mary Ray reported no amnesia, and no recurring after-affects. She never felt another overwhelming compulsion to commit suicide, nor any compulsion to keep her experience secret.

In June of 1958, William F. Chaffin was a sergeant in the U.S. Air Force, stationed at Dover Air Force Base in Delaware. He had been a basic training instructor in biological, chemical, and radiological (CBR) warfare earlier in his career and thought, when he read the bulletin offering volunteers a thirty day tour of duty at Edgewood Arsenal, that it would be easy duty. It would be a nice break in his dull routine and a thirty-day leave at government expense. He assumed that he'd be involved in a program much like the one he'd taught in basic military training on chemical and biological warfare tactics and defenses.

On September 10, 1975, before a joint session of the Senate Subcommittee on Health and the Senate Subcommittee on Administrative Practice and Procedure, Chaffin testified to the *lasting* effects of his volunteer tour of duty at Edgewood.

He told the committee that upon his arrival at Edgewood, he was placed in a barracks with approximately thirty other volunteers. Daily, some of the volunteers were taken to various points on the base, given gas masks, and used in experiments involving DDT and other relatively mild chemicals. But at first Chaffin was simply ordered to report to a certain station each morning, and then he would be released for the remainder of the day to pursue his own interests.

Today Chaffin cannot say with any certainty how long this procedure went on. He can't remember whether he was there for one week, two weeks, or three weeks before he was actually used in a test.

"At some point around the middle of the month of July [1958]," Chaffin told the committee, "myself and four or five other individuals were taken to a hospital on the base. We were, at that time, taken into a room and a psychologist or psychiatrist—I cannot remember which—who I believe was associated with the University of Maryland, informed us that we would be administered a drug or a substance in distilled water. We were further informed that this drug or substance would be odorless, tasteless, and colorless. We were asked to perform certain tests prior to the ingestion of the substance. My best recollection of these tests is that we were simply asked to estimate certain amounts of elapsed time by any means other than a watch or clock. We were then taken back to our various wards and a short time thereafter, I was given a beaker of colorless, odorless, and tasteless substance by an orderly or an attendant.

"I have no recollection whatsoever that I was informed of the nature or qualities of the substance. Certainly, no reference was made to any possibility of detrimental psychological or physical effects on myself, or my future family, by taking of the substance.

"I cannot estimate adequately the length of time that elapsed after I took the drug until I first began to notice the effects, but my best recollection is that it was in the nature of one-half hour.

"At that time, I remember being taken back to the psychiatrist or psychologist and again asked to estimate various lengths of time by any means except observing a clock or watch. It is extremely difficult for me to describe adequately what occurred in the next hours of that day. I have, to this day, distinct recollections of vivid and colorful events that made no sense whatsoever to me. I have distinct recollections of either myself hallucinating or other individuals hallucinating and imagining that they were seeing certain objects and things. I do not recall if they were in fact hallucinating, or if I was simply imagining they were.

"I was obsessed with a feeling that I can only describe as utter and total depression. I don't think these words adequately convey the meaning of that which I experienced, but I simply do *not* have the words to set forth the occurrences of that day.

"Later, I was released from the hospital. I cannot recall if this was after a period of twelve hours, twenty-four hours, or thirty-six hours or more. It is simply impossible to adequately determine what lengths of time elapsed."

Shortly thereafter, Chaffin returned to his base. His life returned to its usual routine, but for some reason, he found it extremely difficult to talk to anyone. He could not even bring himself to tell his wife about his Edgewood experience.

"Since that time," Chaffin said, "I have experienced what I believe to be LSD flashbacks on at least three separate occasions. The feelings that encompassed me on those three different occasions were again what I can only describe as a total depression accompanied by nearly uncontrollable desire to take my life . . ."

After Chaffin's return, his wife became pregnant. In November of 1958, she miscarried. The Chaffins' doctor informed them that in all likelihood the fetus had been deformed. "I do not know at this time if this was attributable to LSD which I was administered at Edgewood, Maryland, or not. We do not at this time know if various other problems which have arisen in one of my children are directly attributable to LSD or not. Conversely, we do not at this time know that there is no relation.*

"After the ingestion of the substance in July of 1958," Chaffin said, "*my personality and behavior began to*

* Actually there is no conclusive scientific evidence that ingestion of even large amounts of LSD-25 can cause genetic malformation. There is only evidence that if laboratory animals and eggs are saturated with a pure concentration of LSD, chromosomal damage can occur.

change [emphasis added]. After seven years of marriage, I was certainly not an individual that tended to depression. However, after the ingestion of LSD, I have undergone, as I mentioned earlier, several occasions of the same total and extreme depression that occurred when I was given the LSD initially. Additionally, my wife has related to me one incident that occurred and which I have no recollection of whatsoever. This incident involved my actually taking a gun and attempting to leave our home for the purpose of taking my own life."

Then Chaffin told the Joint Committee, "I would like to state for the record that I believe that the United States Air Force was always extremely fair to me in my military career. I enjoyed my military career and consider myself to be a loyal member of the United States Air Force, retired. I must also state that the trauma that I have undergone as a result of being surreptitiously administered this drug is something I consider to be totally out of keeping with my concept of the service. I can only hope that the Committee will take every means available to make sure that the other individuals who were administered LSD receive notification and help."

Army records show that William Chaffin was given a drug known only as EA1729. On August 5, 1975, after the Olson disclosure, Chaffin wrote a letter to the army stating that he thought he might have been given LSD. He requested the medical follow-up the army had promised. Michael V. Johnston of the Army Surgeon General's office responded to his letter. "In checking our records," Johnston wrote, "we find that you did receive LSD in the army research program. Medical consultants in the Office of the Surgeon General are now making plans for a follow-up study of persons who took LSD. You will be contacted within the next few months and invited to be examined . . ."

Chaffin was called in for a physical subsequently but he feels the examination was inadequate. He has only the army's word that the drug he received was LSD. Probably it was not. LSD is not known for its abilities to induce amnesia, to cause depression, or to place a lock on the tongue. If anything, LSD could be used in interrogation to loosen the mind and the tongue.

Until that day in Edgewood, William Chaffin had always

had a firm grip on reality. Either he was given one of several drugs far more powerful than LSD, and with different properties to affect the mind, or he was given LSD and put through some extreme behavior modification procedure which programmed him to remain silent, and later, after his connection with the Edgewood experiment had been severed, to wish to take his own life.

Chapter Seven
THE MKULTRANS

Following the release of the Rockefeller Report, John D. Marks, author and former staff assistant to the State Department Intelligence Director, filed a Freedom of Information Act appeal on behalf of the Center for National Security Studies requesting documentation from the CIA. Marks requested documentation for the evidence cited in the Rockefeller Report on the CIA's mind-control activities conducted within the United States.

Seven months later, Marks was given more than 2,000 pages of top-secret and "eyes only" documents by the CIA's Information Review Committee. These pages were said to be the bulk of the information upon which the Rockefeller Commission had based its report. Exempted from release were portions of or entire documents which contained information said by CIA officials to pertain to "intelligence sources and methods which the Director of the Central Intelligence has the responsibility to protect from unauthorized disclosure pursuant to section 102 (d) (3) of the National Security Act of 1947." But in the Xeroxed pages Marks obtained was a statement to the effect that within a few hours of his resignation (forced by the disclosures of the Watergate and Church Committees), Director Richard Helms ordered the records shredded and burned.

The remaining documents, which were judged by the CIA to be "safe" to keep for subsequent release, were all highly sanitized. They contained few names of participating individuals or organizations and none of the details of the long-range experiments designed to mold and control the minds of American citizens.

In addition to offering a superficial review of the CIA's involvement in research on mind control, the documents Marks obtained gave the Agency's own officially censored version of what had happened to Dr. Frank Olson.

According to the CIA, at a "liaison conference" with Fort Detrick personnel at Deep Creek Lake, Maryland, on the eighteenth and nineteenth of November, 1953, Dr. Olson and seven other men were given LSD in glasses of Cointreau, an orange-flavored liqueur. The unsuspecting "guinea pigs" were told twenty minutes later that they had been given LSD.

Olson suffered "serious aftereffects," and later the same day, he was sent at CIA expense to New York City with an escort, Dr. Robert V. Lashbrook. There he was taken to see a psychiatrist, Dr. Harold A. Abramson. After five days of observation and treatment, Dr. Abramson decided that Olson had to be hospitalized. Arrangements were made for his admittance to a private sanitarium near Rockville, Maryland.

Following that consultation with Abramson on November 22, Olson and Lashbrook returned to their rooms at the Statler Hotel and retired for the evening. At 2:30 A.M. the next morning, Lashbrook was awakened by a loud crash. According to the "eyes only" investigation report, he went into Olson's bedroom and found him missing. The window, "glass and all," and the blinds were missing. Lashbrook assumed that Olson had dived through them.

Before Lashbrook notified the hotel desk he called Dr. Sidney Gottlieb, the chief medical officer of the CIA drug project, and informed him of Olson's fate. Lashbrook then called the desk man who called the police.

When the police from the Fourteenth Precinct arrived, Lashbrook told them that Olson was employed by the U.S. Army. He also told them that he, too, was a government employee and a friend of Olson's, but nothing else. Police, however, found Lashbrook in possession of government identification, including a CIA badge, and made note of this identifying data. The CIA and the Department of Defense quickly took over liaison with the police and succeeded in covering up the cause of Olson's "suicide."

Three months later, CIA Director Allen W. Dulles wrote

three notes of reprimand and sent them to the chiefs of the Technical Services Staff, Technical Operations, and Chemical Division. The "eyes only" reprimand to the Chief of the Chemical Division said, "I have personally reviewed the files from your office concerning the use of a drug on an unwitting group of individuals. In recommending the unwitting application of the drug to your superior, you apparently did not give sufficient emphasis to the necessity for medical collaboration and for proper consideration of the rights of the individual to whom it was being administered. This is to inform you that it is my opinion that you exercised poor judgment in this case." It was signed, "Sincerely, Allen W. Dulles, Director."

There was no change of operations. The research on mind control continued unabated.

According to the documents obtained by John Marks, the CIA mind-control program was run under four different project names. "In 1949 the Office of Scientific Intelligence (OSI) undertook the analysis of foreign work on certain unconventional warfare techniques, including behavioral drugs, with an initial objective of developing a capability to resist or offset the effect of such drugs. Preliminary phases included the review of drug-related work at institutions such as Mount Sinai Hospital, Boston Psychopathic Hospital, University of Illinois, University of Michigan, University of Minnesota, Valley Forge General Hospital, Detroit Psychopathic Clinic, Mayo Clinic, and the National Institute of Health.

"This first project, code-named Project BLUEBIRD, was assigned the function of discovering means of conditioning personnel to prevent unauthorized extraction of information from them by known means. It was further assigned to investigate the possibility of control of an individual by application of special interrogation techniques, memory enhancement, and establishing defensive means for preventing interrogation of agency personnel."

In August, 1951, Project BLUEBIRD was renamed Project ARTICHOKE, and was subsequently transferred from the Office of Scientific Intelligence (OSI) to the Office of Security (OS). OSI, however, retained the responsibility for evaluating foreign intelligence aspects of ARTICHOKE. In 1953, the OSI proposed that experiments be undertaken to test LSD on Agency volunteers. Records do not indicate, however, whether or not such experiments were made. According to the information released, OSI's involvement in Project ARTICHOKE ceased in 1956.

The emphasis originally given ARTICHOKE by the OS became focused on the use of drugs such as sodium pentothal in connection with interrogation techniques and with the polygraph. During this period there was an informal group known as the Artichoke Committee which had representatives from OSI, OS, Medical Services, and Technical Services. True to form, only brief records were kept, so that the details of the exchanges of this committee are still secret.

A CIA memo to the Director of Central Intelligence dated July 14, 1952, cited a successful application of narco-hypnotic interrogation undertaken by a team of representatives from the CIA. This memo revealed that by that date two successful interrogations had already been conducted using drugs and hypnosis. The subjects were Russian agents suspected of being double agents. The cover was called "psychiatric-medical" (they were admitted to a hospital). The control methods were by narcosis, by hypnosis, and by a combination of both. The subjects were regressed by hypnosis and made to relive past experiences. When the interrogation was completed posthypnotic suggestion succeeded in giving the subjects amnesia of the actual interrogations. The interrogations were regarded by the CIA as being very successful.

"In each case," the CIA memo read, "a psychiatric-medical cover was used to bring the ARTICHOKE techniques into action. In the first case, light dosages of drugs coupled with hypnosis were used to induce a complete hypnotic trance. This trance was held for approximately one hour and forty minutes of interrogation with a subsequent total amnesia produced by posthypnotic suggestion. In the second case (an individual of much higher intelligence than the first), a deep hypnotic trance was reached after light medication. This was followed by an interrogation lasting for well over an hour. However, a partial amnesia only was obtained at this time, although a total amnesia was obtained for a major part of the test. Since further interrogation was desired, a second test was made on this individual in which the ARTICHOKE technique of using a straight medication was employed. On this test, highly successful results were obtained in that a full interrogation lasting two hours and fifteen minutes was produced, part of which included a remarkable regression. During this regression, the subject actually 'relived' certain past activities of his life, some dating back fifteen years while, in addition, the subject totally accepted Mr. (deleted) [the case officer and interpreter at this time] as an old, trusted, and beloved personal friend whom the subject had known in years past in Georgia, USSR. Total amnesia was apparently achieved for the entire second test on this case."

The memo revealed that sodium pentothal and the stimulant desoxyn were the drugs used to aid the hypnotic trance. The memo continued: "For a matter of record, the case officers involved in both cases expressed themselves to the effect that the ARTICHOKE operations were entirely successful and team members felt that the tests demonstrated conclusively the effectiveness of the combined chemical-hypnotic technique in such cases. In both cases, the subjects talked clearly and at great length and furnished information which the case officers considered extremely valuable."

According to Agency Inspector General Chamberlain, "There is reference in papers in the records held by the Office of Security, of something referred to as an ARTICHOKE Team traveling overseas in 1954, with indications of operational applications to individuals representing a Communist Bloc country. There is no record of the operation or its results."

A summary of a conference on July 15, 1953, offered a clue to other kinds of operations conducted under ARTICHOKE. The report, addressed to the Chief of Security, CIA, said, "Mr. (deleted) then discussed the situation of a former Agency official who had become a chronic alcoholic and who, at the present time, was undergoing operative treatment in (deleted) for a possible brain tumor. This individual had called the Agency prior to the operation and warned that when given certain types of anesthetics (sodium pentothal), previously he had been known to talk coherently. The matter was taken care of by placing a representative in the operating room and by bringing the various personnel participating in the operation under the Secrecy Agreement. Mr. (deleted) stated that the subject did talk extensively under the influence of sodium pentothal and revealed internal problems of the Agency. Dr. (deleted) added that he was acquainted with the details in the case.

"(Deleted) then commented that this type of thing had been a source of great concern to himself and others in the operations work and stated that he hoped that the ARTICHOKE efforts to produce some method that would perhaps guarantee amnesia on the part of those knowing of Agency operations in vital spots would be successful. He stated that some individuals in the Agency had to know tremendous amounts of information and if any way could be found to produce amnesias for this type of information—for instance, after the individual had left the Agency—it would be a remarkable thing. Mr. (deleted) stated the need for amnesia was particularly great in operations work. Mr. (deleted) and Mr. (deleted) both explained that work was continually being done in an effort to produce controlled amnesia by various means.

"Mr. (deleted) called attention to the fact that at the preceding conference, Colonel (deleted) had advanced the idea of testing new methods, new chemicals, and new techniques (and combinations thereof) on certain carefully selected employees of the Agency, probably individuals in the training groups . . ."

One of the documents John Marks obtained was dated July 30, 1956. Under the heading "Schizophrenic Agent" the memo stated that bulbocapnine, an alkaloid, could cause catatonia or stupor from its affects on the central nervous system and the cerebral cortex. The report stated: "We desire to have certain psycho-chemical properties tested on man, using the bulbocapnine which we were fortunate to obtain from (deleted), a sample being enclosed herewith. More bulbocapnine is available if needed."

Along with the sample was the request that subjects be tested for "loss of speech, loss of sensitivity to pain, loss of memory, and loss of will power."

Another memo in 1956 authorized psychiatrists in universities and state penitentiaries (the names were deleted) to test these drugs on unwitting subjects.

An even earlier memo said "it was essential to find an area where large numbers of bodies would be used for research and experimentation. Dr. (deleted) stated that in connection with the testing of drugs, he was quite certain a number of psychiatrists all over the United States would be willing to test new drugs, especially drugs that affect the mind . . ."

ARTICHOKE evolved to become Project MKULTRA which, according to CIA documents, was "an umbrella project for funding sensitive projects . . . approved by Allen Dulles on April 3, 1953. Cryptonym MKDELTA covered . . . policy and procedure for use of biochemicals in clandestine operations . . ."

Besides drugs, MKDELTA and MKULTRA experimented with radiation, electroshock, psychology, psychiatry, sociology, anthropology, harassment substances, and what were called "paramilitary devices and materials." Contacts were made with individuals at prominent hospitals and drug "safe houses" under Bureau of Drug Abuse control. Through the Bureau of Narcotic and Dangerous Drugs (BNDD) and federal institutions such as prisons, drugs could be administered to unsuspecting individuals.

One hundred thirty-nine different drugs, including various amnesia potions, were first tested under laboratory conditions (see Appendix B). Then, beginning in 1955, the most promising drugs were given to unwitting subjects "in normal social situations" through the informal arrangement made between the CIA and the BNDD. The CIA Inspector General's report indicates that this part of the mind-control program was terminated in 1963, but that a project to test various drugs "in an inquiry into improvement of learning ability and memory retention" did continue until 1972.

Document 32 in the MKULTRA file, sheds a more direct light on the CIA's involvement in mind-control research. The "Memorandum for the Record" was written by an unidentified intelligence officer. It is reproduced below in its entirety.

17 January 1975

MEMORANDUM FOR THE RECORD

SUBJECT: MKULTRA

1. The following represents the best of my unaided recollection regarding the MKULTRA program. I was first briefed on it in 1962. At that time it was in the process of a significant decrease in activity and funding. As Chief, Defense and Espionage (C/D&E), I

continued to decrease funds significantly each year until the program was phased out in the late 1960s.

2. MKULTRA was a group of projects most of which dealt with drug or counter-drug research and development. The Director Central Intelligence (DCI) and the Deputy Director of Plans (DDP) were kept informed on the program via annual briefings by Chief Technical Services Division (C/TSD) or his Deputy. Most of the research and development was externally contracted and dealt with various materials which were purported to have characteristics appealing for their covert or clandestine administration under operational conditions. The objectives were behavioral control, behavior anomaly production and counter-measures for opposition application of similar substances. Work was performed at U.S. industrial, academic, and governmental research facilities. Funding was often through cut-out arrangements. Testing was usually done at such time as laboratory work was successfully completed and was often carried out at such facilities as the (deleted) and the (deleted). In all cases that I am aware of, testing was done using volunteer inmates who were witting of the nature of the test program but not the ultimate sponsoring organization.

3. As the Soviet drug use scare (and the amount of significant progress in the MKULTRA program) decreased, the program activities were curtailed significantly as budgetary pressure and alternate priorities dictated.

4. Over my stated objections the MKULTRA files were destroyed by order of the DCI (Mr. Helms) shortly before his departure from office

CI OFFICER
By Authority of 102702

As for the unidentified intelligence officer's claim that the experiments "in all cases that I am aware of" were performed on "volunteer" and "witting" subjects, one can only suggest that this man may not have had the "need to know" about the unwitting subjects. Records of court proceedings indicate that many "guinea pigs" in federal institutions were not fully informed of the long-range consequences of drug-enhanced behavior modification.

One such experiment on human "guinea pigs," conducted at the California Medical Facility at Vacaville, involved the use of the drug anectine, a strong muscle relaxant which leaves the victim totally without involuntary muscle control. The body lets loose its waste, breathing stops, and without proper attendance, death can result.

Whether or not the subject dies, he experiences the feeling that he is dying. According to chief Vacaville psychiatrist Dr. Arthur Nugent, anectine induces "sensations of suffocation and drowning. The subject experiences feelings of deep horror and terror, as though he were on the brink of death." While in this condition a self-styled therapist scolds him for his misdeeds and tells him to reform or expect more of the same. Dr. Nugent told the *San Francisco Chronicle,* "even the toughest inmates have come to fear and hate the drug. I don't blame them, I wouldn't have one treatment myself for the world."

Writing about the anectine therapy program, Jessica Mitford noted that of those given the drug, nearly all could be characterized as angry young men. "Yet some seem to have been made even angrier by the experience, for the researchers said that of sixty-four prisoners in the program, nine persons not only did not decrease, but actually exhibited an increase in their overall number of disciplinary infractions."[1]

Experimentation with drugs and behavior modification became so widespread in prisons and mental institutions that in the middle and late 1960s court dockets became crowded with lawsuits filed on behalf of the "human guinea pigs" who were victims of such research. By 1971 the number of lawsuits had reached such proportions that the Senate Subcommittee on Constitutional Rights began an investigation. Three years later, the Senate Committee on the Judiciary, chaired by Senator Sam Ervin, released a report entitled "Individual Rights and the Federal Role in Behavior Modification." It was largely ignored by the press, yet it revealed some interesting information.

Two years before the CIA and its subcontractors owned up to their mind dabbling, a large number of behavior modification projects were already underway. The report disclosed that thirteen projects were run by the Defense Department; the Department of Labor had conducted "several experiments"; the National Science Foundation conducted "a substantial amount of research dealing with understanding human behavior"; even the Veterans' Administration participated in psychosurgery experiments, which, in many cases, were nothing more than an advanced form of lobotomy.

One of the largest supporters of "behavior research" was the Department of Health, Education and Welfare, and its subagency the National Institute of Mental Health. The subcommittee said that HEW had participated in a "very large number of projects dealing with the control and alteration of human behavior." Largest of all the supporters of behavior modification was the Law Enforcement Assistance Administration (LEAA) which, under the Department of Justice, funded hundreds of behavior modification experiments. All the above agencies were named in secret CIA documents as those who provided research "cover" for MKULTRA.

The subcommittee found that controls and guidelines, where they existed, were at best loose. The poorly organized and loosely accountable research operations included not only traditional conditioning techniques, but also more advanced modifiers such as chemotherapy, aversive therapy, neurosurgery, stress assessment, electric shock, and the well-known form of psychological indoctrination popularly called "brainwashing."

Another of the documents released to John Marks was one dated February 10, 1951 entitled "Defense Against Soviet Mental Interrogation and Espionage Techniques." It began: "International treaties or other agreements have never controlled the experimental development and actual use of unconventional methods of warfare, such as devices for subversive activities, fiendish acts of espionage, torture and murder of prisoners of war, and physical duress and other unethical persuasive actions in the interrogation of prisoners."

According to this document, the Technical Services division of the CIA contracted with officials of what was then known as the Bureau of Narcotics to have mind-influencing drugs given to unwitting subjects. The CIA felt that the drugs needed to be tested in "normal life settings," so that the "full capabilities to produce disabling or discrediting effects" of the drugs would be known.

With the full approval of Allen W. Dulles, an arrangement had been made with the Bureau of Narcotics whereby the CIA financed and established "safe houses" in which federal narcotics agents could dispense the drugs and record the reactions of those who took them. No CIA men were present when the drugs were administered. The report did not reveal the number of "unwitting" subjects given drugs nor the identities of any but Olson. But it did acknowledge, for the first time, the scope of the cryptocracy's interest in mind control.

The CIA Inspector General, Donald F. Chamberlain, was stimulated by Olson's death to investigate the above-cited drug program himself. In a summary dated February 5, 1975, he wrote "Records do not permit a description of such relationships as may have existed between these various activities; it is apparent that there was some sharing of information between these various components in the Agency, and some overlap in time, but there also are indications of independent approaches to the problem."

Naturally, the CIA allows itself to be questioned and examined only by loyal employees. But even the in-house inspector general could not avoid reporting that the CIA had had a recurring interest in behavioral drugs for more than twenty-five years. The earliest record of this interest dated to the post-World War II period, when the CIA, heir to the OSS mind control research and perhaps the victim of its own motivating propaganda, thought that the Soviets were using drugs and other behavior-influencing techniques.

In 1949, Irving L. Janis of the Rand Corporation, wrote: "Defense against these [mind control] actions will depend largely upon knowledge of enemy capabilities. Reports of experimental and actual use of illegitimate interrogation techniques by the Soviets to obtain intelligence and court confessions against the interrogatee's will indicate clearly the need for medical investigation," the report claimed.

"The implications referred to above embrace several categories. The behavior of defendants in Soviet courts and in those of the satellite countries, together with the whole pattern of Soviet trial procedure, makes it essential for us to consider Soviet use of drugs, hypnotism, hypno-narcoanalysis, electric and drug shock, and possibly the use of ultrasonics."

The report continued, "There is documentary evidence to support the belief that the Soviets have been conducting medical research, have actually used various techniques, and have made provision for large-scale productions of uncommon drugs known for their speech-producing effects . . ." Only a few drugs with which the Soviets were supposed to be experimenting are named. No hard evidence is presented that they were in fact experimenting with such drugs. The report goes on to point to the trial of Joseph Cardinal Mindszenty, who was accused of collaborating with the enemy (the United States), as an example of the Russians' use of drugs in obtaining forced confessions in court procedure. "Behavior patterns, rapport, symptoms of residual effects of treatments, and the physical condition of the defendants all indicate the use of drugs. Several documents refer to memorized testimony and departures from text, indicating forced false confessions."

It was later learned that the elicited confessions were false. By Mindszenty's own admission, they were not induced by drugs or sophisticated techniques of mind control; they were simply forged, and rather poorly forged at that. Mindszenty's foggy mental state at the trial had resulted from psychological indoctrination, isolation, and interrogation, and generally can be regarded as standard police procedure, for most countries of the world.

The report clearly stated that "the use of these drugs does not usually result in amnesia of past interrogations unless the victim's mental faculties have been destroyed by their effects." Thus, even if drugs *were* used on Mindszenty, by the CIA's own conclusion he would have remembered getting the drugs and something about the subsequent interrogation sessions. The fact was he remembered neither. It is surely not a coincidence that the CIA "eyes only" report which claimed Mindszenty was narcohypnotized was issued the same year that Edward Hunter, the CIA "propaganda specialist," released *Brainwashing in Red China*. Most newspaper reporters would never go to press on the kind of sourceless, generalized information provided in the CIA report; yet are we to believe the cryptocracy had launched a thirty-odd-year research and development project based on evidence which amounted to hearsay?

Another CIA report uncovered by Marks, "Defense Against Soviet Medical Interrogation," revealed the alarming statistics that "although susceptibility to narco-hypnosis varies from person to person, skilled operators can readily hypnotize about twenty-five (25) per cent of a given group of average persons." It added "at least eighty (80) percent, however, would be susceptible following the use of certain drugs . . ."

This second document also discussed the plan of the CIA's organization of "a Special Defense Interrogation Program." In addition to outlining the use of drugs and hypnosis, the report brought up two other mind-bending possibilities: electroshock and ultrasonic sound.

"Psychiatrists in many nations," the report said, "have used insulin and electric shock as methods of choice under certain circumstances in their psychiatric work. Electric shock is more rapid than any of the above techniques [drugs or hypnosis]. It is instantaneous. It can be applied with or without the recipient's knowledge. Amnesia of interrogations equals that of hypnosis. If the enemy uses electric shock for interrogation purposes and the victim is available after recovery from the shock, highly trained specialists should be able to reveal the past use of electric shock by electroencephalographic analysis."

The report went on to recommend that groups within the CIA, the armed forces, and the FBI be organized and coordinated to give high-level direction to this project. "Civilian capability for solution of some of the problems should be utilized," the report said. "Close liaison between CIA and the Armed Services has been established, but it is not as effective as it should be. Liaison within the Armed Services appears to be inadequate, and they do not seem to be aware of some civilian sources of knowledge. Liaison with the FBI on this subject may be described as 'cooperative,' although somewhat mutually evasive. A satisfactory guiding organization could be set up under high-level direction for the development of an integrated program. If feasible, a committee to accomplish this purpose should be appointed." The report concluded by recommending that "a technical committee should include medical intelligence representatives from the CIA, Navy, Army, Air Force, probably the FBI and *ad hoc* Government and non-Government consultants."

From the first days of Project BLUEBIRD, and throughout all the ensuing CIA projects the goal was the same—find answers to the following questions:

"Can accurate information be obtained from willing or unwilling individuals?

"Can Agency personnel (or persons of interest to this Agency) be conditioned to prevent any unauthorized source or enemy from obtaining information from them by any known means?

"Can we obtain control of the future activities (physical and mental) of any individual, willing or unwilling, by application of [mind-control] techniques?"

Beyond the laboratory and operational research on unwitting subjects, the CIA set up training teams which included polygraph operators, interrogation specialists, hypnotists, and others in what was a long-range, all-out effort to develop reliable mind-control and counter-mind-control techniques. In all, fifteen separate research areas were defined by the CIA planners.

Most of the drug projects came under the operating authority of the U.S. Navy. At Bethesda Naval Hospital, under the direction of a Dr. Gaefsky, the drug project that was begun in 1947 continued until 1972. The CIA reports defined the project as one which sought to "isolate and synthesize pure drugs for use in *effecting psychological entry and control of the individual*" (italics added).

Also under the navy's direction was a project headed by a Dr. Ellson at the University of Indiana called "Detection of Deception." This project was aimed at determining the physiological changes which occur when a person is engaged in deception. Mechanical and electrical devices were developed to measure these changes.

At the University of Rochester, again under navy direction, a Dr. Wendy investigated motion sickness. The CIA report describes that study as one to determine "the effect of drugs on the vestibular function of the ear and the development of side effects which indicate the possibility of psychological entry and control."

Besides mind-control drugs and techniques, also investigated were tools which might be effective in compromising individuals. One report stated that in spite of the intensive research, as late as 1960, "no effective knock-out pill, truth serum, aphrodisiac, or recruitment pill was known to exist." Towards that goal under the auspices of the U.S. Army Surgeon General's Office, a Dr. Beecher at Harvard University was given $150,000 to investigate "the development and application of drugs which will aid in the establishment of psychological control."

And, under air force guidance, a Dr. Hastings at the University of Minnesota was engaged to research the effects of LSD on animals. His research area, as defined by CIA, also included the use of electric shock in interrogation, with particular emphasis placed on the detection of prior use of electric shock and the "guaranteed amnesia" it produced.

According to the documents, the investigation of hypnosis as a mind-control tool was kept under the aegis of the CIA. Their prime research interest was the "investigation of the possibilities of hypnotic and post-hypnotic control."

While MKULTRA was the code name for the research and development period of mind control, MKDELTA was the code name for the operational phase, during which all of the techniques of mind control were applied to individuals.

What followed next was the MKULTRANS, acting out their "mindless" roles at the behest of the cryptocracy.

Chapter Eight
THE MATA HARI OF MIND CONTROL

Candy Jones was a sex symbol during World War II. Born Jessica Wilcox, with her catchy stage name and shapely legs she rose to a standing second only to Betty Grable as America's most popular pinup. Like other pinup girls, she was a favorite of the troops at the front, and she felt it a duty to entertain them near the battlefields. After her advertised beauty faded and she could no longer serve to raise the morale of the troops with her appearance, she served her country in another way. She served under MKULTRA as a hypno-programmed CIA courier for twelve years.

While on a USO tour in the Pacific in 1945 Candy contracted a case of undulant fever and, shortly thereafter, malaria. On top of that, she caught the contagious fungus known as "jungle rot." Within a week, her hair had begun to fall out, and her complexion had turned a sickly yellow.

The combination of these diseases sent her to a military hospital in Manila, where she met a young medical officer whom she identifies only by the pseudonym "Gilbert Jensen." He would, later, offer her the opportunity to become a CIA courier.

In 1959 Candy started a modeling school in New York. She rented office space in a modern skyscraper across the hall from an office occupied by the one-time heavyweight boxing champion, Gene Tunney. One night Candy noticed a "cleaning lady" fumbling for keys to open Tunney's door. The next day Tunney reported that his office had been burglarized, but that nothing important had been stolen.

Later the same week Candy observed a young couple approaching Tunney's door. She watched as the young man took out a set of keys and went through the same trial-and-error process that the cleaning lady had performed a few nights earlier. Candy went into the hallway and asked the young man what he was doing. He told her that he was supposed to meet Tunney there. Candy informed him that Tunney had left hours before and was not expected back that evening. The couple hurriedly left.

The next day Candy told Tunney about the incident. He was not alarmed nor did he even seem to be interested that a second burglary of his office had been attempted.

One day later, in the lobby of her building, Candy ran into a retired army general she'd known in the South Pacific. The general had not known her well in the past, but now he was more than courteous. He mentioned that he was on his way to have lunch with Tunney so Candy invited him to her office first and showed him around. Then she brought him across the hall to Tunney. Tunney seemed quite surprised that Candy had known the general, and, after a brief conversation, the two men went to lunch and Candy continued with her business.

A few days later Candy was visited by a man who introduced himself as an FBI agent. He asked her about the burglary of Tunney's office, and Candy told him what she had told both Tunney and the superintendent of the building. The FBI man then unexpectedly went over to the window ledge and picked up a microphone Candy had obtained from Allen Funt of "Candid Camera" fame. The agent wanted to know what use Candy had for the microphone. She explained that she used it to tape her models' voices to help them develop their speech. The agent said that he'd been looking for just such a microphone to use in a surveillance job on Fifty-seventh Street. He asked Candy if she would mind if he borrowed it. Flattered that she'd been asked to help the FBI, Candy offered it for as long as it was needed. The FBI man thanked her and left with the microphone.

When he returned a month later, he was accompanied by another agent. After making casual conversation for a few minutes, the FBI men asked Candy if she would allow them to have some of their mail delivered to her office. There would be letters addressed to fictitious names in care of her modeling school. Some of the letters, he said, might be mailed from Europe and addressed to her, or to a specified fictitious man's name. If that happened she was supposed to call a number and report the arrival of the mail. Candy, once again flattered, said she'd be happy to help.

Two weeks after Candy took the job with the FBI, Gene Tunney moved out of his office. The general, however, kept in touch with her all during that year. He invited her to several parties, and even sent her a Christmas card.

In the summer of 1960, Candy received a letter at her apartment from the first FBI man, and the next day the general called her at her office. Somehow he knew that she was taking a trip to speak at the all-male Tuesday Night Supper Club in Denver, and afterwards going on to San Francisco to attend a fashion show. The general wondered if, since she was going to California anyway, she would mind carrying a letter from a government agency. He told her the letter was to be delivered to a man who would call at her hotel and identify himself.

Again flattered to be called upon to serve her country, Candy agreed to act as a courier. The important letter was hand-delivered to Candy's office a few days after the general's phone call. There were two envelopes—a large one inside of which were her instructions and a smaller one which contained the actual letter. Candy carried the letter with her to Denver, then on to San Francisco where she waited for her contact.

Within a few days she received a call at her hotel from a man who identified himself as Gil Jensen; it was the same man who had been Candy's doctor in the Philippines.

Jensen invited her to dinner that evening at the Mark Hopkins Hotel. During dinner Candy brought up the subject of the letter, but Jensen avoided the subject, saying that they could better talk about it at his office the next day.

Candy protested that she had to go back to New York the next day, but Jensen would not take no for an answer. He told her that it would be worth her while to stay on for a few days. "There's some interesting work you could do for the Central Intelligence Agency, Candy, without interfering with your business."

He told her that the work could be quite lucrative and since at that time she needed money, she decided to stay and find out what the CIA was offering.

The next day a car picked Candy up at her hotel and drove her across the Bay Bridge to the Oakland office of Dr. Jensen. That was the beginning of what Candy's biographer Donald Bain (who told Candy's story in the book *The Control of Candy Jones*) described as twelve years of adventure which would eventually take her to the Far East as a covert operative of the CIA.

"She would be harassed, badgered and even tortured." Bain wrote. "Her role was small, a carrier of messages, and the fact that she chose initially to perform such duties, for pay, renders the misfortunes that befell her 'occupational hazards.'

"What Candy hadn't bargained for, however, was becoming a human guinea pig in a secret CIA scientific project in which mind control was the goal.

"She was an unwilling and unknowing laboratory subject for twelve years, and only her chance marriage saved her from the final stage of her adventure—her own suicide as choreographed by Dr. Gilbert Jensen."

In 1973 Candy Jones married an old friend, "Long John" Nebel, the host of a New York all-night radio talk show. Candy had met John in 1941, at the height of her career, when he was working as a free-lance photographer assigned by a magazine to photograph her. After losing contact with each other for more than a decade, they accidentally renewed their acquaintance and were married twenty-eight days later.

On their wedding night, John noticed that his bride was suddenly acting out of character. She had left the bed and gone into the bathroom to look in the mirror. When she returned, John said, "I saw somebody who only *resembled* the woman I'd married." He stressed the word "resembled" because, although the body which walked out of the bathroom belonged to Candy, the being inside it did not. Her voice was cold and distant, and her expression was cruel. Soon the strange bitter mood passed and the warm and loving Candy returned.

The next evening Candy's strange "mood" returned. John naturally became curious about his wife's psychohistory and began asking questions about her past. Candy told him about her contact with the FBI in 1959. She also told him that from time to time she would still have to take little trips for the government.

On June 3, 1973, John and Candy came home early in the morning after doing one of his all-night talk shows. Candy tried to sleep, but found that she could not. She tossed and turned and when she complained to John of her sleeplessness, she was near tears.

John told Candy that he'd read that hypnosis could relax insomniacs, and although he never had tried to put anyone into the trance state, he'd read a lot about it and he suggested perhaps they ought to try it. Candy laughed and said, "I can't be hypnotized, John." But a short while after John began to hypnotize her, Candy was deeply asleep.

Although John had no way of knowing it then, Candy was already a highly suggestible subject since she had been hypnotized on many previous occasions by the CIA. Because of this, whenever John sought to induce trance in Candy, she rapidly became relaxed and was able to get a full night's natural sleep.

One night, while under John's hypnosis, Candy suddenly and spontaneously began to relive her childhood. During these age regressions, she revealed many terrible incidents in what had been, obviously, a lonely and troubled past. In dreamlike monologues she related how her father had abused her. Once when she was eleven he'd crushed her fingers, one by one, in a nutcracker because she wouldn't cry when he was about to leave.

Candy's portrayal of her mother depicted a person only a little less cruel than her father. A calculating woman, she often locked Candy inside a closet as a form of punishment.

In several hypnotic monologues Candy revealed how she had developed an alter ego named Arlene to defend her from the blows of her formative years. Later, John was to discover that the despicable personality which he had observed taking over his wife's consciousness on their wedding night was the same alter ego she'd developed in her childhood.* John Nebel began tape-recording his wife's hypnotic monologues.

One day, while under hypnosis, Candy told John about working with Dr. Jensen in California. She revealed that

* Bain fails to say whether or not Candy's alter ego playmate was a manifestation of true schizoid behavior, or if Jensen developed a monster from a harmless childhood fantasy.

Jensen worked for the CIA and she did, too, but John was not interested in the CIA story.

John became interested, however, when his wife described how Dr. Jensen had tried to hypnotize her. According to Candy, when Jensen had suggested that she submit to hypnosis and she had told him with great certainty that she couldn't be hypnotized, he had agreed with her that this was probably true, judging from what he knew of her personality.

John had read that the best way to deal with a subject who believes he cannot be hypnotized is first to agree with him, then to proceed to demonstrate how a hypnotist might *try* to induce trance. John's subsequent hypnotic sessions with Candy verified that that was exactly what Jensen had done. But he'd gone one step further.

According to the memories dredged up from Candy's subconscious, Jensen had regularly given her injections of "vitamins." John thought these might actually have been hypnotic drugs. Although Candy had probably always been a good hypnotic subject, narco-hypnosis provided access to greater depths in her already pliable personality.

When John began asking Candy about Jensen in her conscious state he found that she could provide little information about him. She could only recall visiting Jensen on that first trip for the CIA. She had no memory of what had happened in his office, nor of the events of her life which *immediately* followed that visit. John began to fear that the CIA doctor still possessed a hold over his wife's mind.

Over the course of many hypnotic sessions with Candy, John Nebel gathered up her fragments of memory and wove them into a picture of a satanic CIA doctor. But, reports Donald Bain, "the major difficulty in dredging up this material is that Candy Jones was programmed by Jensen *not* to remember, and this programming proved frighteningly effective."

John later discovered that on that first visit, Jensen had obtained from Candy the important piece of information that she had had an imaginary playmate named Arlene. This single fact provided the basis for the methodical splitting of her personality, for it was Arlene that Jensen wished to cultivate as a courier, not Candy.

Candy's willingness to carry messages was the extent of her conscious cooperation with the CIA. But from the first visit to Jensen's office she had become an unwitting victim of Operation Mind Control. Jensen had her sign a security oath which officially made her an employee of the government, and as such she forfeited her right to legal compensation for the harm done her by the ruthless mind-control operation.

Jensen also placed her against a large sheet of paper and traced her silhouette. Then he photographed her and asked her to pick a pseudonym for a new passport. She suggested her actual middle name, Arline.

In answer to Jensen's questions she revealed that her imaginary playmate had spelled her name A-r-l-e-n-e. Jensen said that he didn't care which way she spelled it and asked her to pick a last name as well. Candy suggested the name Grant, which was the last part of her grandmother's name, Rosengrant and "Arlene Grant" was agreed upon. It would be an easy name for Candy to remember since that was the very name she had given her alter ego in childhood.

As time went on, John found that he was talking more to Arlene than to Candy. In one session John asked Arlene if she thought Jensen had in any way crippled her. Arlene scornfully replied that Candy had not wanted to be programmed, but that she "didn't know what end was up."

John asked Arlene who had developed her, and she replied, "Mother Jensen. He hatched me like a mother hen." Jensen had told her to come up through Candy's stomach, she said. He'd say, "A. G.! A. G.!" and Candy would experience a severe stomach pain before Arlene took over her personality. When she refused to come when she was called, Jensen would give Candy an injection, and one day he miscalculated and gave her three injections, which put Candy to sleep for fourteen hours. Jensen had quite a scare because he had a difficult time reviving her.

Under John's hypnosis, Candy revealed that she had been given a number of drugs by Jensen: possibly aminazin, reserpine, and sulfazin, as well as the "truth drugs" sodium amytal and sodium pentothal. She was programmed not to allow any doctor except Jensen to treat her, and never to allow anyone to give her thorazine, the powerful tranquilizer.

The details of Candy's role as a mind-controlled CIA courier were pieced together from hundreds of hours of tapes of her hypnotic monologues. She worked for the CIA under her professional name Candy Jones, under the name Arlene Grant, and under her given name, Jessica Wilcox. She was first ordered to lease a post-office box at Grand Central Station in the name of Jessica Wilcox in August of 1961. She maintained this box until 1968 or 1969 and paid for it herself. Mail seldom arrived at the box, but when it did Candy would take it to her office and hold it for an unidentified man who always made the pickup, or sometimes, a phone call would order Candy to deliver certain letters to various locations around the city.

Slowly it began to dawn on Candy that some of the people she was delivering mail to might be just the kind of people who could kill her for reasons of their own. To protect herself, she wrote a letter to her attorney and put two copies in safe deposit boxes at different banks. The letter stated that for reasons she couldn't disclose she often used the names Arlene Grant, Jessica Wilcox, and Candy Jones. She wanted to put on record the fact that these different names all referred to her. In the event of her death, she wrote, whether it was due to accident or sudden illness, whether it happened in the United States or outside the country, there should be a thorough investigation. She wrote that although she was not at liberty to divulge her sideline activities, she was not performing illegal, immoral, or unpatriotic acts.

Candy holds that assumption to this day, even after hearing her own voice under hypnosis tell tales of physical torture, of illegal entries and exits from the country, and of the most shocking kind of abuse at the hands of the CIA. Candy probably still would do almost anything out of this hypno-cultivated sense of patriotism.

Eventually John tried to get his wife to see a psychiatrist, but she refused, saying that if she did so she would get very sick and might even have a convulsion. Evidently Jensen had told her this. Even talking about possible therapy gave Candy severe stomach cramps.

Candy had been programmed so that she would not only be protected from foreign intelligence operations, but from *everyone,* the CIA included. Jensen planned to use her for some evil design of his own.

Candy Jones was, in fact, not one, but two zombies, Candy and Arlene, sibling rivals trapped inside the same skin.

They would talk *to* each other but never *about* each other to anyone but Jensen. They traveled together on CIA assignments, Candy Jones being the person who acted within the United States, and Arlene Grant, the persona who took over once the airplane left the country.

Usually when Candy arrived in San Francisco from New York she would immediately go to Jensen's office. There she would change clothes, don a black wig, and pick up her fake passport in the name of Arlene Grant. Jensen would call forth the Arlene personality and send her off to Southeast Asia to deliver her messages. In his book, Donald Bain writes that Arlene often carried an envelope, but he wonders, wisely, if in fact there was anything in the envelope. The possibility is strong that Candy carried her secret messages within her mind, locked behind posthypnotic blocks which could be released only by hearing the proper cue.

In 1966 she was sent on several missions to Taiwan, where three businessmen were her contacts.

On her first mission to Taiwan, Arlene was met at the airport by one of them. She immediately offered him the envelope, but he insisted that she accompany him to his home, which turned out to be a large and institutional-like structure located on an impressive estate twenty miles outside Taipei. In front of the house a long row of trees lined the driveway which circumscribed a lush green lawn. There were other buildings on the property some distance from the main house.

As he escorted Arlene into the house she noticed two Chinese women dressed in lab coats on the lawn. She asked him who these women were, and he explained that they were only household help. During that first three-day visit, the man entertained Arlene royally. He took her to extravagant dinners and on an extensive sightseeing tour of the island.

When she returned to San Francisco, Jensen met her at the airport and drove her back to his office. There he gave her an intravenous injection of drugs and restored her to the Candy Jones personality. She turned in her Arlene Grant passport and put her black wig, dark makeup, and clothing in a closet in Jensen's office On that trip she also turned over to Jensen several rolls of exposed film which she had taken on her sightseeing tour. On her return to New York, she found her staff at the modeling agency very upset because she had forgotten to tell anyone where she was going or how long she would be gone.

A month later, Candy was again summoned to San Francisco. Jensen put her through the same procedure as before, having Arlene Grant emerge and travel to Taiwan. Again, the same man met her at the airport and took her to his country home. Again she stayed for three days. But this time she was not a guest but a prisoner.

Candy recalled, through John's questioning under hypnosis, that she was hooked up to an electric box of some kind and was shocked repeatedly on her shoulders, arms, and breasts. The Chinese grilled her about the contents of the envelope she'd just delivered. She protested that she did not know anything about its contents, but that answer did not satisfy her torturers.

When she wouldn't change her story, they turned to questions about Dr. Jensen. Arlene maintained that she did not know Dr. Jensen. Obstinately, she stuck to her programmed cover story, even though she was severely and repeatedly shocked.

Although the real event had taken place almost ten years earlier, the physical impressions revived by reliving these experiences under her husband's hypnosis were so strong that her lymph system responded protectively and pumped fluid to her skin producing blisters in the exact places where the electrodes had been attached.

According to Candy's recollection, the torture stopped only after the Chinese man talked with someone on the telephone. Following his conversation he unstrapped her from the chair and seemed most friendly and apologetic. He told her that the electrodes had been used not to torture her but to try and jog her memory. After lunch he drove her to the airport and put her on a plane for San Francisco. She remembers that on the return flight she wore gloves in order to hide the blisters. She also recalls that her hands smelled of sulfuric acid, although she has no recollection of having been burned with it.

At San Francisco, Jensen met her and gave her the customary injection after they reached his office. He told her that the torture had been a mistake, the result of a typographical error in the message she had carried.

In 1968 Candy was again sent to Taiwan. Normally an individual would not knowingly and willingly place herself in a position to be tortured a second time, but Jensen's control over Candy was so complete that she did his bidding without the slightest hesitation.

The final trip to Taiwan brought her into contact with other Taiwanese. She delivered her envelope, this time to a girl in an art gallery. She remembers that after the girl took the envelope from her, she spit in her face. Under hypnosis Candy could not recall any reason why the girl had done so.

After delivering the message, Arlene was picked up by the same man and driven to his home. Again she was tortured with electrodes and questioned about the contents of the message she'd delivered. When she would not, or could not, answer, her torturers put her hand in a box which contained a scorpion. This apparently was supposed to be a scare tactic, for when the scorpion bit her, the torturers immediately stopped the shocks and gave her antibiotics and administered other medical treatment.

Candy told her husband that on another occasion her thumbnails had been cut to the quick in an attempt to make her talk. She remembered that this had taken place on January 24, 1968. On still another occasion, something had been put in her ears to cause pain. But throughout all this torture, Jensen's programming held. She said nothing.

In another hypnosis session Arlene told about getting dizzy in a Taiwan hotel after having one drink. She began to sweat profusely and went to a bathroom which had a little dressing room and a bed in it. An attendant accompanied her and took her clothes and hung them up since they had become drenched with perspiration. She was given a dressing gown and allowed to lie down. Eventually a doctor came to see her. He gave her an injection and she drifted off to sleep.

After the doctor left the room, the female attendant came over and began to pinch her on different parts of her body, asking her where "the papers" were. When the attendant began to pinch Arlene's nipples, she fainted from the pain. The woman persisted, repeatedly pulling her to a sitting position and severely pinching her nipples.

When the woman finally left the room, Candy remembers, she tried to crawl under the bed to hide. The doctor came back and gave her another injection. The next day when she awoke and dressed, she was courteously escorted to the airport by her torturers as if nothing had happened.

When she got back to Jensen's office, she reported the incident to him. He seemed most concerned about it, but when he asked to see her bruises, she refused to show him her black and blue nipples.

On a number of occasions Candy was sent to the Central Intelligence Agency's training ground called "The Farm." Known to the outside world as Camp Peary, it appeared to be an ordinary military installation. There Candy learned how to search a room, and various guerrilla warfare tactics including how to commit undetectable arson. She was taught how to use a poison lipstick to take her own life, and how to use the same lipstick to kill someone else by sticking a pin inside it, then jabbing the intended victim. She learned how to use acid as a defensive and offensive weapon. She learned how to fire various weapons, how to climb ropes, and how to write coded messages on her fingernails and cover them with polish. The training at "The Farm" was known as 3-D: "Detect, Destroy, and Demolish."

At one point Candy told her husband of an especially outrageous incident which took place at CIA headquarters in Langley, Virginia. She had been taken to an amphitheater where more than two dozen CIA men were gathered to witness a performance of Dr. Jensen's stable of zombies. There were eight subjects scheduled for the performance and Candy was the first.

In a deep hypnotic trance, she was made to lie naked on a table. The table was wheeled before the CIA audience and Candy was introduced to the group as Laura Quidnick. She wore her Arlene wig during the entire performance.

Dr. Jensen demonstrated his complete control over the prone, disrobed figure of Candy Jones. He lit a candle and told his nude subject that she would not feel a thing. Then he shoved the burning candle deep into her vagina.

Several of the witnesses tried to break through Jensen's control, but they all failed. "Candy is perfect," Arlene told John. "Jensen proved in Virginia how impossible it was to break his control."

Piecing together such fragmented incidents of Candy's secret CIA past, John Nebel discovered that his wife had been programmed to commit suicide once she was no longer useful to the CIA. The self-destruct program was to be activated in Nassau. She was to check into the Paradise Beach Hotel on December 31, 1972. She'd stayed at the hotel many times before on normal business trips, so there was nothing unusual about that. But on this occasion Arlene was primed to spontaneously take over Candy's body upon receiving a phone call from Jensen. She was programmed to walk Candy's body to a steep cliff overlooking the sea and there to make a high dive. This was to be the last dive of Candy Jones' life, for from that location her body would certainly have crashed into the rocks on the beach below.

It was extremely fortunate that Candy married John Nebel on the very day she was supposed to check into the hotel. The marriage, by putting off the Nassau trip, had short-circuited Jensen's program of suicide, which was scheduled for the same month.

But today, despite John's help in countering much of Jensen's programming, Candy is still not completely free of his control over her mind. Still, whenever she looks into a mirror, she feels Arlene struggling to take over her consciousness.

Although Candy told Jensen that she was through working for the Agency in the middle of 1972, more than six months after she and John were married a strange phone call was recorded on their telephone-answering machine. The message was: "Japan Airlines calling on the 03 July at 4:10 P.M. . . . Please have Miss Grant call 759-9100 . . . She is holding new reservation on Japan Airlines Flight 5, for the sixth of July, Kennedy-Tokyo, with an open on to Taipei. This is per Cynthia that we are calling. Thank you."

A check with Japan Airlines disclosed that the number 759-9100 was indeed the reservation number for the airline. There was, however, no record in the airline's computer of the reservation or a record of who made it. Neither was there a reservation clerk named Cynthia, or anyone else at the airline by that name. The "per Cynthia" phrase may have been a code which was supposed to trigger Candy's automatic program, or it may have been a thin disguise for the Agency represented by Cynthia's first and last two letters.

Today, Candy's controlled mind and John Nebel's sense

of patriotism still prevent the whole truth of the story from emerging. For some reason John Nebel, Candy Jones, and Donald Bain conceal the real names of Candy's programmers. In Bain's book the name Gilbert Jensen is said to be a pseudonym.

Another doctor, who supposedly conditioned Candy to hate and distrust people, is given the name "Dr. Marshall Burger" in the book, though at one point there is a footnote stating that Nebel wondered if Burger wasn't a cover name for the California hypnotist, Dr. William Jennings Bryan.

Bryan, as noted in an earlier chapter, was the hypnotist and physician who offered the long-distance, instant diagnosis that Gary Powers had been "Powerized" by the Soviets. He was formerly a hypnotist for the air force and has been linked to the CIA. He was also the technical consultant for the film *The Manchurian Candidate.*

According to the April 22, 1969, *Los Angeles Times,* the California State Board of Medical Examiners found him guilty of "unprofessional conduct in four cases involving sexual molesting of female patients." For this offense Bryan was only placed on five years' probation—the lightness of the penalty might well have been accomplished through his connections with the CIA.

Alan W. Scheflin, an attorney who for five years has been researching the subject of mind control for his book *The Mind Manipulators,* says he has evidence which suggests that the Nebels and Donald Bain may be concealing the fact that the "doctor" who programmed Candy is the same doctor who programmed Lee Harvey Oswald, James Earl Ray, and Sirhan Beshara Sirhan.

In early 1976 Candy Jones and I both spoke on a KSAN radio special on mind control. I was interviewed via telephone and Candy was interviewed in the studio. We did not meet, but KSAN provided all the participants with duplicate tapes of the program.

On the KSAN program Candy Jones and Donald Bain both insisted, despite my own evidence and arguments, the testimony of Jessica Mitford, and the evidence provided by two other investigative reporters, that Candy had been only a human guinea pig used for experimental purposes. The records of the CIA mind-control project clearly show, however, that during the 1960s the cryptocracy's mind control had gone far beyond the experimental stage. On that radio show, Candy Jones herself revealed that Sir William Stephenson *(A Man Called Intrepid)* believed that she was no guinea pig. She reported that Stephenson wrote her that as far back as the early days of World War II he had used zombie agents like her in the service of British Intelligence.

Shortly after the program was aired I called Nebel's office to try and make contact with Candy or John. They had ignored my previous letters and my calls were taken by their producer, who tried to help me but finally had to report that the Nebels were not interested in being interviewed. I subsequently learned that neither would they grant an interview to John Marks of the Center for National Security Studies. They turned him down as flatly as they'd turned me down.

My attempt to clarify the question of whether or not Dr. William Jennings Bryan had anything to do with programming Candy Jones was also frustrated by his avoidance of me. I persisted in trying to get an interview with him until March of 1977, when Dr. Bryan died prematurely at the age of fifty, allegedly of a heart attack. He was a rather flamboyant man who toured the country holding "conferences" where he would lecture on the uses of hypnosis in police interrogation. He died at one such conference in Las Vegas, Nevada, only months after his name was raised in connection with Candy Jones.

A few of the questions which beg for the Nebels' answers are: What are the real names of the men who programmed Candy? Why weren't they included in the book? What are Candy's and John's personal political affiliations? Why are they not outraged by Candy's manipulation? Why are they attempting to protect the guilty and justify the rape of Candy's body and mind by the "national security" rationale?

In light of Candy's disclaimer, and the Nebels' refusal to clear up these questions, I can only ask the reader to decide whether or not Candy Jones was a courier in a fully operational sense, or only an experimental guinea pig, as she still maintains.

Chapter Nine
THE SLAVES WHO BURIED THE PHARAOH

The CIA uses thought reform, programming, and indoctrination on its own employees. Patrick J. McGarvey, a veteran of fourteen years in U.S. intelligence service, described the cryptocracy's more ordinary indoctrination procedures in his book *CIA: The Myth and the Madness.* McGarvey said that his indoctrination was carried out in a classroom which was "right out of *The Manchurian Candidate.* It was a cavernous room not unlike a nineteenth-century surgical exhibition pit."

That training, he said, consisted of "an admixture of common sense, insanity, old-time religion, and some of the weirdest lectures you can imagine." The most important result of this early training, as far as the CIA was concerned, McGarvey said, "was the attitudes they managed to inculcate" among the recruits.

"Many among us believed in the intelligence establishment simply because we were part of it. This attitude lingered for years among us, and today, in middle age, most of us still talk about the mind-bending job they did on us during the training period. I am convinced that this manipulation of attitudes has been responsible for keeping silent the many men who have since left the craft of intelligence. Because of my indoctrination, I still get a visceral twinge—and have qualms of conscience about writing this."

McGarvey was referring to behavior modification when he said, "CIA has a wonderful informal system of rewards and punishments for the faithful and unfaithful."

Other fragments of information have leaked through the

memory blocks and security oaths of former CIA employees. They can be found scattered throughout the "true confessions" literature of former spooks. They offer further glimpses of the CIA's interest in mind control—but they are only glimpses.

"The most impressive part of this initial CIA indoctrination," writes Miles Copeland, "is the attitude toward loyalty, security, precision, attention to detail, and healthy suspicion that it manages to implant in the minds of the trainees . . . The fact is that this aspect of the indoctrination has been designed by some of the nation's best psychologists, employing the most modern techniques of 'motivational research.' Certainly it achieves its purpose. The psychologists resent the insinuation that they are engaged in 'brainwashing,' arguing that the effect of what they have contributed to the training is exactly the opposite of brainwashing as practiced by the Chinese. Instead of conditioning a person so that he can accept only 'approved' ideas, it sharpens his instincts and critical faculties so that he can recognize specious political reasoning when he encounters it. Also the psychologists believe their course imparts a strong sense of mission, which is lacking in other branches of government."[1]

Despite the CIA psychologists' defense of their reverse "brainwashing," terrible damage has been suffered by the people who have matriculated from the CIA's mind-control projects. Those techniques employed for indoctrination and "loyalty training" of CIA personnel are but the beginning of a mind-control operation which is the most effective security device short of assassination.

Institutionalized secrecy came to America on the eve of World War II. From the beginning, psychology was both the most important external weapon against the Nazis and Japanese *and* the internal control mechanism for the wartime government.

Psychological warfare was used in World War I, but by the beginning of World War II it had taken on a new dimension. Previously the inspiring, depressing, persuasive, or misleading messages of propaganda had been delivered to target populations via the printed page or by word of mouth. In World War II, for the first time it became possible through radio to address the entire population of a country at the same time. The effects of propaganda, so magnified, became an important tool in warfare.

After the war, electronic propaganda became the staple weapon for waging the Cold War. Persuasion, argument, propaganda, and indoctrination went out over the airwaves not only to "enemy" populations but to our own civilian populations as well.

The full story of the OSS and the beginnings of the CIA was not known until 1976 when a government report, *The War Report of Strategic Services,* was declassified. In 1940 Gen. William J. Donovan was appointed President Franklin D. Roosevelt's special emissary. Upon his return from a Mediterranean tour he reported that "neither America nor Britain is fighting the new and important type of war on more than the smallest scale. Our defenses against political and psychological warfare are feeble, and even such gestures as have been made toward carrying the fight to the enemy are pitifully inadequate." Donovan urged the President to prepare for combat in the field of irregular and unorthodox warfare, as well as in the orthodox military areas.[2]

Five months before the Japanese attacked Pearl Harbor, President Roosevelt added one more new bureau to the New Deal bureaucracy. It was tagged COI, perhaps a fitting acronym for the publicity-shy Office of the Coordinator of Information. Its leader was, of course, William J. Donovan.

Donovan has been called "a queer figure who comes off three-quarters Machiavelli and one-quarter boy." According to Anthony Cave Brown, he recruited "Communists to kill Krauts. He feared and distrusted Communists in places where they counted. In Italy and France, he could never quite make up his mind what to do politically; and, since political belief was the clandestine's primary motive, his policies often failed and, even when they succeeded, led to interminable muddles. Likable, even admirable on occasions, he was in fact an Elizabethan man, swaggering about capitals in beautiful cord, displaying a fine calf for a riding boot, but forever dependent really upon the British for the finesse which that secret struggle demanded."[3]

The British Secret Intelligence Service had developed espionage and intelligence to a fine art during World War I.

They were already masters of sabotage, guerrilla warfare, political warfare, deception, crypto-analysis, irregular maritime warfare, technical intelligence, and secret intelligence when World War II began. During that war they took intelligence into the vanguard of psychology, using drugs and hypnosis to program couriers to carry secret messages locked behind posthypnotic blocks.

The British were the first to employ a financing device known as the "Secret Vote," or unvouchered funds. This was money made available without recourse to legislation and accounted for only by personal signature. As Anthony Cave Brown observed, "plainly, almost unlimited opportunities for fraud existed in this arrangement."[4]

Donovan's COI copied the unvouchered funds financing idea, as well as many others, from the British. He put great emphasis on the psychological warfare arm of intelligence. The British had also emphasized "psy-war," but Donovan promoted it to the degree that he made the psychological warfare division the central control organ of the entire espionage agency.

In 1941, after the birth of COI, President Roosevelt asked Donovan to make specific proposals for the implementation of his ideas for psychological warfare and the development of an intelligence plan. Donovan submitted to the White House a paper entitled "Memorandum of Establishment of Services of Strategic Information." In it he clarified his idea of the relationship of information to strategic planning in total war.

Pointing out the diplomatic and defense inadequacies of the then-existing intelligence organization, Donovan said, "It is essential that we set up a central enemy intelligence organization which would itself collect either directly or through existing departments of government, at home and abroad, pertinent information." Such information and data should be analyzed and interpreted by applying the experience of "specialized, trained research officials in the related scientific fields (including technological, economic, financial and psychological scholars)." He emphasized that "there is another element in modern warfare, and that is the psychological attack against the moral and spiritual defenses of a nation."[5]

In June, 1942, the Office of Strategic Service (OSS) was created to replace COI. Some time passed between the formation of the OSS and the issuance of its charter. The delay was created by Donovan's controversial idea that the psychological warfare unit should be in charge of the entire intelligence operation. The intellectuals hovering around OSS argued with the Joint War Plans Committee about what exactly psychological warfare was, and who should direct it in the name of the United States of America.

Finally a definition was agreed upon. The official definition of psychological warfare read: ". . . it is the coordination and use of all means, including moral and physical, by which the end is to be attained—other than those of recognized military operations, but including the psychological exploitation of the result of those recognized military actions—which tend to destroy the will of the enemy to achieve victory and to damage his political or economic capacity to do so; which tend to deprive the enemy of the support, assistance, or sympathy of his allies or associates or of neutrals, or to prevent his acquisition of such support, assistance, or sympathy; or which tend to create, maintain, or increase the will to victory of our own people and allies and to acquire, maintain, or increase the support, assistance, and sympathy of neutrals."

And, as Donovan had wished, the Joint Chiefs of Staff decreed that "All plans for projects to be undertaken by the Office of Strategic Services will be submitted to the Joint U.S. Chiefs of Staff through the Joint Psychological Warfare Committee for approval. The Joint Psychological Warfare Committee will refer such papers as it deems necessary to the Joint Staff Planners (JSP) prior to submission to the Joint U.S. Chiefs of Staff. The Joint Psychological Warfare Committee will take final action on all internal administrative plans pertaining to the Office of Strategic Services."[8]

The lifespan of OSS was less than three years. During that short period of time it developed psychological warfare into an effective weapon against the minds of civilian and military populations foreign and domestic alike. To wage effective psychological war the OSS needed background information on United States citizens. Thus the burglary of private files was sanctioned. The pattern of illegal clandestine activities within the United States, which became public knowledge with Watergate, began in 1945 when the OSS broke into the office of *Amerasia* magazine, an alleged Communist publication. The OSS illegal entry was followed by a legal FBI search three months later, but no evidence that *Amerasia* was engaged in subversive activity was ever found.

Throughout the war Donovan never lost sight of the fact that while OSS was a wartime expedient, it was also an experiment to determine the nature of a peacetime U.S. intelligence structure in the postwar period. Eventually OSS did provide the framework for the peacetime intelligence service through which the United States continued the bitter moral and territorial struggle against the Communists.

By a small, humorous twist of fate, it was on October 31, 1944—Halloween, the traditional day for spooks and dirty tricks—when President Roosevelt once again turned to Donovan for his views. The President asked Donovan to develop a plan for the organization of an intelligence service which would function after the cessation of hostilities. In November, Donovan submitted to the President his proposal for the creation of a "central intelligence service." In his memorandum, Donovan proposed liquidation of OSS once the wartime necessity had ceased. He was anxious, however, to preserve the intelligence functions developed by OSS, so he repeated his original COI concept of a central authority, reporting directly to the President, which would collect and analyze intelligence material required for planning and implementation of national policy and strategy.

"Though in the midst of war," Donovan wrote, "we are also in a period of transition which, before we are aware, will take us into the tumult of rehabilitation. An adequate and orderly intelligence system will contribute to informed decisions. We have now in the Government the trained and specialized personnel needed for the task. This talent should not be dispersed."[7]

On September 20, 1945, OSS was officially terminated by Executive Order 9620. "Research and Analysis" functions and "Foreign Nationals Recruiting" were transferred to the Department of State. The remainder of the OSS functions were transferred to the Department of War. That same day, the new President Harry S Truman sent a letter to Donovan informing him of the executive order to close OSS, and thanking him for his outstanding service.

The President wrote, in part, "You may well find satisfaction in the achievements of the Office and take pride in your own contribution to them. These are in themselves large rewards. Great additional reward for your efforts should lie in the knowledge that the peacetime intelligence services of the Government are being erected on the foundation of the facilities and resources mobilized through the Office of Strategic Services during the war."

Hidden behind the President's compliment was the fact that Donovan was shut out from the formation of the CIA because of a major character flaw: he had a strong dislike of organization. Whether Donovan was really the right man for the job of chief of America's first intelligence service is debatable. Success in covert operations depends upon an efficient bureaucracy and good judgment in authority. In many cases Donovan displayed neither. At heart he was an activist who did not even like the personalities of conventional administrators. Stewart Alsop said that he ran OSS "like a country editor."

"In every respect, OSS was Donovan's child," OSS historian R. Harris Smith wrote. "He nourished the agency in its infancy, and it bore the stamp of his personality."[9] That stamp carried over into the new peacetime intelligence agency, the CIA, the first in American history.

But while Donovan was the grandfather of the cryptocracy, its techniques and much of the rationale behind them were the work of the Dulles brothers. The following review of the Dulles' rise to prominence shows the manner in which cryptocrats form their liaisons.

On the evening of the day South Korea was invaded, President Truman had hastily returned to Washington from his home in Independence, Missouri. He gathered his principal advisors together at the White House to discuss the emergency. Unanimously, his advisors recognized the gravity of the situation and agreed with Gen. Omar Bradley, then the head of the Chiefs of Staff, who said the intelligence reports indicated Russia was "not yet ready for war, but in Korea they are obviously testing us, and the line ought to be drawn now."

Quickly, Truman ordered Gen. Douglas MacArthur to provide military protection for the delivery of arms to the South Koreans and to evacuate American dependents. He instructed the military chiefs "to prepare the necessary orders for the eventual use of American units." On the following day he said he was convinced that "the Republic of Korea needed help at once if it was not to be overrun."

Truman was given CIA reports which indicated that Korea was a repetition, on a larger scale, of the Berlin blockade. The intelligence reports further indicated that North Korean Communists would eventually prove to be a threat to Japan, Formosa, and the American base on Okinawa. It was the first time the "domino theory" was used.

The President, acting on the advice of the CIA, ordered MacArthur to give immediate naval and air support to the South Korean army, without allowing him to order his troops to cross the Thirty-eighth Parallel. (This act of drawing a political rather than a strategic boundary set the precedent in Asia for the use of the same tactic later in the Vietnam campaign.)

MacArthur's zeal and military instinct disposed him to blindness concerning such arbitrary boundaries. His expressed urge to attack China with nuclear weapons eventually led to his unprecedented dismissal by Truman. MacArthur may have had the knowledge and the skill to win the Korean conflict unconditionally, but such a military victory in the light of history did not fit into the long-range war of attrition the cryptocracy supported as a tool of the military-industrial complex, against the Communists.

Domestic politics also served to compound the power of the new cryptocracy, which was then cutting its teeth in Southeast Asia. In 1952, when Dwight D. Eisenhower was elected President of the United States, he appointed John Foster Dulles as Secretary of State, and allowed Foster's brother Allen, who was then the CIA's "deputy director for plans"—the clandestine operations branch of CIA—to take over directorship of the CIA one year later.

According to Townsend Hoopes, who served in both the Truman and Johnson administrations, though the seeds were sown by Truman, it was under the Eisenhower administration that the Cold War was "pervasively institutionalized in the United States." He described the Cold War's chief manifestations as ". . . a strident moralism, a self-righteous and often apocalyptic rhetoric, a determined effort to ring the Soviet Union and China with anti-Communist military alliances, a dramatic proliferation of American overseas military bases, and a rising flow of American military equipment for foreign armies accompanied by

American officers and men to provide training and advice. The posture of imperative, total confrontation," he said, "thus came to full development during the Eisenhower period. By 1960, the United States government was not only positioned and determined to restrain the major Communist powers, but also determined—through an implicit extension of logic and the inertial momentum generated by a large and powerful military–foreign affairs bureaucracy—to control the pace and character of political change everywhere."[9]

In the chill of the Cold War, few Americans remembered that John Foster Dulles had been pro-Nazi before Hitler invaded Poland. No one thought, either, to question the fact that while John Foster Dulles was running the State Department, and therefore dealing with friendly governments, his brother Allen was running the CIA, which he once described as a State Department for dealing with unfriendly governments. No one seemed at all disturbed by the Dulles dynasty, and only a handful of people realized to what extent the Dulles brothers held power in the Eisenhower administration.

Lieutenant Colonel L. Fletcher Prouty (USAF) was the Pentagon's chief briefing officer assigned to the White House during the Eisenhower administration. He worked closely with Allen Dulles in coordinating military support for the various clandestine political operations undertaken by the CIA. He knew the intimate working arrangements of the Dulles brothers and of the cryptocracy they were building.

In his book *The Secret Team,* Colonel Prouty gave a glimpse of how the Dulles brothers "worked" the President: "That evening, before his usual tennis game on his backyard court, Allen Dulles dropped by his brother's secluded house just off Massachusetts Avenue and discussed the operation [which involved an amphibious plane and a Polish pilot to be run under a CIA business cover]. Foster agreed that Eisenhower would go along with it. He walked over to the wall lined with bookshelves and picked up the special white telephone that connected directly with the White House operator. All he said was 'Is the man busy?'

"Foster Dulles opened with, 'Boss, how did you do at Burning Tree today? . . . Well, six holes is better than nothing . . . Yes, I've been talking here with Allen. He has a proposal he wants to clear with you. He feels it is very important, and it will lift the morale of Frank's boys. [Frank Wisner was then Director of Intelligence Clandestine Operations.] You know, since Korea and Guatemala you haven't had them doing much. Will you see him tomorrow morning? Fine. How's Mamie? O.K. boss, I'll speak to Allen . . . 9:30 . . . Thank you—good night!'

"There was not much left to do," Prouty said, "the flight would be scheduled."

A relevant analysis of "the brother act" is provided by David Wise and Thomas Ross. "[The Dulles brothers] embodied the dualism—and indeed the moral dilemma—of United States foreign policy since World War II . . . Foster Dulles reflected the American ethic; the world as we should like it to be. While he took this public position, his brother was free to deal with nastier realities, to overturn governments and to engage in backstage political maneuvers all over the globe with the CIA's almost unlimited funds . . .

"This is not to say that the same two-sided foreign policy would never have evolved had the director of the CIA and the Secretary of State not been brothers. It very likely would have. But the natural friction between the objective and methods of the diplomats and the 'spooks,' between the State Department and the CIA, was to an extent reduced because of the close working relationship of the Dulles brothers. There was consequently less of a check and balance."[10]

John Foster and Allen Dulles had worked together before coming to government. Foster was the star attorney of the international law firm of Sullivan and Cromwell. He persuaded his partners to take Allen in "to soften up customers," which Allen had a great gift for. Eventually, Sullivan and Cromwell sent Allen to Berlin to negotiate private affairs with the German industrial barons before the war. After the war broke out, he was sent to Switzerland with OSS, where, under cover, he used his former business contacts inside Germany to supply information for his many spectacular single-handed intelligence coups against the Axis.

Though Allen Dulles was more gifted as a diplomat than his elder brother Foster, it was Foster who can be considered the mastermind of the Cold War Aberration. Foster played upon the fear of Communists and implemented the world-policing foreign policy of the Pax Americana which eventually led to our involvement in Vietnam. It was his Cold War campaign at home that made citizens tremble in fear of Communist attack and their children crouch under school desks in atomic air-raid drills. It was John Foster Dulles, in the company of men like Senator Joe McCarthy and Richard Nixon, who presented the specter of the Communist menace to the American public. They convinced the nation that the communists were about to unleash a global war and even a direct nuclear attack upon the United States.

During Eisenhower's 1952 campaign for the presidency, he promised to "peacefully bring about freedom for the captive nations." John Foster Dulles later repeated Eisenhower's promise, omitting, however, the word "peacefully."

Lest we judge John Foster Dulles unfairly by the standards of our own time, it must be said that, to his mind, there must have *seemed* to have been good reasons for invoking the Communist threat. As Senator Frank Church's (1976) Senate Committee to Study Governmental Operations said: "The extent to which the urgency of the Communist threat had become shared perception is difficult to appreciate."

More likely, there was another, more insidious reason for the Cold War: the economy. A glance at a historical graph of the American business cycle will show that since the Civil War, economic depressions tend to precede and follow U.S. wars. Dulles' generation came to power in World War II after having suffered the longest and deepest depression in American history. It could be considered natural for them to overreact to the recessions of 1945–46 and 1949–50 by fomenting war—hot or cold—to feed the military-industrial base of the economy. The research and development of death-dealing technology created the need for unprecedented secrecy. The instrument of keeping those secrets was the cryptocracy.

The Cold War strategy proved to be economically successful. Without having to risk a full-scale nuclear war and simply by *arming* the world against communism through weapons marketing, propaganda, and the psychological warfare of the Cold War scheme, the United States achieved a capital goods boom unequaled in modern history. In the most simple terms, arms constituted the bulk of United States exports from World War Two to the present and figured as the single most important industry which maintained the United States trade balance.

The central core of the Dulles brothers' American containment policy grew from the CIA's covert operations and propaganda efforts. The mood of those times is reflected in a top-secret report submitted by the second Hoover Commission to President Eisenhower in September, 1954, and made public by former CIA man Harry Rositzke. The report urged the United States to make its ". . . aggressive covert psychological, political, and paramilitary organization more effective, more unique, and if necessary, more ruthless than that employed by the enemy . . . We are facing an implacable enemy whose avowed objective is world domination by whatever means and at whatever cost. There are no rules in such a game . . . We . . . must learn to subvert, sabotage, and destroy our enemies by more clever, more sophisticated, and more effective methods than those used against us . . ."

According to Rositzke "The next year a National Security Council directive reaffirmed the Executive's commitment to covert operations. It instructed the CIA to continue creating problems for 'International Communism,' to reduce its strength and its control worldwide, and to 'increase the capacity and the will of peoples and nations to resist International Communism. It specifically reaffirmed CIA's authority to develop underground resistance and facilitate covert and guerrilla operations.' "[11]

Although the Cold War is generally said to date from 1948, with the Berlin Blockade and the Greek civil war, John Foster Dulles contributed to its architecture before he came to office in 1953. He epitomized the fearful gestalt of his generation, took hold of the floundering Cold War strategy, and molded it with his personality. He was fond of quoting Alexander Hamilton, who wrote in the *Federalist Papers,* "safety from external danger is the most powerful director of national conduct." Hamilton's statement, when taken at face value, seems quite innocent. But in the context of John Foster Dulles' materialistic and puritan upbringing, it is not difficult to see how he construed it to mean something quite different than Hamilton intended. Hamilton's thoughts gave Dulles the moral rationale to try to motivate national political, industrial, and economic conduct by posing an overwhelming external danger—the threat of a nuclear war initiated by the "international Communist conspiracy."

If, at the end of World War II, the growth of our economy, still the strongest and richest in the world, did depend upon the military-industrial complex for sustenance, then Dulles' Cold War saved the U.S. from certain recession. Without the *threat* of communism, what could the free world have armed against? And if the health of the U.S. economy *continues* to depend on that merger of military and industrial interests, then we may well expect to see efforts at détente collapse and the Cold War resume as the already inflated armaments industry expands.

In his farewell address to the nation in 1960, President Eisenhower issued his famous warning about the military-industrial complex:

"Our military organization today bears little relation to that known of any of my predecessors in peacetime—or, indeed, by fighting men of World War II or Korea. Until the latest of our world conflicts, the United States had no armaments industry. We annually spend on military security alone more than the net income of all United States corporations.

"Now this conjunction of an immense military establishment and a large arms industry is new in the American experience. The total influence—economic, political, even spiritual—is felt in every city, every state house, every office of the federal government. We recognize the imperative need for this development. Yet we must not fail to comprehend its grave implications. In the councils of government, we must guard against the acquisition of unwarranted influence, whether sought or unsought, by the military-industrial complex. The potential for the disastrous rise of misplaced power exists and will persist.

"We must never let the weight of this combination endanger our liberties or democratic processes. We should take nothing for granted."

Eisenhower accurately predicted the course of history.

"The prospect of domination of the nation's scholars by federal employment, project allocations, and the power of money is ever present and is gravely to be regarded.

"Yet, in holding scientific research and discovery in respect, as we should, we must be alert to the equal and opposite danger that public policy could itself become the captive of a scientific-technological elite."

The Cold War *was* World War III—a war waged largely with words. Yet the men who had won World War II with advanced weaponry were less artful in the use of the new psychological warfare. As the Cold War escalated, propaganda was followed by sabotage, assassinations, "paramilitary" covert operations, and limited "police actions."

America had traditionally been a free and open society. But after the war, U.S. leaders held in their hands an awesome technological superiority. While being the love object of government, the new technologies, especially nuclear energy, made the leaders fearful of losing their monopoly. That fear gave rise to the belief that new secret agencies and operations were needed to guard against technological thefts by foreign governments. The Cold War was a "secret" war in more ways than one.

The psychological war, originally waged only against "enemy" countries, was nevertheless created at home. It was used within the United States, against beliefs and free thought, by a secret bureaucracy which is still supported by all the power of the federal government, but which operates outside the chain of government command. It is a secret bureaucracy become paranoid—a cryptocracy mad with world power.

Although the Central Intelligence Agency has long been the convenient symbol for all those who have committed atrocities in the name of national security, the secret bureaucracy, the cryptocracy, does *not* consist solely of the CIA. It is as well a vast network of alliances between *individuals* in a number of government agencies normally thought to be outside the intelligence field.

Since the cryptocracy violates every constitutional principle as a matter of course, and commits every crime known to man in the interest of "national security," it cannot entirely rely on the patriotism of its agents to keep its secrets. Therefore, no single individual is told more than he has a "need to know."

The cryptocracy is a brotherhood reminiscent of the ancient secret societies, with rites of initiation and indoctrination programs to develop in its loyal membership the special understanding of its mysteries. It has secret codes and oaths of silence which reinforce the sense of elitism necessary for the maintenance of its strict loyalty. It is automated, organized in the mode of a computer, where all have access to general knowledge and the most obvious aims and goals, but where the individual is isolated by tribal rituals and compartmentalization.

It is a technocratic organization without ideology, loyal only to an unspoken, expedient, and undefined patriotism. Its members are anonymous. Its funds are secret. Its operational history is secret. Even its goals are secret. It is a degenerative disease of the body politic which has grown rampantly, spreading so invisibly that after nearly four decades its existence is known only to a handful of "decision makers."

The cryptocracy is designed to function like a machine. It also has the feelings of a machine—none at all. But, unlike a machine, it does have ambition. To it, human beings are so much cheap hardware who perform certain set functions which produce certain predetermined results. They are valued relative to cost and efficiency. The cryptocracy is the perfect cybernetic organism—pure logic at the planning level—nothing but automatic response in the field.

If a prospective agent cannot be recruited by an appeal to patriotism, he is bribed. If he cannot be bribed, he is blackmailed. If he refuses to be blackmailed, he is "programmed." If all these fail, he is killed, for it must not be known that he had ever been approached—so important is "national security."

It is sometimes hard to determine whether the cryptocracy is working for or against the interests of the U.S. President, to whom its constituent agencies are supposed to be accountable. Many of its crimes, now a matter of public record, would indicate that it has often worked against, the President. It *has,* we know, worked against the U.S. Constitution and the American people. It has needlessly caused the death of innocent people who were working for it, just as it has tortured and murdered those who have stood in its way. Documented atrocities and criminal blunders have been revealed by congressional investigations, yet no one has been brought to trial.* Little congressional, judicial, or executive action has been taken to limit its power or ferret out its leaders. Figureheads have been changed, but the *organization* and the National Security Act which has bred this cancer remains in essence *un*changed.

The cryptocracy serves big business and spends a good deal of time and energy supplying American corporations with industrial intelligence. These favors, offered only to those companies friendly to the cryptocracy, may be repaid by such things as political campaign contributions to candidates who are either sympathetic to or compromised by the cryptocracy. In the past the cryptocracy has supported both foreign and domestic politicians with such campaign contributions.

The "old boy network" of retired cryptocrats working within major corporations plays an important role in the cryptocracy's international influence. Secret funds are shunted not only from one agency of government to another, but also from agency to corporation and then, under cover of the corporation's legal business activities, throughout the world, wherever expediency dictates.

Through its authorized functions, the cryptocracy controls the United States government. It feeds the executive branch "intelligence reports" which are often slanted and sometimes falsified, so that the policy decisions which result will be those which fit the cryptocracy's game plan.

Like a fifteenth century Machiavellian princedom that has been computerized and automated, the cryptocracy has systematically manipulated the American consciousness. By justifying its existence by citing an exaggerated danger from communism, it has justified its *own* totalitarianism by convincing key politicians that fire must be fought with fire. The practices of the cryptocracy, once officially sanctioned only in operations outside the U.S., have become internalized. Those practices have included spying, stealing, blackmail, and murder, even within the borders of the country it is supposed to protect and defend.

There is nothing hypocritical about the KGB's employ-

* Since the completion of this book, former CIA Director Richard Helms was given a two-year suspended sentence and fined $2,000 for lying to the United States Congress about the CIA's involvement in the overthrow of Chile's Allende government.

ment of totalitarian, police-state tactics. The Soviet equivalent of the CIA, the KGB, is an extension of the Soviet political system, which *is* totalitarian. Neither is there anything hypocritical about the Chinese use of "brainwashing" on American POWs in Korea. The Chinese have "brainwashed" three and a half million of their own people, though generally they used techniques less drastic than starvation, sleep interruption, and isolation. But the U.S. cryptocracy is the ultimate hypocrisy, subversive to its own government's democratic structure. It operates with methods which are not permitted in most democracies and certainly not permitted by the Constitution of the United States.

In war, a successful campaign greatly depends upon the element of surprise. Since the beginning of human disputes, warriors have found it desirable to keep their strengths and weaknesses concealed.

The use of new technology has been both the strength and the surprise which so often has determined the outcome of war. The first elephant to be outfitted with spikes and used in battle was as great a terror to the bow-and-arrow warrior as the atomic bomb was to the Japanese.

The cryptocracy has long known that the only way it can maintain the upper hand in the global power game is to stay in the vanguard of technology. To that end it has employed all the research and development the federal government can buy.

Since World War II the cryptocracy has used electronic technology to manipulate foreign peoples as well as the American people through a campaign of carefully planned misinformation, disinformation, and propaganda. The cryptocracy's existence depends upon such manipulation of public belief. Since it cannot openly argue its cause, it relies upon persuasion and indoctrination to accomplish its goals and win support for its ends.

The existence of the cryptocracy also depends upon absolute secrecy. Without it they are powerless. Thus the cryptocracy's attempt to control information at its source—the human mind.

It was the CIA which instigated and directed the initial research, and with an invisible hand, kept each group of scientists isolated from the other. Each group researching mind control was kept apart from other groups conducting simultaneous interfacing experiments, so that no one except the Agency would be able to put all the pieces of the puzzle together.

Bases for mind-control techniques already existed in scientific literature, but in a fragmented, incomplete, and unassimilated state. The cryptocracy enlisted the aid of scientists who then developed these fragments into usable techniques. These scientists worked independently, each on only one small part of the overall plan. And, by and large, they were ignorant of the intended use of the final product of their research.

Operation Mind Control was not the plan of a mere cult of intelligence; it did not stop at intelligence gathering, but went on to instigate active operations on its own. Those conspiracies against freedom which were revealed by the investigations into Watergate, the intelligence community, and multinational corporations are minor compared to the conspiracy of mind control which has developed in this country. Although the first victims of Operation Mind Control were, perhaps, especially suitable personality types for such use, with the advances being made in the psychosciences all but a few of us may eventually be victimized.

The power of mind control resides in its use as a superior security technique; as such it is almost as foolproof as that employed by the great Pharaoh of Egypt, who, entombed with the slaves who carried him to his final resting place, had those same slaves killed and buried along with him so that all knowledge of access to the tomb would remain secure for centuries. Mind control arranges that "slaves" of the intelligence community—witnesses, couriers, and assassins—are "protected" from their own memories and guilt by amnesia. These "slaves" may be left alive, but the knowledge they possess is buried deep within the tombs of their own minds by techniques which can keep the truth hidden even from those who have witnessed it. It is the ultimate debriefing, the final security measure short of assassination.

The conspiracy of mind control veils the secret of all secrets. It hides the cabal which possesses its power, so that, even if the CIA and the other intelligence agencies were closed down tomorrow, the cryptocracy would continue to function, for as with the Mafia, "once you are a member, you're a member for life." The power of mind control, and ultimately of the cryptocracy that uses it, resides with those who have culled the fruits of psychoscience since the late 1930s; they now possess the mature body of knowledge upon which the coercive art is built.

To review the labyrinth of events: Out of the natural fear of technology grew an unnatural reliance on secrecy. Secrecy led to covert control and produced a well-organized institution of national security. Institutionalized secrecy directed covert research and produced Operation Mind Control, the ultimate technology of secrecy and control.

Chapter Ten

BRAVE NEW WORLD IN A SKINNER BOX

The cryptocracy's search for reliable mind-control methods was one of the most far-reaching secret projects ever undertaken. In addition to research and development in drugs and hypnosis, CIA funds and cryptocracy guidance gave impetus to a number of behavior modification projects carried out in federal prisons and mental institutions. Most of the projects were arranged secretly so that recipients of the funds would have no way of knowing that the CIA was backing the research.

Even if they *had* known of the CIA's involvement, their interest in behavior modification probably would not have been dampened. Previously called conditioned reflex therapy behavior modification, in the sixties and seventies, was becoming the most popular tool of psycho-science since Sigmund Freud asked his first patient to lie down on the couch.

Behavior modification is based on conditioning, but "conditioning" is a big word for a simple form of learning in which a reaction is evoked by an outside action. The reaction is called a response; the outside action is called a stimulus.

In 1927 Pavlov won the Nobel Prize for his discovery of a method of making dogs salivate at the ringing of a bell. Salivating dogs were not much good to anyone, and it was not for making dogs drool that Pavlov was so honored. He was honored with the world's most prestigious award for making dogs drool *on cue*. He called his process "conditioning." The dogs' involuntary response, he called a "reflex." Pavlov's discoveries provided the breakthrough which behavioral science needed to begin to control the human mind.

Pavlov had begun in 1906 by seeking a simple model of the activity of the brain. He decided that the salivary reflex in dogs could be just such a model, so he raided the dog pound and cut holes in the animals' cheeks to implant measuring devices for the flow of saliva.

By regularly ringing a bell just before feeding the dogs, he found that the stimulus—the sound of the bell—intrinsically unrelated to food, began to evoke the salivation that had initially been observed only when the dogs were eating. His patient studies revealed that the quality, rate, and frequency of salivation changed depending upon the quality, rate, and frequency of the stimuli.

Pavlov's experiments with dogs have been repeated numerous times by different scientists with the same results. Science now agrees that when a hungry dog is given a piece of meat immediately after a bell rings, and when this procedure is repeated a number of times the bell alone will produce the flow of saliva almost as if the bell and not the meat were activating the glands. When the bell rings, not only will a properly conditioned dog salivate but his ears will stand up, he'll turn toward the food source, and even make anticipatory chewing movements. Conditioned reflexes in dogs, however, are a long way from the conditioning of *volitional* thinking in humans.

But Pavlov established the groundwork by which anyone's emotional stability (Pavlov called it "perpetual equalibration") and sanity could be reliably balanced or *unbalanced.* To that end the Soviets, and later the People's Republic of China, employed Pavlov's new science for the creation of the totalitarian state.

While the general public in the West may continue to associate behavior modification with Pavlov's conditioning of dogs, the science is actually an ancient one In its modern form it has its roots in the works of Descartes who, in 1664, put forward the idea that every activity of an organism is the reaction to an external stimulus. Experimental studies to test Descartes' idea did not begin until several centuries later. Then, simultaneously experimentation began in a number of different countries.

At the same time Pavlov was experimenting with dogs

in Russia, John B. Watson was experimenting with humans in the United States. Watson was the founder of the behaviorist school psychology in the 1920s. His most notorious accomplishment was his series of experiments on an eleven-month-old infant known to history as Little Albert.

Watson showed Little Albert a white rat and the child reacted naturally and tried to pet and cuddle the animal. After Albert had established a playful rapport with the rat, Watson began to aversely condition the lad. Each time the rat would come into Albert's view, Watson would beat the floor with a steel bar and produce a deafening sound. Quite naturally, whenever Albert heard the sound he would jump with fright. Eventually Albert associated the loud sound with the white rat and became frightened of it. Every time the rat came into his view he would begin to cry.

Albert became so aversely conditioned to the rat that he would exhibit fear whenever any small animal came into his view. He became so conditioned that he reacted with equal fear to rabbits, dogs, and a sealskin coat—in short, to anything with fur.

Quite proudly Dr. Watson exclaimed, "Give me the baby, and I'll make it climb and use its hands in constructing buildings of stone or wood . . . I'll make it a thief, a gunman or a dope fiend. The possibilities of shaping in any direction are almost endless. Even gross differences in anatomical structure limits are far less than you may think . . . Make him a deaf mute, and I will still build you a Helen Keller . . . Men are built, not born."[11]

Watson saw things, as Pavlov did, in physical and chemical terms. He was not interested in anything beyond overt and observable behavior. And Watson was only the first in a long line of American psycho-scientists who were to take the mechanistic path to control of the mind.

Pavlov and Watson's classical conditioning did not, however, go far in producing a reliable science of mind-control. In the late thirties Harvard psychologist Burrhus Frederick Skinner discovered new principles of conditioning which allowed more complete control.

Skinner came up with what he called *operant conditioning*. It was based on the idea that reinforcement (the repetition of either a positive or a negative response to an action) was at the root of all learned behavior. The distinction between *classical* and *operant* conditioning was made only because different techniques were used to elicit the responses. In essence, the effects of either kind of conditioning were the same.

The three most common methods of modern behavior therapy are operant conditioning, aversion therapy, and desensitization.

Operant conditioning is the reinforcement of certain behavior by reward (usually food), often accompanied by simultaneous sound or light stimulation. Reinforcement is contingent upon the occurrence of the response, and the reinforcing mechanisms are often built into the environment. When rats are used as subjects, the device to be operated is a bar which, when depressed, delivers the reward of food or water. In this situation the behavior which is reinforced is the pressing of the bar. It makes no difference how the bar is pressed, whether the rat presses the bar with its paw, nose, or tail. Once the bar is pressed, the operation has been performed and the animal is rewarded. The dependent variable in operant conditioning is the response rate—the number of times the bar is pressed. Response rate, or the frequency of the response, is an important factor in judging the success of the operant conditioning.

Aversion therapy is a technique in which an undesirable response is inhibited by a painful or unpleasant reinforcement such as electric shock, noxious odors, or any technique which produces fear and avoidance. It is an ancient form of counter-conditioning, or punishment, which has been widely used in the treatment of homosexuality, stuttering, and alcoholism.

In desensitization the subject is first trained to relax beyond his normal state. He is then presented with images which evoke mild anxiety. At first the images are very mild, and they are repeated until the subject shows no anxiety. Then a stronger image is introduced and the process is repeated. Finally the subject becomes desensitized to even the strongest image. Desensitization has been used to relieve people of phobic fears and anxieties.

Skinner began his experiments by building a number of boxes in which pigeons were required to run mazes and press levers to receive the rewards of birdseed. By manipulating the way the reward was given, Skinner found that he could control the rate and the style of the lever pressing.

Eventually Skinner was able to get pigeons to bob and

weave in prescribed ways. He was even able to get birds to distinguish colors by having them peck only at levers of specific colors for food. He soon learned to obtain just about any kind of behavior he desired from a number of different animals.

Skinner concluded that every action is determined by the environment and that all behavior is "shaped and maintained by its consequences." The behaviorists' mechanistic view of man was summed up by Skinner when he said, "If by 'machine' you simply mean any system which behaves in an orderly way, then man and all other animals are machines."

Skinner's subsequent research, however, showed that behavior which is supported by continuous rewards stops when the rewards are withheld. Further experimentation showed that by shifting from continuous to intermittent rewards, the behavior could be kept going even though the rewards became less frequent. This discovery made behaviorism a practical science, for now it could explain how behavior was maintained in the real world.

With unshakable faith in his own science, Dr. Skinner built a large box with a glass window on one side. It was a soundproof cage, much like the ones he'd used in experiments with pigeons and monkeys. But this box was for children, and into it Skinner put his own child.

This "Skinner box" was about as large as a spacious crib. The temperature of the box was carefully controlled, and Skinner testified proudly that "crying and fussing could always be stopped by slightly lowering the temperature." With the soundproof box, Skinner was "never concerned lest the doorbell, telephone, piano, or children at play wake the baby . . ." And, he added, "soundproofing also protects the family from the baby."[2]

Apparently Skinner's scheme to produce "socialized" children was not so successful. In the opinion of the kindergarten teacher of Skinner's youngest daughter, who had received the "benefits" of spending her early childhood in her daddy's box, she was not an obedient automaton, but a rather independent and even rebellious child.[3] Somehow Skinner's programming of his offspring must have failed in his own terms, for it would appear from his writings that Skinner's ideas are quite in line with the dreams of the cryptocrats who would seek to control us all.

In his popular work *Beyond Freedom and Dignity,* Skinner wrote: "The problem is to free men, not from control, but from certain kinds of control, and it can be solved only if our analysis takes all consequences into account. How people feel about control . . . does not lead to useful distinctions."

Skinner is not only concerned with controlling individuals, he desires to build a controlled society, ruled from crib to coffin by behavior modification. "The intentional design of a culture and the control of human behavior it implies are essential if the human species is to continue to develop," he said.

Today B. F. Skinner is the center of a personality cult. He is the guru and founder of the modern psycho-philosophy which holds that it is morally and ethically permissible to change the behavior of others as well as to modify others' belief. About belief Skinner writes, "People must believe that what they are doing has some chance of obtaining what they want or avoiding something to which they are averse. But the chances are in the contingencies. The relation of beliefs to other conditions, such as wants and needs, can be easily stated: to say that desires enter into the causation of beliefs is simply to say that the probability of behavior with which a belief is associated depends not only upon reinforcement but upon a state of deprivation or aversive stimulation."[4]

Aversion stimulation was the process upon which the Cold War faith was built. The Cold War faith, in turn, loosed the cryptocracy upon the world to murder, maim, or rape the minds of any who posed a real threat to its goals of "defending the free world from communism."

In the words of Lewis Andrews and Marvin Karlins, "The world is, in a sense, one large 'Skinner box' . . ."[5] And if this is not already true, it soon may be, because there are behaviorists at work in practically every federal and state institution, as well as in the private sector.

Using federal and state institutions for testing purposes provided many benefits to the cryptocracy. They functioned as recruitment centers, where selected criminals were released to the custody of career spooks who could apply their skills in undercover work. Prisons were also valuable testing grounds.

Philip Hilts, describing the attitude prevalent in both the

cryptocracy and prison bureaucracies, wrote: "There are three possibilities for criminals. The first is deterrent: Keep them from doing it again. The second is punishment: Knock the hell out of the bastards; they deserve it. The third is treatment: They're defective; let's fix them."[6] Behaviorists who work the prison circuit hold that the last is the only humane way of reducing recidivism. Perhaps. But one also begins to sense in such theorizing a preview of what is to come for the whole society.

"These behavioral engineers are growing mightily in numbers and influence, nourished by a law-and-order administration that though riddled by corruption itself, can still deliver the material goods," wrote David Rorvich. "They are not out to change the world but to make man adjust to it; they seek results, not understanding. A thick-skinned lot they are, not loath to admit the crudity of some of their techniques, claiming results that would take the more elegant psychotherapies and social reforms years to attain . . . What the world needs now in the service of 'curing' its deviant and miserable masses, proclaim the new psychotechnologists, is not more prison reform, urban renewal, and nude group gropes but a few well-placed corrective kilovolts in the collective brain."[7]

The California Medical Facility at Vacaville was the center of a number of behavioral research projects funded by various agencies, including the Veterans Administration, HEW, the Bureau of Prisons, private drug companies, and others. Many of these agencies were fronting for the CIA.

In 1973, there was a "flap" in the press over the testing of drugs by these agencies under the guise of behavior modification. It was revealed that tranquilizers, depressants, sedatives, narcotic antagonists, and hypnotics were being tested in the hospitals and prisons (see Appendix B).

Dr. Leo E. Hollister, a medical investigator for the Veterans Administration, defended the practice: "The exemplary Medical Facility at Vacaville is one of the few places in the country where such [drug] studies are possible . . . at a time when the demands for such facilities are increasing, in response to an urgent public health problem, it would be sad to see them denied to responsible and highly reputable clinical investigators."[8]

It is debatable whether you can characterize the scientists who participated in all the projects as "responsible and highly reputable." It appears from the evidence that some may rather have been, as Philip Hilts playfully suggests, ". . . hunchbacked wart-infested evil scientists . . ."[10]

Perhaps the greatest danger to freedom of thought and behavior is posed by the breed of psycho-scientists who call themselves "behaviorists." While most psychologists once concerned themselves with the study of human thought and the rich life of the mind, the behaviorists believe that man's problems can best be understood by studying his actions. What a man thinks, sees, feels, wants and knows—everything that a man *is*, behaviorists believe, can be most easily understood in terms of what he *does*.

Behaviorism would appear to be a predictable expression of materialistic cultures, East and West, which value externals above all else. You will seldom hear a behaviorist speak of "will" or even "mind." These are considered unscientific, subjective terms. Instead, the behaviorists speak only of "reflexes" which are reinforced by conditioning from the environment. They look forward to the day when they can conclusively prove that conditioning begins at the moment of conception, and that reflexes are ultimately the very stuff of what was once called the soul! The science of behaviorism portrays the human being as mechanistic protoplasm. The most *avant-garde* behaviorists have developed an unholy alliance with biochemists who together are exploring genetics, hoping to find the key for breeding selected behavioral characteristics. Certainly a person born with all his limbs will behave differently from a person who is born with genetic damage and without limbs. But beyond that, what some behaviorists are looking for is a genetic factor which controls anger, docility, and other personality tendencies. While many new scientific insights have come from behaviorism, so have many new dangers—especially to the freedom of choice.

"The day has come," said Professor James V. McConnel, head of the Department of Mental Health Research at the University of Michigan, "when we can combine sensory deprivation with the use of drugs, hypnosis, and the astute manipulation of reward and punishment to gain almost absolute control over an individual's behavior." Dr. McConnel expressed the sentiments of behavior modifiers who, like cryptocrats, believe that mankind's salvation resides in the control of individual behavior in an engineered society. But engineered by whom?

". . . We want to reshape our society drastically," McConnel said, "so that all of us will be trained from birth to want to do what society wants us to do. Today's behavioral psychologists are the architects and engineers who are shaping the Brave New World of Tomorrow."[10]

In the practical American way—stripped for action—the psychology profession appears to be turning away from psychotherapy and is becoming dependent upon the time- and labor-saving practical mechanics of behavior modification depending upon principles developed largely through laboratory experimentation. Voluntary as well as involuntary actions can be conditioned. Once a reflex is trained into a subject, he becomes an automaton, responding to the artificial stimulus to which he has been programmed.

When light shines into the pupil of the eye, it contracts, and when the light is removed, it dilates. This pupillary reflex is involuntary; the individual has no conscious control over it, but it can be conditioned.

C. V. Hudgins demonstrated this by conditioning the pupil to a bell using a light as the unconditioned stimulus. He would turn on the light, which shone directly into the subject's eyes at the same instant he rang a bell. The light made the pupil contract every time just as meat made Pavlov's dog drool.

Hudgins then taught his subjects to use their own hands to operate the bell and light mechanisms. Then he would say "contract" and the subject would press the switch. When he said "relax" the subject would relax and turn off both bell and light. After only a few hours' training, Hudgins found that he could do away with the bell, the hand switch, and the light. He had only to say the word "contract," and the pupil would contract.

A modern apologist of conditioning, Andrew Salter, asserts that hypnosis in essence is the same as conditioning. Salter said that after he had conditioned the reader of his book to contract his pupil, as Hudgins had done, he would take him to an ophthalmologist.

"Doctor," Salter would declare, "here is a splendid hypnotic subject. I control this person so thoroughly that at my command his pupil will contract, and perceptibly."

"Come now," the doctor would say, "you know very well that pupillary contraction is involuntary. You need light for that."

Salter would then tell his conditioned reader "contract," and the reader's pupil would obey every time, and the doctor would be perplexed.

"How do you like hypnotism?" Salter would ask the doctor.

"It's amazing," he would answer, but his interest would diminish after Salter explained how, paralleling Pavlov and Hudgins, the reader's pupil had been conditioned. "Well," he would say, "come back next time when you have some real hypnotism."

"Our doctor is wrong," Salter said. "There, in the conditioned reflex, he had seen the essence of hypnosis. (And parenthetically, when we see that the essence of hypnotism is conditioning—or quite loosely, that the essence of the 'unconscious mind' is conditioning—we are in a strategic position to develop a sound understanding of the deepest wellsprings of human behavior)."[11]

The cryptocracy, having discovered the wonders of hypnosis, drugs, behavior modification, and even more revolutionary electrical and sonic manipulations of the brain, learned how to reliably control individual behavior. Whether or not the Constitution protects the individual's free thought and speech, and whether one regards mind control as bondage or a necessary tool for social engineering, one must recognize that the power to control the mind exists—and is being used.

Did Philip Hilts know how close he'd come when he offered his chilling description of the crypto-behaviorists? He wrote: "Suppose a dozen controllers with that incurable twitch for power are meeting, now, in some secret mountain cabin. There, amid piles of rat-behavior charts, rows of cumulative recorders, and reams of human-foibles data, they are designing an environment. They are creating blueprints for a system that would produce the most terrible, violent, and antisocial people possible.'"[12]

Chapter Eleven
A SCHOOL FOR ASSASSINS

The cryptocracy recruited their assassins from among people who had already demonstrated a violent nature, people who had few reservations about taking human life. No homicidal maniacs were recruited because they could not be controlled. The cryptocracy needed killers who would not murder on impulse, but only upon command.

Once selected, the assassin candidates were turned over to the military, where, under the guise of "combat readiness" training, they underwent a complete program of conditioning. Graduates of the program would forever after act with ruthless efficiency. They would eliminate local political leaders in a foreign country, or undertake "search and destroy" missions in violation of national and international laws. They would be given the cover that would allow them to enter the Foreign Service; or they would pose as embassy marine guards.

In July, 1975, the *Sunday Times* in London quoted a U.S. Navy psychologist who admitted that U.S. Naval Intelligence had taken convicted murderers from military prisons, conditioned them as political assassins, and then placed them in American embassies around the world. This admission came shortly after the Senate Intelligence Committee had scolded the CIA for plotting a number of political assassinations around the world. From the congressional reports, however, one got the feeling that the cryptocracy was being chastised not for the assassinations it had successfully accomplished, but for those which it had attempted, but failed. The attempts on the life of Fidel Castro drew the greatest notice from the congressional committees and the press.

According to the *Sunday Times* story, naval psychologist Lt. Comdr. Thomas Narut was assigned to the U.S. Regional Medical Center at Naples, Italy. When he first made public the navy's part in programming assassins, he was attending a NATO conference in Oslo on "Dimensions of Stress and Anxiety." In attendance at that conference were 120 psychologists of all descriptions and from many countries. Many of them were involved in research on how to improve man's ability to cope with stress, but none of them felt compelled, as Narut did, to discuss their work so fully or so frankly.

The stated objective of the conference was to exchange information on how soldiers and people in difficult jobs could cope with stress. Dr. Narut's talk was on "The Use of a Symbolic Model and Verbal Intervention in Inducing and Reducing Stress." His speech began with a plug for the navy. He knew, he said, that many of the scientists present had often encountered problems in their purely scientific research because of the military's inclination to research that would yield quick and useful results. He sympathized with those who had trouble getting subjects, funds, or both, out of the military for their purely scientific research. But things were different *in the navy* he said.

In the navy, Narut bragged, there were plenty of captive personnel who could be used as guinea pigs. In the navy there was a computerized record of each man's background and psychological profile, so that a quick selection of men with suitable psychological inclinations for experiments could be made. Navy psychologists not only had access to computerized records, but also to psychological tests and background data on a large number of people. In the navy, Narut said, funds were plentiful, and there were no problems with transporting subjects for study to nearly any place in the world. Narut stated proudly that the U.S. Navy provided scientists with the most advanced research facilities in the world.

A Canadian psychologist at the conference later remarked, "Narut's message was loud and clear—'Join the navy and study the world.'"

In his brief discourse, Dr. Narut did no more than hint at the work he had been doing in teaching "combat readiness units" to cope with the stress of killing. Later, however, during private questioning with a small group of listeners (reporter Peter Watson of the *Sunday Times,* a former psychologist, among them), Narut unfolded the amazing story of the navy's programming of assassins on an assembly-line basis.

In his mid-thirties, Dr. Narut had just completed his doctoral dissertation on the question of whether certain films provoke anxiety, and whether forcing a man to do irrelevant tasks while watching violent films would help him cope with the anxiety they produced.

When pressed by Watson to explain the details of this kind of conditioning, Narut said that he had worked with "combat readiness units" which included men being programmed for commando-type operations and for undercover placement at U.S. embassies. These, Narut said, were "hit men and assassins" (Narut's words) made ready to kill in selected countries should the need arise. Dr. Alfred Zitani, an American delegate to the conference, was very surprised by Narut's disclosure. "Do you think Dr. Narut realizes what he has just said?" Zitani asked. "That kind of information must be classified."

The conditioning of Narut's assassins was accomplished by audio-visual desensitization, a standard behavior modification process. These men were "desensitized" to mayhem by being shown films of people being killed or injured in a number of different ways. At first the films would show only mild forms of bloodshed. As the men became acclimated to the scenes of carnage, they would see progressively more violent scenes. The assassin candidates, Narut explained, would eventually be able to dissociate any feelings they might have from even the goriest scenes they viewed.

Narut said that of course U.S. naval psychologists would have first selected the candidates for training by their psychological makeup. Those selected for assassination assignments were often from submarine crews and paratroops. Others were convicted murderers from military prisons who had already shown a proclivity for violence.

Still others were men who had been given awards for valor. World War II Medal of Honor winner Audie Murphy was a subject of extensive research.

The best killers, according to Narut, were men whom

psychologists would classify as "passive-aggressive" personalities. These were people with strong drives that were usually kept under tight control. Such types were usually calm, but from time to time would exhibit outbursts of temper during which they could literally kill without remorse. Narut said that through psychological testing, he and his colleagues were looking for more such men, for further conditioning.

Among the tests used by the navy to determine violent natures was the Minnesota Multiphasic Personality Inventory, which is used widely by educators and businessmen to determine psychological qualities of students and employees. The tests consist of hundreds of questions designed to measure such personality traits as hostility, depression, and psychopathy.

According to Narut, the men selected by the tests, or by evidence of past violence, were taken for programming to the navy's neuropsychiatric laboratory in San Diego, California, or to the Naples medical center which employed Dr. Narut.

Audio-visual desensitization was the major technique used in programming the assassins. Psychological indoctrination completed the programming by instilling the desired prejudicial attitudes.

The audio-visual desensitization began with the subject strapped into a chair with his head clamped so that he could not look away from the screen. A special mechanism prevented the subject's eyelids from closing.

The candidate was then shown a film of an African youth being crudely circumcised by fellow members of his tribe. The youth was circumcised with a blunt knife, painfully and without anesthetic. This well-known film is used widely in psychological experiments to create stress. Afterwards the candidate was asked about details of what he had seen. He was asked, for example, to describe the color of the belt on the doctor's trousers, or the motif on the handle of the knife that cut off the foreskin.

The next film showed a man in a sawmill, where planks were sliced from huge logs. In the operation of the saw the man slipped and cut off his fingers.

As the films progressed in gruesomeness, the reactions of the candidate were measured by sensing devices. Heartbeat, breathing rate, and brain waves were recorded, very much as on a polygraph. If the physiological responses, which might have been great in the beginning, slowed down and resumed normal patterns as the more bloodthirsty scenes were viewed, the candidates were judged to have completed this stage of conditioning.

The last phase of conditioning, Narut said, was to indoctrinate the candidates to think of their potential enemies as inferior forms of life. By this stage, the candidates would have already been selected for assignment to particular countries. They would be shown films and given lectures which portrayed the customs and cultural habits of the foreign countries in a biased fashion. The people of those countries would be portrayed as enemies of the United States and were always spoken of in demeaning terms. They were often presented as if they were "less than human." Their customs were ridiculed, and local leaders were presented as evil demagogues, even if they were legitimate political figures.

According to Dr. Narut it took only a few weeks to indoctrinate susceptible candidates by this process. Those who were not susceptible to the conditioning were dropped earlier in the program and returned to other assignments. Narut admitted that he did not have the necessary "need to know" as to where all the programmed men were sent, although at one point in his conversation with Peter Watson, Narut specified that programmed assassins have been installed in the Athens embassy. He said that his busiest time was when a large group of men went through such training towards the end of 1973, at the time of the Yom Kippur War.

After the Oslo conference interview, Watson returned to London to file his story. Writing up the details, he found a few points which needed clarification but he could not reach Narut either at his home or in his laboratory in Naples. Watson then asked the U.S. embassy in London to comment on the information Narut had volunteered. The embassy passed the buck to the U.S. Navy.

Within a few days the Pentagon issued a categorical denial that the U.S. Navy had ever "engaged in psychological training or other types of training of personnel as assassins. "They also denied that any such training had ever taken place either in San Diego or in Naples. They said they too had been unable to contact Lieutenant Commander Narut, but they did confirm that he was on the staff of the U.S. Regional Medical Center in Naples as a psychologist. But Dr. Zitani later offered to testify about what Narut had told him to "appropriate authorities." Watson was also approached later by a psychologist in Los Angeles who said he had seen the Pentagon denials so thought Watson would like to know that he had lent the San Diego psychologists a copy of his film on circumcision which was used in the desensitization conditioning.

A few days later Narut was located. He flew to London to discuss the matter ostensibly with Watson's paper, the *Sunday Times,* but instead he held a press conference saying only that he had been talking in "theoretical and not practical terms." He then flew back to the Naples base.

After his return to Naples, U.S. naval headquarters in London offered the official explanation for Narut's statement: Narut had "personal problems." A few days later Watson was able to contact Narut at the U.S. hospital in Naples, but he refused to elaborate on his disclosure.

During the Oslo conference interview, Narut had said several times that what he was saying about the assassins was "coming out anyway." He was referring to the congressional disclosures about CIA assassination plots. But the fact that the navy had been operating along lines similar to the CIA was not known to the public nor has it subsequently been admitted. The details of the story that Lieutenant Commander Narut related have been strongly and categorically denied in all subsequent queries of the navy.

It came as no surprise to many that the navy had been interested in psychological research to help its men cope with "stress." Several years before, one of the organizers of the Oslo conference, Dr. Irwin Sarason, had been approached by the navy to work on projects similar to Narut's. At the time, the navy had said nothing to him about programming assassins; it said it wanted him to adapt his work for applications to "spies."

In response to that request, Sarason devised a film which showed how successful students asked questions in school. The film was shown to a group of juvenile delinquents for a period of time until they, too, learned how to pose the right questions. As a result, over the next two years they did much better in their studies and got in trouble less. The control group who had *not* seen the films did just as poorly in school as they'd always done and were just as delinquent.

Since his "symbolic modeling" study had been successful, Sarason wanted to continue his research and applied to the Office of Naval Research for more funding. A few weeks after his application was received, Sarason was called by a navy official who asked him if he would object to having his work classified. Sarason wondered why, and the navy official told him his research would be most valuable to the navy's neuropsychiatric laboratory in California, as spies were being trained there to resist interrogation. The naval official said that if Sarason would allow his work to be classified, he'd get all the funds he needed.

But Sarason was interested in the peaceful scientific nature of his work, not its military applications, so he refused to have the project classified. His goal was the exception rather than the rule.

The federal government supports most scientific research in the United States. Enough psychologists and other social scientists haven't asked questions about what their research is to be used for; their main objective has been to get the grant, so they could support themselves and their scientific curiosity. Since too many of them have been politically disinterested or naive, they have been easy prey for the cryptocracy. Lieutenant Commander Narut was therefore but one in a long line of psychologists being employed for psychological warfare and illegal clandestine operations.

Another such operation was the training of security officers at the Washington-based International Police Academy by psychologists and sociologists. The officers were supposedly being taught interrogation techniques for Third World countries; actually it was a highly sensitive clandestine operation organized for the training of U.S. spies. Congress closed the Academy on January 1, 1974, after its real purpose was disclosed to the press.

Another, uncovered in the late 1960s, was "Project CAMELOT," purportedly a sociopolitical analysis of Chile, but actually designed to keep Chile free of Communist leaders by discrediting them. Project CAMELOT played an important role in the overthrow of Salvador Allende and his democratically elected leftist government.

In 1975 Congress questioned the navy about its development of a questionnaire to survey attitudes toward death.

Congressmen had learned that psychologists were eagerly working on such a questionnaire, known as the "Value of Life" study, that would allow the navy to assess a recruit's willingness and ability to kill from the very first day he entered the service.

In still another government-funded experiment, psychologists working for the Human Resources Research Organization in Alexandria, Virginia, had conducted a brutal series of "stress-training" experiments in the early 1960s.

In one experiment army "volunteers" were taken on an airplane flight. Suddenly, the airplane's engines failed and the plane was forced to land abruptly on a rough airstrip. The soldiers were later tested to see if this incident had caused a fear of flying. In another experiment soldiers were taken out and "lost" in a forest. Suddenly, a huge forest fire engulfed them, so that the men found themselves "off course" and surrounded by fire. These men were tested to see if that experience had given them a fear of fire.

In yet another experiment, soldiers were allowed to "stray" into an artillery target area. Shells were exploding all around them, and they had to get out of the area by keeping cool and following orders. Since artillery shells fired from a distance of twenty-five miles away are hard to control, the explosions were created by detonating underground charges triggered by remote control from a lookout point. After the realistic shelling was over the men were tested to see if they suffered any discernible "shell shock."

During all these experiments the men were under visual observation. In some, they also wore telemetry devices which allowed scientists to measure their pulse rate, respiration, and other vital signs to determine the level of stress they were experiencing at the time they were exposed to the dangers.

As this battery of experiments became known to the outside world, public opinion and congressional pressure brought a stop to them. The military was not deterred, however, from other kinds of cruel and dangerous experimentation; it continued its stress research in spite of the bad publicity.

While military "stress testing" may have developed useful insights into the psychology of warriors, its primary goal, as Lieutenant Commander Narut pointed out, was the programming of assassins. These experiments were most useful in programming those men who were already inclined to kill. Hypnosis was *still* the only effective tool for motivating those who were not inclined to kill, then for erasing the memory of their crimes or eliciting false confessions.

Alarmed by evidence found in the assassinations of John and Robert Kennedy and Martin Luther King, Dr. Joseph L. Bernd of the Virginia Polytechnic Institute in 1968 questioned leading authorities on hypnosis about the possible use of hypnosis to motivate assassins.

Bernd wanted to know if political influences could be induced by hypnosis; could people be hypno-programmed to operate unconsciously and take what seemed to be independent action? Could people be influenced to commit political assassination as a consequence of hypnotic influence?

In his query Bernd asked authorities to assume that a skilled hypnotist found a subject who was both a good hypnotic subject and highly capable in the use of weapons. They were to assume that the subject also had a deep hatred for some political personality prominent in the news. Bernd's first question to the authorities was: "Could the hypnotist use hypnotic suggestion to persuade the weapons expert to kill the hated political personality at a time and under conditions suggested by the hypnotist?"

His second question was: "Could the hypnotic suggestion of this action be achieved in a way which could leave the subject assassin unconscious of and unable to recall to consciousness the fact that his violent act was made as a consequence of hypnotic suggestion?"

The authorities who responded to Bernd's questions stated that they did think it possible to induce a subject to kill. One expert said, ". . . I would say that a highly skilled hypnotist, working with a highly susceptible subject, could possibly persuade the subject to kill another human . . ." Another expert went further, saying that it was possible through posthypnotic suggestion to make a subject unable to recall his act. "There could be a conspiracy," one expert wrote, "but a conspiracy of which the principal was unaware."

It may well be that Bernd hit a nerve in the cryptocracy. His report, "Assassination and Hypnosis: Political Influence or Conspiracy," was never published.

But despite all the efforts of the cryptocracy, slowly, the

secrets of mind control began to emerge. Soon there surfaced other evidence that there were indeed such things as programmed assassins. One such assassin made bold headlines on the front page of a newspaper in the Philippines.

Chapter Twelve
THE FOUR FACES OF A ZOMBIE

On March 2, 1967, twenty-four-year-old Luis Angel Castillo was arrested by the Philippine National Bureau of Investigation (NBI) on suspicion of conspiring to assassinate President Ferdinand Marcos in Manila. In a series of interrogation sessions, the NBI and Philippine Army investigators gave him truth serum (at his request) and put him under hypnosis. During one of these sessions, Castillo revealed that he had been involved in an assassination four years earlier.

Castillo told the NBI, both under hypnosis and truth serum and also in a normal state, that he had been hypno-programmed to kill a man riding in an open car. Although Castillo did not know the identity of his target, the scene of his supposed "hit" was in Dallas, Texas. The date was November 22, 1963.

After revealing this information, Castillo asked for political asylum in Manila. He was quoted in the *Manila Times* as saying, "I am afraid to go anywhere anyway. I am as good as dead now."

"I don't know how I got into Dallas and how I got out," Castillo told reporters, "but I am sure I did not carry a gun."

The *Manila Times* story reported that Castillo had arrived in Manila carrying a Philippine passport which identified him as Antonio Reyes Eloriaga, a returning resident who had been expelled from America for overstaying his visa and stealing a car. While in the U.S. Castillo had traveled under the aliases Angelo Rodriguiz, Razo Hernandez,

Mario Rodriguez, Ignacio Gonzales Gradjeda, and Antonio Eloriaga.

Castillo told investigators that a woman had given him his initial instructions in Dallas. According to Castillo, she was just one of many individuals who worked on him to place him in a deep hypnotic trance for the Kennedy job. Castillo said that he had been a private in the Cuban militia, the Segunda Organizacion Defensiva in Santiago, Cuba, when he was initially chosen for training in espionage work. He was subsequently trained by the Defensiva at a camp located about fifteen miles from the Bay of Pigs. Among the members of the training cadre, Castillo said, were a communications expert, along with some other Cubans and a handful of Americans.

Three years later, on October 2, 1966, Castillo was arrested in New Mexico and charged with driving without a proper auto registration. His arrest was made under the Eloriaga identity. Castillo was brought before New Mexico Justice of the Peace Elmer Bassett and sentenced to four days in jail. "The reason I gave him a jail sentence," Bassett said, "was, I figured when a fellow has a hard time remembering what his name is, there's something wrong with him." After serving his sentence Castillo was turned over to U.S. immigration authorities because he had no proof of U.S. citizenship.

Bassett reported that "Castillo said he was from Madison, Wisconsin, but was born in the Philippines. He couldn't show that he *was* from the Philippines or that he *wasn't*."

Bassett also revealed that someone had called him a few hours after Castillo had appeared before him and asked that the man be released. "I don't know who it was," Bassett said, "I just told them I couldn't do that."

According to the NBI, Castillo had Antonio Eloriaga's Philippine passport on his person when he was arrested in Manila. Based on information provided by the intelligence service of the Philippine armed forces, the NBI had been searching for him since February. They had evidence that Castillo, in the guise of Eloriaga, had made contact with a guerrilla group that was constantly plotting to assassinate Marcos and overthrow the Philippine government.

The NBI set to work grilling their captured suspect. They knew something of his criminal past. They knew, for example, that he had been arrested in 1962 for carrying a concealed weapon; they also knew that two years later he had been sentenced to a state reformatory in Bordentown, New Jersey, for larceny. But nothing prepared them for the shocking story implicating him in the events of Dallas.

They asked Castillo to submit to a lie detector test and were surprised when he said that he preferred truth serum. Suspicious of both his strange story and his behavior, NBI officials called in a psychiatrist to examine him. But even after the psychiatrist judged Castillo normal, the NBI investigators still refused to take Castillo's bizarre and contradictory story at face value.

Later, reporters connected with the *Manila Times* were equally dumbfounded by Castillo's strange behavior.

One reporter described him as a "now-talkative, now-reticent cloak-and-dagger man." He clammed up when he was asked whether he was in the Philippines to help implement an assassination plot against President Marcos. In his truth serum statement, he claimed he had worked with a "cell of Reds" to end someone's life. But during his interview with the press he said, "neither do I admit or deny it." When quizzed about Lee Harvey Oswald, he drew a blank.

As a member of the Warren Commission, Gerald Ford was queried by the Philippine authorities about Castillo's revelations concerning the JFK assassination. Ford said that he would not comment on the Castillo story until he had more information. A spokesman for the Dallas Police Department said that they had no record on Castillo.

Nevertheless, the U.S. embassy did agree to a closed-door meeting between embassy officials and NBI Director Serafin Fausto on the subject of Castillo. After the meeting, Fausto refused to comment further on the story, but he did tell reporters that, "although publication of the story has prejudiced investigation of the case, one good thing has come out of it; needed information is coming in from the United States to shed light on the case."

Fausto also made it clear that leads obtained from the U.S. embassy justified continuing the investigation of Castillo's link to the assassination of President Kennedy.

After making an official request for assistance from the FBI, the NBI clamped a news blackout on the story, and nothing further was published in the press. Private investigations later revealed that Castillo was spirited out of the Philippines, but not before a series of hypnotic sessions had taken place, at the request of the FBI.

The FBI wanted to have Castillo, while under hypnosis, place the time of the Kennedy assassination. They wanted to know when Castillo had come to Dallas, what time he arrived at the building, and from what location he was supposed to shoot. They wanted to know the time he left the building, the names of any people involved, and any information which might indicate how the plot was hatched, and by whom.

It came as a surprise to the NBI that the FBI also wanted Castillo questioned about the Boyeros airport, eight miles south of Havana, Cuba. The FBI requested that the tightest possible security be kept on any testimony obtained from the hypnotic sessions.

In the last of three sessions requested by the FBI, Castillo was induced into deep hypnotic trance by the ordinary talking method in an NBI interrogation room in Manila. While in that trance state he was questioned for more than three and one-half hours.

The hypnotist's report stated, "Initially, the subject indicated an admixture of desired susceptibility to hypnosynthesis but deep-seated resistance due to the presence of a posthypnotic block. The total removal of this block may pave the way for maximum results."

The hypnotist reported that during the pretrance warm-up he examined Castillo and found little scars on his forehead, chest, stomach, and fingers. Castillo told him that the scars were the result of a car accident in the U.S., which happened when some men were chasing him while he was trying to deliver "an envelope of some kind." Castillo mentioned that after the crash he'd awakened in bandages in a hospital bed.

Names which were presented to Castillo in the pretrance interview were repeated while he was under hypnosis. He recognized the names of several individuals who were then gaining notoriety in connection with New Orleans District Attorney Jim Garrison's JFK assassination investigation. But Castillo revealed that he knew some of the people by other names.

Throughout his recollections Castillo suffered stomach

cramps, said he felt a "weight on his legs," and cried out in pain a number of times. Through the manipulations of the hypnotist, he was able to recall that on many different occasions he had been taken to a factory. He had always driven to the factory in a woman's car, and they had always entered through the front door. Castillo could not remember the exact location of the factory, other than that it was located "way outside Chicago." He spoke of a romantic relationship with the woman, but while one moment he spoke of her as "nice" and "kind," in the next breath he said that he hated her.

According to the hypnotist's report one thing was certain. Whoever the woman was, she "controlled the subject's activities and consciousness like a nightmare."

Eliciting information from Castillo was no easy task. Over the course of many interrogations, the hypnotist discovered that Castillo could be taken to four different hypnotic levels. It appeared to the hypnotist that each level came closer to the truth. He labeled these states "Zombie I, Zombie II, Zombie III, and Zombie IV." Depending upon which "Zombie" state Castillo was in, his mannerisms and identity changed.

In the first state, "Zombie I," Castillo believed he was Eloriaga, and he told tales of anti-American espionage. During "Zombie II," he took on the identity of a tough-talking CIA agent in trouble. While in "Zombie III," again Castillo emerged as an agent whose cover had been blown. At this level, however, he experienced a compulsion to kill himself. On the day he was to have assassinated Marcos, Castillo responded to a program he had revealed in an earlier interrogation. He attempted suicide in his jail cell by swallowing a bottle of epoxy glue.

The "Zombie IV" state revealed that "Castillo's" true name was Manuel Angel Ramirez, a twenty-nine-year-old native of the Bronx, New York. In this state he had no recollection of his youth, except for a hazy memory of his father, who "Ramirez" believed was a highly placed official at "the Agency."

As "Ramirez," Castillo said that most of his life had been spent in training with, or on missions for, the Special Operations Group of the CIA. He remembered one training camp where he learned clandestine and martial arts.

Throughout the interrogations the theme of "programmed agent" emerged. Castillo's testimony under hypnosis was that of an individual whose identity had been completely erased and reconstructed several times over.

On May 30, 1967, Castillo spontaneously went from his normal state into a "Zombie" state. In answering Castillo's question about transfer from the hospital to jail, the hypnotist unknowingly said, "That depends entirely on the big chief, you know." Upon hearing these words, a blank look came over Castillo's eyes and all efforts to wake him were at first unsuccessful. The hypnotist then called out a series of phrases from Castillo's notebooks and found that the phrases "I will win if I don't lose my nerve" and "I must believe myself or no one else will believe me" awakened him.

The next day was Castillo's birthday. The NBI planned to give him a birthday party as an excuse to get him drunk to see if his behavior changed. Castillo, it seemed, had a huge capacity for liquor. Drunk to the eyeballs, he saluted one of the NBI agents and called him "Colonel." "Where do we fly tonight, Colonel?" he asked.

The agent quickly told him that he was to fly the same mission as the last one. Castillo said, "Haiphong," then drunkenly fell into bed. He dug his fingers into his throat and vomited. He cried out for a doctor and between vomit spasms, rattled out his mission to the hypnotist.

He said his real name was Manuel Angel Ramirez, his rank was sergeant, and he was assigned to the Strategic Air Tactical Command in South Vietnam.

He was in Saigon in January, 1966, he related, and had flown B-26 missions over Haiphong and Hanoi. He came to Manila, he said, to kill President Marcos in June, when the president would make a public speech. If his assassination attempt failed someone else would get Marcos before the end of 1968, Castillo added.

"I am dying," he groaned, and pleaded again for a doctor. He thought he was dying from a heart attack. "If I die today," he warned, "my secrets die with me."

When the NBI doctor arrived, he examined Castillo and pronounced him fit, except for his obviously drunken state. He tried to give him a shot to calm him down, but Castillo protested violently. The doctor then asked him to take a pill, which he did without resistance.

Two days later, Castillo was given another medical examination by Dr. Alexis Guerrero of the NBI. A series of tests were given to measure his breathing rate, pulse rate, sweat production, and other functions. All of these tests were performed in "Zombie" states I, II, and III. The doctor noted that in each state there was a vast difference in pulse rate, and assumed, because of what Castillo said, and the reactions of his heart and respiration, that he was experiencing some emotional agitation.

Sodium amytal was administered while he was in the "Zombie III" state. According to the hypnotist, Castillo did not even notice he'd been given the injection. Soon he began to talk as he'd done previously while in the drunken state. "I'm Sergeant Manuel Ramirez of the Tactical Air Command," he said. When asked to reveal his base he said, "You'll never know," adding, "I am a pilot. I've flown a B-26."

"The NBI are suckers," he said a little while later. "They thought they arrested me. But there I was, waiting for them to get me. I know of a great plot. I am supposed to expose it, after I'm arrested. I know I will eventually return to my country [the U.S.]. I'll go through the motions of a trial, conviction, and jail as a criminal. After a couple of months, I will be released for my next assignment."

Awakened from the "Zombie" state, Castillo was told all about these various states and his strange behavior while in them. The hypnotist explained how he thought Castillo had been programmed. Castillo seemed baffled by this news. He said that he was not told by anybody about being programmed. He said that "Papa" didn't even know about the "Zombie" state. He grew agitated, saying that if he were in the "Zombie" state he might even kill "Papa," and then "the Agency would go to blazes. Hell will break loose on the guy responsible for the Zombie."

Asked in a trance to identify "Papa," Castillo said that he was not just a "guy," but was his *real* father. He described him as having a moustache and smoking a pipe. He said he was the only one who could send the Agency to "blazes" if he, Castillo, was killed on this mission. He said that he would personally tell "Papa" about the "Zombie" when he got back.

After more than forty hypnotic sessions lasting from one to five hours each, covering the period from April 3 to June 25, 1967, the hypnotist reviewed the data and summarized it for the Chief of the Defense Intelligence Division of the National Bureau of Investigation. The summary report not only involved Castillo in the assassination of John F. Kennedy; it disclosed that Castillo was a hypno-programmed "Zombie" who would kill on cue.

The summary report stated: "The Zombie phenomenon referred to here is a somnambulistic behavior displayed by the subject in a conditioned response to a series of words, phrases, and statements, apparently unknown to the subject during his normal waking state. While under the influence of such a Zombie state, the subject closed his eyes, rose bodily, walked, triggered a pistol, stared blankly, and fell to the floor with no apparent sense of physical pain. As far as could be determined experimentally, the Zombie behavior had for its objective the assassination of President Ferdinand Marcos of the Republic of the Philippines."

The report also added: "Neither the presence nor the discovery of the Zombie states in our subject should be regarded as noble or unique. If anything, the only remarkable character of the Zombie state in our subject is its deeply ingrained and systematic presentation, indicating a certain disturbing degree of conditioning."

In a lengthy summary, the NBI hypnotist and deprogrammer of Castillo recounted the details of exactly how he had uncovered the key that unlocked the programmed assassin's mind.

The letters "XBGUMIDUTYBX" were found scribbled on the white surface of a cigarette package which was in Castillo's possession at the time of his arrest. The paper had been folded carefully and tucked into the back of his watch. Castillo had told investigators that this piece of paper was given him by a man named Luis Mauricio. Castillo said that Mauricio also gave him money. Mauricio was known to the NBI as a member of the Huk guerillas.

Placing Castillo in a trance, the hypnotist called out the series of letters on the cigarette package. Castillo did not react. He then tried calling out the letters, pausing at different places. He found that when he paused between the G and the U, saying "XBG,UMIDUTYBX," Castillo would reply with "I am myself to kill."

The hypnotist then tried the letters one at a time, and then in different combinations. While many of the combinations produced no response, the following were significant:

When the hypnotist said "X," Castillo quickly answered, "Mauricio."

When the hypnotist said "BGU," Castillo slowly said, "I am myself."

When the hypnotist said "MI," Castillo answered, "to kill."

In another session the hypnotist experimented with saying "Luis Castillo" as a command. The hypnotist reported, "A pathetic sight takes place after this. The subject turns his pistol to his own temple and squeezes the trigger, as many times as his name is repeated."

Whenever the hypnotist would say, "June 12, 1967, 12 o'clock," "June 22, 1967," "July 4, 1967," or "January 1, 1968," Castillo would invariably aim the pistol and squeeze the trigger.

The hypnotist found that after the preparatory command to put him in a trance, if Castillo's eyes were open and he saw a photograph of President Marcos, he would, with no verbal instructions, aim and repeatedly squeeze the trigger of his pistol, following the photo wherever it was taken around the room. If the hypnotist said the word "kill" while Castillo was following this program, he would drop heavily to the floor and remain motionless.

The hypnotist's report also includes Castillo's amazing story about his participation in yet another organized assassination attempt. Under hypnosis, Castillo said that the assassination had happened "before noon." He remembered being with a tall man, weighing about 190 pounds, with a hawklike nose, black hair, and Oriental eyes set in a long face. He spoke with a foreign accent which Castillo could not identify. He said that he remembered meeting the man along with four or five other men in an airport. They then drove together in a black car to a building. Castillo said that he thought the group included both Americans and foreigners, and he thought one man was Spanish.

When the group arrived at the building, Castillo said they climbed to a second-floor room which he described after some uncertainty as brown. The room contained packing crates, a short brown table, a typewriter, and two "lift-up glass windows overlooking a street."

The first man opened a black suitcase, which Castillo described as a bowling bag with a zipper and lock. It contained a scope and pieces of a rifle, which he assembled. He set the scope at 500 yards and gave the rifle to Castillo. Castillo did not seem certain about the make or caliber of the rifle, but finally said that he thought it was Russian.

The man told him to shoot a man in the back seat of an open car in the middle of the caravan. He said that the man would be seated with a lady or another man. A mirror was to be flashed twice from a building across the street, so that Castillo would know when he was to shoot. When he saw the two flashes he was supposed to shoot at the next car coming into view. When he was questioned about the identity of the man riding in the open car, Castillo said that he did not know who the victim was.

After the man had assembled the rifle and had given Castillo his instructions, he went downstairs. Later he rushed into the room. "They got him already," he told Castillo. "Let's get out of here." He then grabbed the rifle away from Castillo, dismantled it, and stuffed it and the scope into the black bag.

Castillo and the man rushed downstairs, got into a car with two other men, and drove away from the building. They picked up a bald-headed, skinny man after they turned the first corner. Three or four blocks later the car stopped and picked up another man.

Castillo said he was riding in the back seat between the first man and the man who had joined them at the second stop. As the car drove away from the scene of the crime, this second man gave Castillo an injection while he wasn't looking. He went immediately to sleep and woke up in a Chicago hotel room with the woman hypnotist.

He and the woman got into a blue car and drove to Milwaukee, Castillo said. While driving there, they heard the news of the assassination of John F. Kennedy on the car radio.

Within a few days after the hypnotist submitted his final report, Castillo was out of the NBI jail and had left the

Philippines for parts unknown. It was later uncovered that Castillo was returned to the United States in 1967 and questioned by the FBI, whose spokesman said, "We talked to Castillo and he told us that he'd fabricated his story about the Kennedy assassination. Said he'd made it up in Manila."

The official record says that Castillo was sentenced to six years in the Missouri Penitentiary for robbery in June, 1971. On August 1, 1974, he was released after serving thirty-seven months. Castillo's last known contact was with his mother shortly after his release from prison. Since then he has disappeared, from both his family and those researchers who would like to question him further.

If Castillo had indeed "made it up in Manila," as the FBI spokesman claimed, then he would have had to have had a phenomenal memory, an incredibly high tolerance to sodium amytal and alcohol, and virtuoso acting ability. Neither the psychological profile nor the life history of Luis Angel Castillo supports the conclusion that he possessed any of these talents.

Chapter Thirteen
THE LONE NUTS

MKULTRA was fully operational when Luis Castillo was programmed. It was active that same decade when events blamed on three "lone assassins" changed the course of history.

In a well-executed, mass indoctrination campaign employing all the honor, prestige, and power of the U.S. government, Americans were told over and over again that the lives of John Kennedy, Martin Luther King, and Robert Kennedy were all taken by lone assassins—men operating without political motivation. These three assassins—Lee Harvey Oswald, James Earl Ray, and Sirhan Sirhan—conveniently left diaries, underlinings in various books, and other self-incriminating clues to establish their guilt.

The evidence gathered on the assassinations remains fragmented and incomplete. Any event of such magnitude as political assassination is bound to invite a large number of interpretations. While there has not as yet surfaced any single, conclusive proof of a conspiracy, more than eighty percent of the American public *believe* there was a conspiracy. A string of circumstantial evidence, and a knowledge of the fundamentals of mind control invites further speculation.

In each case the method was the same—death by the bullet. In each case the circumstances were the same—murder in a public place in view of many witnesses. All three assassins were men whose personal histories can be interpreted to indicate that they were mentally unstable.

Evidence suggests that all three had been hypnotized at one time or another.

But the similarity in their psychological profiles, and the "coincidence" of each having left a trail of evidence, did not seem suspicious to the government investigators of the assassination. That three assassins, from three different parts of the country, with three different ethnic backgrounds (and three different victims in three different cities), could all have had the same *modus operandi* did not seem improbable to the investigators. Those "coincidences" did not even warrant their notice.

A good detective would immediately have suspected that the M.O. of each assassin was a cover laid down by a professional hit team.

The cryptocracy which grew up after World War II was composed of a cadre of professionals, trained during the war. Professional intelligence agents in both the KGB and the CIA are trained to stick to the cover story that works, and use it as long as it does work. Even if the cover story is blown, the agent is supposed to stick to it and, if necessary, die with sealed lips. The "lone nut" theory—that the assassins of King and the Kennedys had acted alone—and the evidence planted to support that theory, stands out as a typical professional intelligence "cover."

The *modus operandi* or method of a murder is the first of two major clues detectives use to solve crimes. The second clue is the motive.

Those who support the "lone nut" theory point to the fact that no clear political motive could be attributed to any of the three assassins. Yet even to a casual student of history each of the three murders was of obvious political benefit to the extreme right: John and Robert Kennedy and Martin Luther King were all independent thinkers who could not be bought off. They worked for expanded civil rights in a manner the right wing interpreted as being Communist, e.g., it involved *government legislation* of civil rights. J. Edgar Hoover is known to have had a personal vendetta against Dr. King, and it has been reported that he lost no love for the Kennedy brothers. The Kennedys were not only on the wrong side of Hoover's FBI, they were on the wrong side of the CIA as well. JFK fired several top intelligence officers (he asked for Allen Dulles' resignation) and at the time of his death he was privately talking about reorganizing the entire U.S. intelligence service. Robert Kennedy, as attorney general, was waging a tireless campaign against organized crime. His campaign cut across the alliance the CIA had formed with gangsters who had lost their gambling and drug concessions in Cuba. Robert Kennedy was a close friend of Dr. King, and one rumor persists that the assassins had issued a dire warning that RFK not run for president, and that King was sacrificed to show that the group meant business. A similar threat was issued against Ted Kennedy when he was entertaining presidential thoughts. Robert Kennedy's knowledge of the CIA-Mafia link and the CIA assassination teams might have been a motive behind the motive, assuming that fanatical right-wing operators were "contracted" for the "Executive actions" against the three.

The obvious results of all three assassinations would indicate that the extreme right wing, known to be widespread in the cryptocracy, had the most to gain. By their deaths, the civil rights movement was severely crippled, the conflict in Vietnam escalated, and the corrupt leaders of the cryptocracy stayed in power.

More recently a rumor has been put forth by CBS News and others that Castro and/or the KGB were behind the assassinations. That theory smells like more disinformation from the cryptocracy. The motives of the Communists seem much less clear than the motives of misguided patriotic right-thinking Americans. The cryptocracy was in a better position to benefit from the deaths of the three charismatic and humanitarian leaders than were the Communists.

Following the assassination of President Kennedy, his successor appointed a now notorious commission to investigate the crime. Headed by Chief Justice Earl Warren, it included Sen. John Sherman Cooper (R., Kentucky), Sen. Richard B. Russell (D., Georgia), Rep. Hale Boggs (D., Louisiana), Rep. Gerald R. Ford (R., Michigan), former CIA Director Allen Dulles, and John J. McCloy.

After nine months of deliberation, the Warren Commission concluded that Lee Harvey Oswald acting alone, had shot President Kennedy. Although Oswald was in turn assassinated by Dallas thug Jack Ruby, and although Ruby's connections with organized crime and the anti-Castro movement were well known, the Commission found no evidence of a conspiracy.

The twenty-six volumes of evidence which made up the commission's final report left so many questions unasked that by December, 1976, a Harris Survey concluded that 80 percent of the U.S. population did not believe the commission's conclusion.

From the beginning, the investigation was slanted towards proving that Oswald was guilty and that he had acted alone. The commission had proceeded with haste to put to rest forever the question: Was there a conspiracy behind the Kennedy assassination? In its haste it had overlooked key facts and ignored witnesses who did not support the foregone conclusion that there was no conspiracy—that Oswald was just a "lone nut."

Throughout the Warren Commission hearings there was conflicting testimony about Oswald. There was testimony that Oswald did not drive a car. There was other testimony that he *did* drive, and very well. Some of his acquaintances said he was a poor shot, too poor to have accomplished the feat of marksmanship in Dealy Plaza. Others said that he was a fine marksman. Some said, by turns, that he was a Communist, a pro-Castro and an anti-Castro sympathizer. His own mother said that he performed undercover work for the U.S. government. Out of this mass of conflicting evidence, the Warren Commission simply took what was needed to support its foregone conclusion, and relegated the rest to published transcripts or to top-secret files in the National Archives.

There were so many conflicting descriptions of Oswald that many independent assassination investigators subsequently concluded that there must have been at least *two* Oswalds—the "real" one and an intelligence double. If, however, one considers that Oswald might have been controlled in the same way as Candy Jones or Luis Castillo—split into multiple personalities—another explanation for the conflicting descriptions of the assassin becomes credible. He might have been an excellent shot in one zombie state, and in another he might have been blocked so that he could not even aim a rifle. In one state he might have had the ability to drive a car, while in another state he might have had a posthypnotic block so that he could not drive.

Oswald *said* that he didn't kill anybody. His statement

was recorded in the basement of the Dallas Police Station on the day after the assassination. Captured on film by a local CBS film crew, Oswald told reporters, "I positively know nothing about this situation here. I would like to have legal representation." In answer to an inaudible question from one reporter Oswald said, "Well, I was questioned by a judge. However, I protested at that time that I was not allowed legal representation during that very short and sweet hearing. I really don't know what this situation is about. Nobody has told me anything, except that I'm accused of murdering a policeman. I know nothing more than that. I do request someone to come forward to give me legal assistance."

"Did you kill the President?" another reporter asked.

"No," Oswald answered, "I have not been charged with that. In fact, nobody has said that to me yet. The first thing I heard about it was when the newspaper reporters in the hall asked me that question."

Ten years after Oswald made that statement, George O'Toole applied a newly developed "truth detector," the Psychological Stress Evaluator (PSE), to the soundtrack of the film which recorded Oswald's protestation of innocence. The PSE, unlike the polygraph, does not have to be connected to the body to measure stress. It measures subaudible micro-tremors in the human voice which occur whenever an individual experiences even mild anxiety or stress. The micro-tremors form a distinct pattern on the PSE chart and can then be compared to stress patterns in other parts of the statement. A deliberate lie, especially one which involves personal jeopardy, stands out clearly from the other stress patterns that might represent situational stress or vague anxiety.

Oswald was in a situation of high stress that day. He had been grilled for hours by police. He had been manhandled and accused of killing not only a police officer but also the President of the United States.

Yet the PSE analysis of Oswald's statement showed that he exhibited far more stress when he was talking about not being represented by a lawyer than he did when he denied murdering the President or the police officer. George O'Toole concluded, as have many other investigators, that Oswald was innocent. He could not have been consciously involved in the assassination as a fall guy—a patsy—or he would have shown stress in his answers to these key questions on the PSE.*

But what if he had been hypno-programmed so that he could remember nothing of his involvement in the assassination plot? Then every lie-detector test in the world would prove him innocent, since consciously he would *believe* that he was innocent. Hypnosis is the only reliable way to defeat a lie detector, whether it be a polygraph or the more advanced PSE.

Among evidence concealed from the commission was a CIA document obtained under the Freedom of Information Act in 1976, which quoted an unidentified CIA officer reporting to his superiors on Oswald. According to that memo, which had been written only three days after JFK's assassination, Agency officials had discussed interviewing Oswald for intelligence purposes in the early 1960s. The same document revealed that Allen Dulles had secretly coached the CIA on how the Agency should deny having any connection with Oswald. According to one of the memos, Dulles strongly recommended that CIA Director Helms deny under oath that the CIA had any material in its files which suggested an Agency relationship with Oswald. Later disclosures revealed that Oswald did indeed have a CIA "201 file."

In sworn testimony before the Warren Commission in 1964, Richard Helms applied the artful deception which came from a lifetime of CIA training; he testified that the Agency had "never even contemplated" making any contact with Oswald prior to the assassination. That the CIA *did* make contact with him was never disclosed to the commission.

Despite the attempts of Allen Dulles to steer commission investigators away from other information which linked Oswald to both the FBI and the CIA, the rumor that Oswald

* Posing as a *Look* reporter, former CIA employee O'Toole conducted and recorded interviews with local police officials and FBI men who were the original investigators in the Kennedy case. Too many of their PSE patterns showed levels of stress which could only be interpreted as having been the result of willful deception. In his book *The Assassination Tapes,* O'Toole offers the details of his PSE analysis, and concludes, not surprisingly, that there was a conspiracy behind the assassination of John F. Kennedy.

had been sent to Russia as an intelligence agent persisted.

In an attempt to scotch that rumor, Dulles told the commission that it would be impossible for anyone to prove or disprove that Oswald had or had not been an agent or informer. He said, astonishingly, that Oswald could have been a CIA agent without anyone ever knowing about it!

During one meeting of the commission, Senator Russell asked Dulles, "If Oswald never had assassinated the President, and had been in the employ of the FBI, and somebody had gone to the FBI, would they have denied he was an agent?"

"Oh yes," the ex-CIA chief replied. "They would be the first to deny it."

"Your agents would have done the same thing?" Senator Russell asked incredulously.

"Exactly," Dulles answered.

At another juncture, John J. McCloy said that he had received several inquiries about the Oswald-agent rumor. He asked Dulles point blank, "What is there to this story?"

Dulles went in circles: "This is a terribly hard thing to disprove, you know. How do you disprove a fellow was not your agent?"

"You could disprove it, couldn't you?" Congressman Boggs asked.

Dulles replied, simply, "No."

"So I will ask you," Boggs continued, "did you have agents about whom you had no record whatsoever?"

"The record might not be on paper," Dulles said. "But on paper would have been hieroglyphics that only two people knew what they meant, and anybody outside the agency would not know and you could say this meant the agent, and somebody else could say it meant another agent."

The discussion then turned to U-2 pilot Francis Gary Powers. Dulles explained that Powers was a different kind of agent. He had signed a contract with the CIA.

Alluding to the Oswald-CIA relationship, Boggs asked Dulles, "Let's say Powers did not have a signed contract but was recruited by someone in CIA. The man who recruited him would know, wouldn't he?"

"Yes," Dulles replied, "but he wouldn't tell."

"Would he tell it under oath?" Chief Justice Warren wondered.

"I wouldn't think he would tell it under oath, no," Dulles replied matter of factly.

"Why?" asked Warren.

"He ought not to tell it under oath," Dulles said, offering Warren a lesson which years of legal training made him incapable of learning: the cryptocracy operates completely outside of the law and, because of the power of the "national security" rationale, it operates completely above the law.

Dulles admitted later, while responding to a question from McCloy, that a CIA operative might not tell the truth even to his own superior.

"What you do," Boggs indignantly said, "is you make our problem, if this be true, utterly impossible because you say this rumor [that Oswald was a CIA agent] can't be dissipated under any circumstances."

"I don't think it can," Dulles admitted, "unless you believe Mr. Hoover, and so forth and so on, which probably most of the people will."

Hoover, of course, had written a carefully worded response to a Commission inquiry about Oswald's FBI connections. He denied all association between Oswald and the FBI.

Also ignored by the Warren Commission was information about the cryptocracy's attempts to assassinate Fidel Castro. Dulles presumably knew about the plots which took place during his tenure with the Agency, but he remained mute. Richard Helms was the only CIA official on active duty to have direct contact with the Warren Commission, and although he provided them with information on a number of things, he volunteered nothing about the unsuccessful plots against Castro—plots which would have been within the commission's "need to know" since they showed that the cryptocracy had practical experience in assassination planning.

Testifying before the Senate Select Committee to Study Governmental Operations with Respect to Intelligence Activities, Helms revealed how the cryptocracy evaded and withheld information from the Warren Commission. His testimony illustrated the cryptocracy's contempt for the helpless commission, the American people, and above all the truth.

During the Church Committee's investigation of the

CIA's involvement in assassinations, Senator Church asked Helms: "Since you had knowledge of the CIA involvement in these assassination plots against Castro, and knew it at the time . . . I would have thought . . . that ought to have been related to the Commission, because it does bear on the motives, whatever else."

Helms: ". . . Mr. Allen Dulles was a member of the Warren Commission. And the first assassination plot happened during his time as director. What he said to the Warren Commission about this . . . I don't know. But at least he was sitting right there in [the commission's] deliberations and knew about this, and I am sure that the same thought that occurred to you must have occurred to him."

Senator Morgan: "You were charged with furnishing the Warren Commission information from the CIA, information that you thought was relevant?"

Helms: "No sir, I was instructed to reply to inquiries from the Warren Commission for information from the Agency. I was not asked to initiate any particular thing."

Morgan: ". . . In other words if you weren't asked for it, you didn't give it?"

Helms: "That's right sir."

Nevertheless, despite the denials of Dulles and Hoover, the rumor persisted that Oswald had defected to Russia on a clandestine mission for the CIA. Some believed he had been uncovered by the KGB and subsequently programmed like the Manchurian Candidate to return to the U.S. and act as an unconscious "sleeper agent," a programmed assassin.

Following up on this rumor, J. Lee Rankin, General Counsel to the Warren Commission, wrote a letter to CIA Director Helms requesting all information the CIA had on Russian "brainwashing" capabilities.

In response, Helms claimed that there were "two major methods of altering or controlling behavior," and the Soviets were interested in both. He said the first was psychological and the second was pharmacological. "The two may be used as individual methods or for mutual reinforcement," Helms wrote. "For long-term control of large numbers of people the former method is more promising than the latter.

"In dealing with individuals, the U.S. experience suggests

the pharmacological approach (assisted by psychological techniques) would be the only effective method."

Helms told the Warren Commission that while Soviet drug research was extensive, *it had consistently lagged about five years behind Western research.* That was an interesting admission, for in the MKULTRA files which were declassified over a decade later the CIA was using the Soviet success in mind control to motivate our own scientific program.

Helms's memorandum told the commission that the Soviets had adopted a multidisciplinary approach to mind control, integrating biological, social, and what he called "physical-mathematical research" in attempts to control human behavior in a "manner consonant with national plans."

But while attempting to tell the Warren Commission what the Soviets were up to, Helms was, at the same time, revealing the cryptocracy's own intentions. His conclusions stated that "there is no evidence that the Soviets have any techniques or agents capable of producing particular behavioral patterns which are not available in the West." Appended to the memorandum (Commission Document 1113, reproduced here as Appendix A) were several hundred pages of reports on Soviet mind-control techniques and an extensive bibliography on brainwashing, which for some reason remained classified even after the main body of the memorandum was declassified.

The question of whether Oswald had been hypnoprogrammed was raised in another context when New Orleans District Attorney Jim Garrison began his independent investigations of the Kennedy assassination.

Garrison told an anxious press he was going to crack the Kennedy case wide open: "The plain fact is that our federal intelligence agencies are implacably determined to do whatever is necessary to block any further inquiry into the facts of the assassination.

"The arrogant totalitarian efforts of these federal agencies to obstruct the discovery of the truth is a matter which I intend to bring to light when we have finished doing the job they should have done."

One of the central targets of Garrison's investigation was David William Ferrie, who was both a hypnotist and a CIA operative. Coincidentally, Ferrie had been in a New Orleans Civil Air Patrol group in the fifties with Lee Harvey Oswald. One witness said that Ferrie had been the man who had instructed Oswald in markmanship.

When New Orleans police raided Ferrie's apartment, they confiscated a number of weapons, various drugs, and three blank U.S. passports—things that any good CIA operative would keep at his elbow. Much later researchers realized the importance of some of the evidence obtained in the raid—several voluminous abstracts on posthypnotic suggestion and a library on hypnotism.

A salesman for the Equitable Life Insurance Company, Perry Raymond Russo, told a New Orleans grand jury that Ferrie's apartment had been the scene of many "parties" where hypnosis had been used as "entertainment." One evening, Russo said, Ferrie hypnotized a young man to whom he apparently had a strong homosexual attraction. Another evening, Russo said, he himself hypnotized a young woman and made her immobile. He struck pins in her hand and burned her arms just to demonstrate the extent of the control he had over her.

At Russo's request, his story was tested by Garrison's investigators. Under both sodium pentothal and hypnosis, Russo told the identical story he had told to the grand jury. He testified that he had been with Ferrie, a man named Leon Oswald, and a third man named Clem Bertrand in Ferrie's apartment during the summer of 1963. The three had discussed an assassination attempt in which diversionary tactics were to be used.

Russo quoted Ferrie as saying that "there would have to be a minimum of three people involved. Two of the persons would shoot diversionary shots and the third . . . shoot the 'good' shot." Ferrie said that one of the three would have to be the "scapegoat." He also said that Ferrie discoursed on the "availability of exit," saying that the sacrificed man would give the other two time to escape.

On February 23, 1967, a few days before Luis Castillo was arrested by the NBI in the Philippines, Garrison subpoenaed David Ferrie. That evening George Lardner of the *Washington Post* went to Ferrie's apartment for an interview. Ferrie, in remarkably good spirits, told Lardner, "A President is no better than anyone else . . . If I were killed, I'd expect my death to be investigated just as thoroughly."

Lardner left Ferrie at 4:00 A.M. Seven hours and forty minutes later Ferrie was found in bed with a sheet pulled over his head. He had been dead for several hours.

On the dining room table was a note which read in part: "To leave this life is for me a sweet prospect. I find nothing in it that is desirable and on the other hand, everything that is loathsome." Fifteen empty medicine bottles littered the apartment. The medicine bottles had contained a prescription drug for a vascular disorder.

Garrison immediately jumped to the conclusion that Ferrie had committed suicide because of the subpoena. The autopsy, however, revealed that Ferrie had not died from an overdose of drugs, but from a ruptured blood vessel at the base of his brain.

Dr. Ronald A. Walsh, Louisiana State University School of Medicine pathologist, stated in his autopsy report that David Ferrie died of a "berry aneurysm." Several forensic pathologists later concluded that such an aneurysm could have been caused by a karate expert inflicting a blow to the back of the head in such a manner that no external damage would be discernible.

A number of Ferrie's friends began to fear for their lives. One, Jack Martin, came out of hiding long enough to suggest that Oswald had been programmed by Ferrie to go to Dallas and kill the President. Immediately following the assassination, Martin had reported to Assistant District Attorney Herman S. Kohlman that Ferrie and Oswald had been friends, and that Ferrie had instructed Oswald in the use of a telescope sight on a rifle. But in 1963 no one followed up on Martin's story.

Another of Ferrie's friends was a Reverend Raymond Broshears, who had roomed with Ferrie three years before Ferrie's death. Broshears stated in a television interview: "David admitted being involved with the assassins. There's no question about that."

The Warren Commission must have had *some* suspicions about Ferrie, for in Volume 24, Exhibit 2038, of the *Warren Commission Report,* NBC cameraman Gene Barnes is quoted as saying, "Bob Mulholland, NBC News, Chicago, talked in Dallas to one Fairy [sic]. . . . Fairy said that Oswald had been under hypnosis from a man doing a mind-reading act at Ruby's 'Carousel.' Fairy was said to be a private detective and the owner of an airplane who took young boys on flights 'just for kicks' . . ."*

Bob Mulholland later came forward to say that he had been misquoted by the Warren Report. What he had actually overheard were FBI agents saying that Ferrie might have been involved in the assassination with Oswald; he had merely relayed that information to his reporters in Dallas.

In any event, there was enough substance to the David Ferrie angle to cause both the FBI *and* the Secret Service to have interviewed him immediately following the assassination. Yet there were no reports, official or otherwise, as to the outcome of that interview.

Those not disposed to believe in conspiracies against the American people by its own government might well ask, "If there is a conspiracy by a cryptocracy, why wouldn't we, by now, have proof of it? Why wouldn't there have been at least one deathbed confession by one of the conspirators?"

Two such confessions to the JFK assassination conspiracy may well have been made—and overlooked.

* Ferrie did own an airplane, and he is alleged to have worked for Guy Bannister, the New Orleans private eye and CIA contract agent.

Chapter Fourteen
THE IGNORED CONFESSIONS

Only an understanding of the techniques and applications of mind control could begin to bring meaning to the fragmented ramblings of Jack Ruby.

On June 7, 1964, Jack Ruby was questioned in jail in Dallas, Texas, by Earl Warren and Gerald Ford. In that session Ruby continually pleaded for a lie-detector test or for sodium pentothal. He desperately wanted to prove his honesty so that Warren and the commission would know he was telling the truth.

Said Ruby: "I would like to be able to get a lie-detector test or truth serum of what motivated me to do what I did at that particular time, and it seems as you get further into something, even though you know what you did, it operates against you somehow, *brainwashes* you, that you are weak in what you want to tell the truth about, and what you want to say which is the truth."

"As I started to trial," Ruby continued, "I don't know if you realize my reasoning, how I happened to be involved—I was carried away tremendously emotionally, and all the time I tried to ask Mr. Belli [Melvin Belli, Ruby's first lawyer], I wanted to get up and say the truth regarding the steps that led me to do what I have got involved in, but since I have a spotty background in the nightclub business, I should have been the last person to ever want to do something that I had been involved in. In other words, I was carried away tremendously. You want to ask me questions?"

Warren asked Ruby to just "tell us what you want, and then we will ask you some questions."

"Am I boring you?" Ruby replied.

He pleaded with Warren to be taken to Washington where he could be questioned in safety. Possibly either his control agent was in the room, or Ruby *felt* that he was, for again and again he hinted to Warren that he had something quite important to say but could not say it at that moment in Dallas.

"Gentlemen, unless you get me to Washington, you can't get a fair shake out of me. If you understand my way of talking, you have to bring me to Washington to get the tests. Do I sound dramatic? Off the beam?"

"No, you are speaking very, very rationally," Warren replied, "and I am really surprised that you can remember as much as you have remembered up to the present time. You have given it to us in great detail."

Again Ruby pleaded with Warren: "Unless you can get me to Washington, and I am not a crackpot, I have all my senses—I don't want to evade any crime I am guilty of." Then Ruby asked that the sheriff and the law enforcement officers leave the room, and after they were gone he said, "Gentlemen, if you want to hear any further testimony, you will have to get me to Washington soon, because it has something to do with you, Chief Warren. Do I sound sober enough to tell you this?"

"Yes, go right ahead," Warren said.

"I would like to talk to you in private," Ruby told him.

Warren seemed to miss the import of Ruby's statement. "You may do that when you finish your story. You may tell me that phase of it."

"I bet you haven't had a witness like me in your whole investigation, is that correct?" Ruby asked.

"There are many witnesses whose memory has not been as good as yours. I tell you that honestly," Warren replied.

"My reluctance to talk," Ruby went on, "you haven't had any witnesses in telling the story, in finding so many problems."

"You have a greater problem than any witness we have had," Warren retorted.

"I have a lot of reasons for having those problems," Ruby explained. Then after another exchange about going immediately to Washington, Ruby said, "Gentlemen, my life is in danger here. Not with my guilty plea of execution. Do I sound sober enough to you as I say this?"

Warren assured him that he did sound sober. "From the moment I started my testimony, haven't I sounded as though, with the exception of becoming emotional, haven't I sounded as though I made sense, what I was speaking about?" Ruby asked.

"You have indeed," Warren again assured him. "I understand everything you have said. If I haven't, it is my fault."

"Then I follow this up," Ruby blurted out. "I may not live tomorrow to give any further testimony. The reason why I add this to this, since you assure me that I have been speaking sense, then I might be speaking sense by following what I have said, and the only thing I want to get out to the public, and I can't say it here, is, with authenticity, with sincerity of the truth, of everything, and why my act was committed, but it can't be said here.

"It can be said, it's got to be said amongst people of the highest authority that would give me the benefit of the doubt. And following that, immediately give me the lie-detector test after I do make the statement.

"Chairman Warren, if you felt that your life was in danger at the moment, how would you feel? Wouldn't you be reluctant to go on speaking, even though you request me to do so?"

Warren again reassured Ruby that he was making perfect sense. "I wish that our beloved President, Lyndon Johnson, would have delved deeper into the situation, hear me, not to accept just circumstantial facts about my guilt or innocence, and would have questioned to find out the truth about me before he relinquished certain powers to these certain people . . . Consequently, *a whole new form of government is going to take over our country* [emphasis added], and I know I won't live to see you another time. Do I sound sort of screwy in telling you these things?"

"No," Warren said, "I think that is what you believe or you wouldn't tell it under oath."

"But it is a very serious situation," Ruby said, "I guess it is too late to stop it, isn't it? Now maybe something can be saved. It may not be too late, whatever happens, if our President, Lyndon Johnson, knew the truth from me . . . But if I am eliminated, there won't be any way of knowing.

"Right now, when I leave your presence now, I am the only one that can bring out the truth to our President, who believes in righteousness and justice. But he has been told, I am certain, that I was part of a plot to assassinate the President. I know your hands are tied; you are helpless."

Earl Warren said, "Mr. Ruby, I think I can say this to you, that if he has been told any such thing, there is no indication of any kind that he believes it."

When it became apparent that Warren did not realize Ruby had intended to confess to being a part of the plot to kill President Kennedy, Ruby exploded. "I am sorry, Chief Justice Warren, I thought I would be very effective in telling you what I have said here. But in all fairness to everyone, maybe all I want to do is beg that if they found out I was telling the truth, maybe they can succeed in what their motives are, but maybe my people won't be tortured and mutilated . . ."

Warren could find no meaning in Ruby's testimony. He merely assured him that neither he nor his family would be tortured or mutilated by anyone. "You may be sure of that," the Chief Justice added.

"No," Ruby answered. "The only way you can do it is if he knows the truth, that I am telling the truth, and why I was down in that basement Sunday morning, and maybe some sense of decency will come out and they can still fulfill their plan, as I stated before, without my people going through torture and mutilation."

Warren assured Ruby that the President would know everything he had said. "But I won't be around, Chief Justice," Ruby said. "I won't be around to tell the President."

Then one of the aides asked the first intelligent question of the day, "Who do you think is going to eliminate you, Jack?"

Ruby replied, "I have been used for a purpose, and there will be a certain tragic occurrence happening if you don't take my testimony and somehow vindicate me so my people don't suffer because of what I have done . . ."

Jack Ruby was subsequently given a polygraph test which proved to be inconclusive due to high levels of stress.

In 1965 syndicated columnist Dorothy Kilgallen interviewed Ruby in his Dallas cell. She was the *only* major journalist allowed to interview him. She told a few friends that from what Ruby had told her, she was able to obtain evidence that would "blow the JFK case sky high." Within a few days, Dorothy Kilgallen died of a massive overdose of barbiturates combined with alcohol. Her apartment was found in shambles. The transcripts of her interview with Ruby were missing. Her death was ruled a suicide.

In early 1967 Ruby complained that he was being poisoned. He was diagnosed as having cancer, but a few weeks after complaining of being poisoned, he died not of the cancer, but of a "stroke" similar to the one that had killed David Ferrie.

Another deathbed confession supports what Jack Ruby was trying to tell the Warren Commission. That confession was made by Professor George de Mohrenschildt, a former intelligence agent who was also a friend of Lee Harvey Oswald.

De Mohrenschildt was born in 1911 in the Ukraine. Following the revolution, in 1921 he and his parents fled Russia for Poland. He attended a Polish military academy for a year, and later, in 1938, received a doctorate in international commerce. He emigrated to the United States soon thereafter and, in 1949, became a citizen.

After becoming interested in the exploration and generation of oil, de Mohrenschildt received his master's degree in petroleum geology and petroleum engineering. Sometime thereafter he became acquainted with right-wing oil magnate H. L. Hunt. Although the basis of their relationship is unknown, de Mohrenschildt, in a recent interview with Dutch journalist Willem Oltmans, stated, "I knew Hunt, now the late Mr. Hunt, intimately. For some twenty years I was invited to his parties."

FBI disclosures in 1976 suggested that Lee Harvey Oswald was also acquainted with Hunt. And de Mohrenschildt knew Oswald. Apparently he had introduced himself to Oswald after hearing about him through a Russian-speaking group in the Dallas–Fort Worth area.

Marina Oswald told the Warren Commission: "Lee did not have any close friends, but at least he had—here in America—he had a great deal of respect for de Mohrenschildt . . . he considered him to be smart, to be full of joy of living, a very energetic and very sympathetic person . . ."

It was the conclusion of the Warren Commission, after extensive investigation, that de Mohrenschildt had exhibited no signs of subversive or disloyal conduct. The Warren Report stated: "Neither the FBI, CIA, nor any witness contacted by the Commission has provided any information linking de Mohrenschildt to subversive or extremist organizations. Nor has there been any evidence linking them in any way with the assassination of President Kennedy."

It was subsequently revealed, however, that de Mohrenschildt had indeed been associated with various intelligence operations over the years. He was connected with French intelligence during World War II and was also linked to the CIA Bay of Pigs operation.

In late March, 1977, de Mohrenschildt's name was brought before the newly formed House Select Committee on Assassinations. Willem Oltmans told the committee that de Mohrenschildt held the key to the Kennedy assassination; that de Mohrenschildt had privately confessed to him that prior to the assassination he was aware of a conspiracy to murder the President in Dallas. According to Oltmans de Mohrenschildt was about to have a book published which would reveal the details of his knowledge of the assassination.

After Oltmans' testimony, a spokesman for the House Committee on Assassinations said that the committee would investigate his claims and would, if warranted, track down de Mohrenschildt for questioning. He was located a week later in Palm Beach, Florida, but he could not be called to testify. George de Mohrenschildt was found dead, the victim of a gunshot wound in the head. Local officials termed his death a suicide.

Following de Mohrenschildt's death, his Dallas attorney, Pat Russell, supported Oltmans' claims to the Commission. He verified the fact that before his death, de Mohrenschildt had insisted that persons other than Lee Harvey Oswald had participated in the slaying of President Kennedy. The attorney revealed that he had in his possession tapes, a book-length manuscript, and a photograph which de Mohrenschildt had turned over to him earlier. He said the tapes consisted of ten reels of interviews with de Mohrenschildt about the Kennedy assassination, which, he claimed, were firsthand accounts of the late professor's recollections of Oswald.

Russell said that although he did not know if the tapes or the book contained any new evidence, the photograph should be of particular interest to assassination investigators. He claimed that although the photo was similar to a well-known picture obtained by the Dallas police which showed Lee Harvey Oswald holding a rifle and wearing a pistol, what made the photograph interesting was that it was autographed on the back by Oswald and dated May 4, 1963, approximately six months prior to the assassination.

After de Mohrenschildt's death Willem Oltmans released a portion of his interview with the deceased. Oltmans described him as "Oswald's most intimate friend," and, without offering an explanation, said that he had been intimate with Oswald during "the years when Oswald's brain was being programmed toward the murder of the century."

In the interview dated February 23, 1977, de Mohrenschildt told Oltmans "In June, 1976, I completed a manuscript. That's when disaster struck. You see, in that book I played the devil's advocate. Without directly implicating myself as an accomplice in the JFK assassination I still mentioned a number of names, particularly of FBI and CIA officials who apparently may not be exposed under any circumstances. I was drugged surreptitiously. As a result I was committed to a mental hospital. I was there eight weeks and was given electric shocks and as a consequence I sometimes forget certain details temporarily . . ."

De Mohrenschildt went on to say that as a result of the drugs and shocks, he could take no more. "I tried to commit suicide five times . . . One of these days I will put a revolver to my head . . ."

According to Oltmans, de Mohrenschildt left Dallas in the middle of the night on March 3, 1977, telling him, "I don't want anybody to see me." Oltmans reported that at that time de Mohrenschildt was in a state of panic, constantly worried whether "they" would let him leave the country. "He always felt watched and followed," Oltmans said. "I really cannot see how somebody who does not have anything to hide would develop such behavior."[1]

On the day he died, George de Mohrenschildt was being interviewed by author Edward Jay Epstein for his book *The*

Legend of Lee Harvey Oswald. They broke for lunch at one o'clock and Epstein walked de Mohrenschildt to his car. They were supposed to resume the interview at three P.M., and when de Mohrenschildt didn't return, Epstein called his room and heard a distraught maid tell him that de Mohrenschildt had taken his own life. De Mohrenschildt's daughter, Alexandra, told Epstein that she believes her father took his own life after having had a post-hypnotic suggestion triggered by a voice over the telephone in his room.

The last days of George de Mohrenschildt sound strikingly similar to those of the victims of mind control. Could it have been that when drugs and "electric shock" failed to erase his memory, the final solution was prescribed? Or was he programmed to self-destruct?

Chapter Fifteen
ANOTHER HYPNO-PATSY?

On April 4, 1968, Nobel laureate Dr. Martin Luther King was murdered on a second-floor balcony of the Lorraine Motel in Memphis, Tennessee. Half of the six-thousand-man FBI force was assigned to the task of bringing the killer to justice.

The FBI should have had an easy job. There was an abundance of evidence left behind on the second floor of a rooming house a block from the Lorraine Motel. There were fingerprints on the window ledge of a bathroom next to a room which had been rented to an "Eric S. Galt." On the sidewalk in front of the house was a weapon, a high-powered rifle with telescopic sight. Neighbors said they had seen a white Mustang roar away moments after the shooting.

Nevertheless, the killer got away.

A ham radio operator broadcasting from a fixed station posed as a CB operator in a mobile unit. He broadcast a convincing account of a high-speed chase between a white Mustang and a blue Pontiac. He reported that the two cars were shooting at each other. While police concentrated their search in the area described by the ham operator, the white Mustang they were seeking sped away from Memphis in the other direction. The ham operator's actions were explained away by authorities as a hoax. Within a few days local police and federal authorities forgot the incident. While the use of a high-powered ham radio on the eleven-meter CB band and the broadcasting of false emergency information are two clear violations of the Federal Communications Code, the identity and fate of that ham "prankster" are not known.

The FBI soon discovered that the fingerprints left at the scene of the crime belonged to the man who had rented the room, Eric S. Galt. Through a computer search they later found that Galt's real name was James Earl Ray.

The day after Robert F. Kennedy was assassinated in Los Angeles, James Earl Ray was captured in London. He was apprehended by British customs inspectors while attempting to leave the country on a passport issued to a Canadian constable.

Ray was quickly extradited to Tennessee for trial. The lengthy search and investigation, billed as "the most complete manhunt in history," was followed by one of the shortest trials in history. On March 10, 1969, less than one year after the assassination, Ray had his day in court, literally. By most standards his was not a trial but a deal. The deal had been arranged by Ray's attorneys, who had urged him to plead guilty so that he would get ninety-nine years instead of the death penalty.

Under Tennessee law, even if a defendant enters a guilty plea, a jury is required to attend the plea and to "ratify" the plea and the sentence. In a courtroom sealed by the tightest possible security, twelve jurors heard the prosecutor, State Attorney General Phil Canale, explain to Ray his rights to a trial by jury. They heard Ray plead guilty to murder in exchange for the ninety-nine-year sentence. They heard prosecutor Canale say that, as required by law, he would outline the evidence which would have been presented had the case gone to formal trial. Canale then asked the jury if they each could sit as jurors and accept the guilty plea from the defendant. They nodded in unison.

Canale told the jury: ". . . There have been rumors going all around—perhaps some of you have heard them—that Mr. James Earl Ray was a dupe in this thing, or a fall guy or a member of a conspiracy to kill Dr. Martin Luther King, Jr.

"I want to state to you, as your Attorney General, that we have no proof other than that Dr. Martin Luther King, Jr., was killed by James Earl Ray, and James Earl Ray alone, not in concert with anyone else. Our office has examined over five thousand printed pages of investigation work done by local police, by national police organizations, and by international law enforcement agencies. We have examined over three hundred physical bits of evidence, physical exhibits. Three men in my office, Mr. Dwyer, Mr. Beasly and Mr. John Carlisle, the Chief Investigator of the Attorney General's Office. . . have traveled thousands of miles all over this country and to many cities in foreign countries on this investigation, our own independent investigation, and I just state to you frankly that we have no evidence that there was any conspiracy involved in this . . ."

The state had not charged Ray with conspiracy; it had charged him with murder in the first degree. Nevertheless the prosecutor felt compelled to deny that Ray had collaborators.*

Stranger still was the reaction of defense attorney Percy Foreman, a man who had never lost a case, to the remarks of the prosecuting attorney. As soon as Canale had finished issuing his disclaimer of conspiracy, Foreman rose and faced the jury. "It is an honor to appear in this Court for this case. I never expected or had any idea when I entered this case that I would be able to accomplish anything except perhaps save the defendant's life . . . It took me a month to convince myself of that fact which the Attorney General of these United States, and J. Edgar Hoover of the Federal Bureau of Investigation announced last July, that is, what Mr. Canale has told you—that there was not a conspiracy."

Just as the jury was about to rubber stamp "the deal," Ray rose to his feet. "Your Honor," he said, "I would like to say something. . . I don't want to change anything that I have said, but I just want to enter one other thing. The only thing that I have to say is that I can't agree with Mr. Clark."

"*Ramsey* Clark?" Foreman asked.

The judge said, "Mr. *who*?"

"Mr. J. Edgar Hoover," Ray said. "I agree with all these stipulations, and I am not trying to change anything."

The judge said, "You don't agree with *whose* theories?"

". . . Mr. Canale's, Mr. Clark's, and Mr. J. Edgar Hoover's about the conspiracy. I don't want to add something

* Though it was not presented at the "trial," Ray's version of the story had already been published. In a series of magazine articles written by William Bradford Huie, Ray had confessed that he had been the unwitting pawn in a conspiracy to kill Dr. King.

that I haven't agreed to in the past," Ray answered, making sure he didn't blow the deal.

Foreman tried to explain. "I think that what he said is that he doesn't agree that Ramsey Clark is right, or that J. Edgar Hoover is right. I didn't argue *that* as evidence in this case, I simply stated that, underwriting the statement of General Canale [sic] that they had made the same statement. You are not required to agree with it all."

The judge wanted nothing to sidetrack the smooth proceedings. "You still . . . your answers to these questions that I asked you would still be the same? Is that correct?"

"Yes, sir," Ray answered.

And so the proceedings continued with Canale's presentation of a report of what would have been the evidence had this been a real trial.

After hearing from eyewitnesses that Dr. King had been killed on the balcony of the Lorraine Motel, Canale called experts from the Memphis Police Department and the FBI to testify on how they had accumulated physical evidence that linked Ray to the scene of the crime.

In the boarding house room that Ray (a/k/a Eric Starvo Galt) had rented, the FBI and police found a green bedspread, a pair of pliers and a hammer, some shaving articles, binoculars, beer cans, a newspaper, a T-shirt, shorts, a transistor radio, and two leather straps for binoculars. The testimony established that the white Mustang was found in Atlanta, Georgia. It had a sticker on it that indicated it had crossed the border into Mexico. The pliers had been obtained in Los Angeles, California, as had the T-shirt and shorts. In the bathroom from where the shot was supposed to have been fired, the investigators found scuff marks in the bottom of the tub. They found the window of the bathroom opened and the screen forced off.

"This [window] sill was ordered removed, was cut away and was subsequently sent to the FBI for comparison," Canale said, "and the proof would show through expert testimony that the markings on this sill were consistent with the machine markings as reflected on the barrel of the 30-06 rifle which has heretofore been introduced to you."

If this were a trial Canale said, eyewitnesses would be called to testify that Ray had purchased the rifle in Birmingham, Alabama, that he'd stayed at a motel in that city and had checked out on the nineteenth of December and had returned to Los Angeles. Also Dr. Russel C. Hadley of Hollywood, California, would be called by the state to testify that "in his capacity as a plastic surgeon, he did perform an operation on the nose of the defendant under the name of Eric Galt on March 5, 1968."

Canale placed in evidence a photo he said was of James Earl Ray, a photo of a graduating class from the International School of Bartending.

Other evidence Canale said would have been presented in a trial was the expert testimony of FBI fingerprint analyst George Bornebreke. The fingerprint expert would testify that he found "a print of sufficient clarity on the rifle . . . another print of sufficient clarity for identification on the scope mounted on the rifle . . . a print on one of the Schlitz beer cans . . . a print on the binoculars . . . a print on the front page of the April 4th issue of the *Memphis Commercial Appeal* . . ." and "prints of sufficient clarity" on maps of Atlanta, Birmingham, Texas, Oklahoma, Louisiana, California, Arizona, New Mexico, and Mexico, all of which, it could be proved, were the fingerprints of James Earl Ray.

The entire presentation of the case took just under three hours. There was a recess for lunch, after which Ray was ordered jailed for ninety-nine years.

As soon as Ray began to serve his sentence he renewed his protestations of innocence and began working for a new trial. He fired attorneys Percy Foreman and Arthur Hanes, alleging that he had not had a fair trial. He said that he'd been "set up to take the rap" for a crime he didn't commit. At Ray's hearing on a new trial, he stated, under oath, "I personally did not shoot Dr. King, but I may have been partly responsible without knowing it."

If Ray's psychological profile made him a likely victim for anyone who might need a fall guy in a murder, he was equally well suited to be a victim of mind control. The crimes for which he had previously been tried and convicted were all robberies in which no one was harmed. They were all remarkable for one thing—the chase that followed.

Each time Ray committed a crime he left a trail of evidence. Each time he left the scene in either a footrace or a hair-raising car chase, with outraged citizens or police or both in hot pursuit. In each crime, Ray behaved like a little boy who'd just stolen money from his father's pockets and was then daring him to catch and punish him. He was from a deprived family, the eldest of eight children. Many individuals who were once emotionally deprived children learn to seek negative attention since positive attention was unavailable to them in their formative years. James Earl Ray fit that pattern. In the opinion of a psychologist he may have committed his daring daylight robberies not out of a need for money, but out of a subconscious desire to receive love.

The only evidence which cast light on Ray's possible motive for the assassination was an eyewitness report that he had spoken passionately of his hatred of blacks in a Los Angeles bar.

A few years after Ray's sentencing, other evidence came to light which suggested that the FBI had a stronger motivation to kill Martin Luther King than Ray had. On November 19, 1975, the Senate Select Committee on Intelligence made public the fact that the FBI had sent a compromising tape recording with an anonymous letter to Dr. King in late 1964 in a crude attempt to blackmail him into silence. Dr. King had thought the tape and letter were an effort to drive him to suicide.

King received the package thirty-four days before he was to receive the Nobel Peace Prize. The tape was allegedly of a sexual encounter of Dr. King and a young woman. It was accompanied by an unsigned note that read, "King there is only one thing left for you to do. You know what it is. You have just thirty-four days in which to do it. (This exact number has been selected for a specific reason.) It has definite practical significance. You are done. There is but one way out for you."

A month after Dr. King received his copy of the tape, a duplicate was sent to his wife. Mrs. King said publicly that she and her husband had listened to the tape together and had concluded that it had nothing on it that would discredit King.

The Senate subcommittee said that at about the same time Mrs. King had received her copy of the tape, a copy was submitted to FBI Director J. Edgar Hoover. Accompanying that tape was a memorandum written by the FBI Chief of Counter-Intelligence William Sullivan. The memo suggested that the FBI discredit King by "knocking him off his pedestal."

The Senate committee disclosed further that the FBI had kept tabs on Dr. King for six years prior to his death. It had instituted sixteen different wiretap operations and had planted eight room bugs in its attempts to catch him in some compromising situation which could be used for blackmail or public discreditation. The shocked Senate select committee members discovered that the taps and bugs had produced "thousands of hours of tapes."

In addition, it was discovered that Hoover had ordered some of his men to rewrite reports that had originally indicated King was not a threat to the country. Those officials who were ordered to change their reports readily did so, the committee said, because they feared for their jobs.

After the Senate Select Committee on Intelligence made these facts known, Mrs. Coretta King said what she had feared to say before. She said she believed that her husband had been killed by a government conspiracy.

"The way he was documented and followed around by Hoover and the CIA, when he was abroad, it [his assassination] would have to have been attached to the forces of our government that felt he was a threat to the system as it existed," said Mrs. King.

A few days after Mrs. King issued that statement, Maryland private investigator Harold Weisberg used the Freedom of Information Act to obtain previously classified FBI reports. These reports revealed that directly contrary to claims made by Canale at Ray's "trial," the FBI had been unable to find any physical evidence that a rifle had been fired from the window in Ray's rooming house, either on the weapon or in the room from which the assassin had allegedly fired. This was a crucial discovery, in that it was the rifle alone which linked Ray to the killing.

If the rifle was not fired from the second-story room, then, no matter how Ray's fingerprints got on the weapon, reasonable doubt existed that Ray was the assassin. No ballistics evidence links the rifle to the bullets in King's body. The FBI's evidence, which was kept secret, had all the while pointed to the conclusion that the rifle could have been planted in front of the rooming house to implicate Ray while the real assassin had fired from a location outside the rooming house.

A few months after Weisberg's find, *Newsday* published a copyrighted story reporting that a top law-enforcement official in Memphis had removed one particular black detective who had been assigned to protect Dr. King just hours before he was assassinated. The *Newsday* article suggested that Detective Ed Redditt had been pulled from his post because he had developed a contingency plan to apprehend any assassin who might make an attempt on King's life. Redditt's plan was to seal off a four-block area in the event a shot was fired.

Earlier the same week, *Newsday* had revealed that the Memphis Police Department had assigned "provocateurs" to protect King. The paper charged that men who had previously participated in anti-King riots were "protecting" the civil rights leader at the moment he was shot.

The activities of James Earl Ray during the year preceding the assassination could be interpreted to suggest the possibility that Ray was a patsy in the mold of Oswald. Ray had been to Mexico, New Orleans, and Los Angeles, places which had figured prominently in the activities of Oswald and the others who were indicted by Jim Garrison.

Facts which were not presented at Ray's quick "trial" included the following: Ray had escaped from prison, one year before the King assassination. Evidence indicated that he had been helped by someone in his escape. During the year he was "on the lam," he received an estimated $12,000 from a source he identified only as "Raoul." He had no difficulty in obtaining a car and several complete sets of identification. Each set belonged to a living individual, something an intelligence agent would prefer if he were to set up a false identity. Ray had no difficulty traveling all over the United States, Canada, and Mexico with his fake papers.

The contradictory history of Ray's activities in Los Angeles led private investigators to consider, as they had in the Oswald case, that there may have been two James Earl Rays. One, the James Earl Ray who had been in prison, was a painfully shy fellow who seldom opened his mouth and hardly ever raised his voice. Fellow inmates found they had a hard time describing him, since he maintained such a low profile. He had been raised dirt-poor, had never graduated from a school of any kind, and there is no record of his ever having expressed a political idea about anyone. In Los Angeles, the "other" James Earl Ray was described as an outgoing fellow. He enrolled in and graduated from bartending school; he became involved in an altercation with a girl in a bar who objected to his making slurs about the black race; he was very conscientious about his appearance and was an impeccable dresser, who even wore expensive alligator shoes; and he was a right-wing politician who conspicuously campaigned for George Wallace.

One other bit of evidence gives unity to the contradictions—Ray had been hypnotized while in Los Angeles.

It was not mentioned in Ray's "trial," but at the time of his arrest in London, he had in his possession three books on hypnotism: *Self-Hypnotism: The Technique and Its Use in Daily Living* by Leslie M. LeCron, *How to Cash In on Your Hidden Memory Power* by William D. Hersey, and *Psychocybernetics* by Dr. Maxwell Maltz. Ray had told William Bradford Huie, "I took a course in hypnosis while in L.A. I had read a lot about it in prison on how it was used in dentistry and medicine."

On November 27, 1967, Ray appeared in the office of Dr. Mark Freeman, a psychologist who practiced in Beverly Hills. Dr. Freeman remembered that Ray, who'd given his real name, asked to be hypnotized because he wanted to sleep better and remember things better.

"This fellow really wanted to improve his mind," Dr. Freeman said. "He had an awe of learning. He had a bent for reading. He didn't fight hypnosis. He learned something."

Dr. Freeman told George McMillan, author of *The Making of an Assassin*, "You've got to keep in mind that I get a lot of angry people around here. A lot of people who come to me want to teach me how to do it. I get a lot of rough stuff around here. I mean psychotic, that stuff. But I couldn't pick up on any of that with Ray. He made a favorable impression on me. He was a good pupil. I'd show him how to go under, and pretty soon he'd be lying on the couch on his back and start talking. I taught him eye fixation, bodily relaxation, how to open himself to suggestion. I gave him lots of positive feelings of confidence."

It may have been that Freeman found Ray so suggestible because he had been hypnotized before. His contact with Freeman and other hypnotists (he told Huie he'd been to as many as eight) may have been prompted by an unconscious urge to undo what had already been done to him—a hypnotically induced split personality, one which was programmed to kill upon command, or merely one which was programmed to run away, following his normal pattern, but this time on command. It's easy to program someone to do under posthypnotic cue what he normally does. And it's a lot easier to program a patsy than it is to program a hit man.

Chapter Sixteen
CONFESSION BY AUTOMATIC WRITING

The circumstances of Robert Kennedy's death are well known. On June 5, 1968, at 12:15 A.M., Sen. Robert Kennedy was shot in the pantry of the Ambassador Hotel in Los Angeles. Karl Uecker grabbed the gun, a .22 caliber Iver-Johnson revolver. It was smoking in the hand of Sirhan Beshara Sirhan, a Palestinian refugee.

The Los Angeles police immediately took Sirhan into custody. At first they appeared to be taking every precaution so that they wouldn't make the same mistakes the Dallas police had. They taped every interrogation session with the suspect and kept him under surveillance through a closed-circuit TV camera in his cell. They took every measure to protect the life of this man, the second "lone nut" to gun down a Kennedy.

Trying to avoid anything which would be an infringement on the rights of the alleged assassin, the police carefully informed Sirhan of his legal rights before trying to interrogate him.

Through the first hours of questioning, Sirhan chose to remain silent. For some time, no one knew who the curly-haired, swarthy man in custody was.

It wasn't until the police found a truck in the parking lot of the hotel, and traced it to Sirhan Beshara Sirhan, that they were certain of his identity. Police immediately went to his house and searched his bedroom. On the floor next to Sirhan's bed was a large spiral notebook. On the desk was another notebook. There was a third small notebook, a good deal of occult literature, a brochure advertising a book on mental projection, and a large brown envelope from the Internal Revenue Service on which someone had written, "RFK must be disposed of like his brother was." At the bottom of the envelope was scrawled "Reactionary."

In one of the notebooks there was a page which was used later in the trial to prove premeditation: "May 18, 9:45 A.M.—68. My determination to eliminate RFK is becoming more the more of an unshakable obsession . . . RFK must die—RFK must be killed Robert F. Kennedy must be assassinated RFK must be assassinated RFK must be assassinated . . . Robert F. Kennedy must be assassinated before 5 June 68 Robert F. Kennedy must be assassinated I have never heard please pay to the order of of of of of of of of of this or that please pay to the order of . . ." Also drawn on the page were spirals, diamonds, and doodles.

While Los Angeles Mayor Sam Yorty ignorantly told the press Sirhan was "a member of numerous Communist organizations, including the Rosicrucians," Sirhan's neighbors told a different story. One said he was "very religious." Another reported that he was "just a normal kid. He took cars and bikes apart and put them back together again." Neighborhood kids said he was "nice." When asked if Sirhan was the angry type, a black girl in his neighborhood said, "He didn't show it." Arthur Bean, another neighbor said, "Someone talked that kid into gunning down Kennedy."

When Irwin Garfinkel, a deputy attorney in the public defender's office, asked Sirhan about the shooting, he said, "I don't remember much about the shooting, sir. Did I do it? Well, yes, I am told I did it. I remember being at the Ambassador. I was drinking tom collinses. I got dizzy. I went back to my car so I could go home. But I was too drunk to drive. I thought I'd better find some coffee. The next thing I remember I was being choked and a guy was twisting my knee."

George Plimpton, editor of the *Paris Review*, was in the hotel pantry when Kennedy was shot. He was one of the men who wrestled Sirhan down. According to *Newsweek*, Plimpton "offered some eloquent testimony that appeared to some to support the defense's contention that Sirhan Bishara Sirhan had, in fact, been in a 'trance' during the shooting. 'He was enormously composed', recalled Plimpton. 'Right in the midst of this hurricane of sound and feeling, he seemed to be almost the eye of the hurricane. He seemed purged.' "

The chief counsel for the Los Angeles chapter of the American Civil Liberties Union, A. L. Wirin, went to Sirhan's defense within hours of his arrest. On his second meeting with the accused, Wirin brought the local papers with him. Sirhan read the headline "KENNEDY'S DEAD," then he dropped his head in grief. After fighting to control his emotions, he looked at Wirin through tear-filled eyes and said, "Mr. Wirin, I'm a failure. I believe in love and instead of showing love. . . ." Then, Wirin recalled, "he muttered something about having betrayed his own primary beliefs."

That night, Sirhan complained of being sick. He became very dizzy and had severe stomach cramps, just as had Castillo and Candy Jones. For several weeks Sirhan was given a half grain of phenobarbital at night to help him sleep.

The Los Angeles police went through the motions of looking into the possibility that a conspiracy was behind the RFK assassination. They looked for the girl in the polka-dot dress who witnesses said had been standing next to Sirhan, smiling and talking to him just before he began shooting in the pantry. Sirhan also said he'd been talking to the girl after he'd drunk several tom collinses. The girl in the polka-dot dress was not found, and conflicting statements cast doubt on whether there had ever been such a girl. Forty-five "top men" from the Los Angeles Police Department (LAPD) were assigned the job of tracking down all leads to a conspiracy, but incredibly, they came up empty-handed.

A bag of women's clothing, which included a polka-dot dress and new undergarments, was found by the LAPD in an alley, but police could not find out who'd bought them or who'd worn them. According to Sirhan's biographer Robert Blair Kaiser, ". . . The police and FBI hardly did all they could [to find the owner of the polka-dot dress]. They used faulty logic and browbeat witnesses to eliminate the girl in the polka-dot dress."[1]

To penetrate Sirhan's amnesia, the defense decided to call in an expert hypnotist, Dr. Bernard L. Diamond of the University of California. Diamond was the associate dean of UCLA's School of Criminology and a professor of both law and psychiatry. No one knew more about law, psychiatry, and hypnosis than Diamond.

In a prehypnosis interview, Diamond asked Sirhan to tell him about his notebooks, and Sirhan said he couldn't recall writing them.

Diamond asked if he thought that what he had done helped things, and Sirhan said, "I'm not proud of what I did."

"What do you mean, you're not proud of it?" Diamond asked him. "You believe in your cause, don't you?" (Sirhan had been contacted by Arab sympathizers and others who insisted that the reason he'd killed Kennedy was out of sympathy for the PLO.)

"I have no exact knowledge, sir, that this happened yet. I'm all, it's all in my mind, but goddamn it, when my body played with it . . . I couldn't understand it. I still don't believe it. My body outsmarted my brain, I guess."

"What did your body do?" Diamond asked.

"Pulled that trigger," Sirhan said.

"Does your body remember it, even if your mind doesn't?"

"I don't give a damn, sir, in a way. Now I don't even care," Sirhan said.

Diamond asked Sirhan if he'd thought about suicide. "Hell, no," Sirhan said, "I couldn't do that."

Then Diamond expressed a thought which contained a significant "Freudian slip." "Why didn't you turn the gas on yourself, ah, why didn't you turn the gun on yourself after you killed Kennedy?"

Sirhan waved his hand in front of his face. "It was all mixed up. Like a dream."

Diamond hypnotized Sirhan on six of eight visits. At one point, reliving the killing, Sirhan grabbed at his belt on the left side. Until then police had no idea where he'd carried the weapon. Under hypnosis Sirhan also created writings similar to those in his notebooks.

In one session Diamond had Sirhan climb the bars of his cell like a monkey. After he'd been brought out of trance, Sirhan explained the reason for his climb. He said he was only getting exercise. Then Diamond played the tape to prove to Sirhan that he, Diamond, had given the instructions to Sirhan to climb the cage. But Sirhan denied that he'd done it because he'd been hypnotized.

At the trial Dr. Diamond, acting as the director of Sirhan's defense, testified that Sirhan was a paranoid schizophrenic. His testimony was supported by several other doctors who had examined the psychiatric "evidence" obtained from tests, interviews, and hypno-interviews conducted by Diamond.

Dr. Diamond did not consider that Sirhan had been other than self-programmed. Having worked for the Army Medical Corps in World War II, he did not realize that the U.S. cryptocracy could develop mind control and use it to control the political destiny of the nation.

Sirhan was given yet another battery of tests by Dr. Eric Marcus, a court-appointed psychiatrist for the defense. Among the tests was the Minnesota Multiphasic Personality Inventory (MMPI), which contains more than 500 questions requiring true-false answers. Psychologists interpret the answers to the MMPI according to a set of statistical norms. Two of Sirhan's nonresponses were significant, since usually nonresponses are considered to be more important than the "yes-no" responses. The questions Sirhan did not respond to were: "291. At one or more times in my life, I felt that someone was making me do things by hypnotizing me . . ." and "293. Someone has been trying to influence my mind."

By the second visit, Dr. Marcus had had time enough to familiarize himself thoroughly with Sirhan's notebooks. On one page of the notebooks Sirhan had written: "I advocate the overthrow of the current President of the fucken United States of America. I have no absolute plans yet, but soon will compose some. I am poor—this country's propaganda says that she is the best country in the world—I have not experienced this yet—the U.S.—says that life in Russia is bad . . . I believe that the U.S. is ready to start declining, not that it hasn't—it began in November 23, '63, but it should decline at a faster rate so that the real Utopia will not be too far from being realized during the early seventies in this country."

In one of the notebooks the name "Peggy Osterkamp" was written over and over. "I love you, Peggy," in one place and in another, "Peggy Osterkamp Peggy Osterkamp Peggy Osterkamp Peggy Sirhan."

When Dr. Marcus asked Sirhan who Peggy Osterkamp was, he said that she was just a girl he'd met a few times at the ranch where he'd worked as an exerciser of horses. Dr. Marcus asked Sirhan if he'd ever dated her, and Sirhan told Marcus the story he'd told the public defender about the night of the assassination.

That night, Sirhan said, he had gone to a shooting range and practiced with his pistol until the range closed. Then he went with a friend, a foreign student named Mistri, to get a hamburger at Bob's Big Boy Restaurant. While eating, they talked about horses. For some reason Sirhan showed his friend a pocketful of bullets. He then was given a current newspaper and in it he read a news item about a Zionist rally in Hollywood. He became very angry over this and made up his mind to go to the rally. When he could not find that rally, he wandered into the campaign headquarters of Senator Kuchel and there heard that there would be a party at the Ambassador Hotel nearby.

When he got to the hotel he was fascinated by the television lights. He went to the bar and ordered two tom collinses. He got dizzy and said to himself that he'd better go home. He was reluctant to drive in his drunken condition, and the next thing he remembered was being choked in the Ambassador pantry.

Dr. Marcus didn't buy Sirhan's amnesia. He thought that it was only a convenient cover-up, and that Sirhan was a paranoid. In his testimony at Sirhan's trial, Dr. Marcus selected another page from Sirhan's notebook to illustrate his psychological evaluation. On June 2, 1967, Sirhan had written:

> A Declaration of War Against American Humanity . . . when in the course of human events it has become necessary for me to equalize and seek revenge for all the inhuman treatment committed against me by the American people. The manifestation of this Declaration will be executed by its supporter(s) as soon as he is able to command a sum of money (2,000) and to acquire some firearms—the specification of which have not been established yet.
>
> The victims of the party in favor of this declaration will be or are now—the President, vice, etc.—down the ladder. The time will be chosen by the author at the convenience of the accused. The method of assault is immaterial—however, the type of weapon used

should influence it somehow. The author believes that many in fact multitudes of people are in harmony with his thoughts and feelings.

The conflict and violence in the world subsequent to the enforcement of this decree shall not be considered likely by the author of this memoranda, rather he hopes that they be the initiatory military steps to WW III—the author expresses his wishes very bluntly that he wants to be recorded by history as the man who triggered off the last war. . .

In mid-August Sirhan's notebooks were analyzed by the FBI crime lab in Washington. The pages were subjected to photo and chemical analysis to establish when each had been written and in what order. The FBI experts concluded that Sirhan had penned the notes in a haphazard fashion, skipping around in the books. The two pages dated June 2, 1967, and May 18, 1968, the lab said, had actually been written on those dates.

An overview of the notes shows that Sirhan had been concerned with three things that appeared over and over in the writing: money, the girl Peggy Osterkamp, and a new Mustang, in that order of importance—as determined by the number of times each was mentioned.

Several times he had written, "please pay to the order of. . . ," but when asked about this he could not remember what it meant. He had written, "Today I must resolve to come home in a new Mustang. Today I must resolve to come home in a new Mustang. Mustang. Mustang."

The FBI and the LAPD located Peggy Osterkamp. She was a tall, willowy blonde, the attractive daughter of an affluent dairyman. A horse lover, she had once worked at the ranch where Sirhan worked. She said she knew him only slightly and had been introduced to him at the Pomona Fair in 1966. She said she had never dated him.

On one page of the notebooks Sirhan had written, "Tom, my warmest salutations. I do not know what has prompted you to write to me. . ." And on another page he'd written, "Hello Tom perhaps you could use the enclosed $Sol perhaps you could use the enclosed $." On yet another page Sirhan had written: "11 o'clock Sirhan 11 o'clock Sirhan Sirhan Sirhan 11 o'clock Sirhan Livermore Sirhan Sirhan

Pleasanton . . . Hello Tom racetrack perhaps you could use the enclosed $."

The FBI guessed that Sirhan had been writing about Walter Thomas Rathke, his first employer at the racetrack. The FBI found him working as a groom at the Pleasanton Race Stables, just east of Oakland.

Rathke told investigators that he had known Sirhan, and that they'd compared notes on the occult. He said he'd written Sirhan twice and had asked him if he needed any money. Later it was discovered that Rathke had far more influence over Sirhan than he cared to admit, but the LAPD and FBI dropped him as uninteresting.

In addition to examining the bizarre notebooks, investigators also made note of Sirhan's unusual behavior after the assassination. Sirhan, like Candy Jones, had a "thing" about mirrors. In his cell he'd stare into a little mirror for hours on end. He also practiced concentrating on candle flames, trying to turn them from red to blue to green. And he was apprehensive about drugs.

When asked by his biographer Robert Blair Kaiser if he thought he'd get the death penalty, Sirhan shrugged and said, "A death penalty would only be vengeance. What would it gain?" After another pause he added, "I know I've killed a man. At least, I'm told of it. I have nothing in my conscience about it, but . . . I'm told I killed a man, so I deserve some punishment, but maybe I could serve humanity by working ten years in a hospital, to pay my debt you might say." Later Sirhan said flatly, "I don't regard myself as a criminal."

Kaiser reported, "Sirhan talked about Gandhi, and the black revolution." He identified with both. "The Negroes," he said, "can see everything, but they can't eat it. Their only solution is to dig in and eat it." Immediately Sirhan added: "I wanted a new car. I always wanted a Mustang. I said, 'All I need is money and how am I gonna get it?' They're not giving Mustangs away.'"[2] Was Sirhan implying that he killed Kennedy for money?

The court ordered that Sirhan be fully tested psychologically to see what his mental state really was. They gave him an electroencephalogram to see if by chance his brain had been damaged by a fall he'd taken from a horse two years earlier. The EEG showed that Sirhan had a normal brain-wave pattern. Then, just to determine if alcohol had any effect on the pattern, the doctor, who'd obtained the recipe for the Ambassador Hotel's tom collins, gave Sirhan the equivalent of four drinks and measured his brain patterns again. Still there was nothing unusual in them.

But even though the EEG showed no unusual brain activity, Sirhan got very drunk and shivered violently for ten minutes. He became irrational, agitated, and restless. He screamed out curses.

When someone told him, "Dr. Marcus is here," Sirhan screamed, "Get that bastard out of here!" The doctor ordered Sirhan taken back to his inner cell, and Sirhan seemed confused. "What the hell is going on here?" he asked, then grabbed his throat violently (as Castillo had), and appeared to be choking. The doctor noted that he was in a state of delirium.

Robert Kaiser again asked Sirhan about his notebooks and Sirhan explained everything he could about them. He said that they were writings about the occult, that he had been studying the objective mind in relation to the universal mind. "If you give your subjective mind an intense command by your objective mind, your subjective mind will gather the information to carry out the commands of the objective mind. . ."

Sirhan said that he'd been sitting in front of a mirror after he'd seen a replay of Robert Kennedy on television reporting in 1948 on the Arab-Israeli war in Palestine. "I concentrated on RFK in the mirror," he said. "I had to stop him. Finally, his face was in that mirror instead of my own. Then I went to my notebook and started writing. It was part of the auto-suggestion necessary to get my subjective mind to get my objective mind moving. I read in the Rosicrucian magazine how if you wanted to do anything, you should write it down. It automatically works toward the realization of what you want.

"With that power," Sirhan said with intensity, "I could have been a millionaire! A millionaire! Ohh shit!"

"Why did I not go to the races that day?" Sirhan asked Kaiser. "Why did I not like the horses? Why did I go to that range? Why did I save those Mini-Mags [the high-powered bullets used on Kennedy]? Why did I not expend those bullets? Why did I go to Bob's? Why did Mistri give me that newspaper? Why did I drink that night? It was," he said, "like some inner force."

"But you wrote in your notebook 'RFK must die,'" Kaiser said.

"After the bit with the mirror," Sirhan told him, "I forgot it all. The idea of killing Kennedy never entered my mind, sir."[3]

During Sirhan's trial for murder, the judge refused to authorize the use of lie detectors or truth serum. Sirhan, like Ray, was quickly "put away" for life.

There were those, however, who refused to let the matter rest. In 1973, while Sirhan sat in prison, Dr. Edward Simpson, the San Quentin prison psychiatrist, submitted an affidavit to the California courts requesting that Sirhan be granted a new trial and that the Robert Kennedy case be reopened.

Dr. Simpson testified that the "expert" psychiatric-psychological testimony at Sirhan's trial was full of numerous factual errors and misleading to the jury. "Most of the doctors testifying," Simpson said, "saw their role as proving why Sirhan killed Kennedy, which required a focus on pathology (mental illness) that I found does not exist. They failed to consider the real facts in a more objective light and failed to consider the possibility, clearly suggested by the ballistic testimony and Sirhan's own testimony under close scrutiny, that perhaps Sirhan did not kill Robert F. Kennedy."

"Sirhan's trial," Dr. Simpson wrote, "was not handled properly by the mental health professionals. In retrospect, a close study of the trial testimony and my own extensive study of Sirhan leads to one irrevocable and obvious conclusion: Sirhan's trial was, and will be remembered, as the psychiatric blunder of the century."

Dr. Simpson knew whereof he spoke. For six years he had worked at San Quentin Prison and had made a study of men on Death Row. For two years he'd been in charge of the prison's psychological testing program. In 1969 he interviewed and tested Sirhan extensively during twenty weekly visits. After these visits were terminated, Sirhan requested that his family contact Simpson for the purpose of reviewing the psychiatric testimony that had been given at his trial.

After examining Sirhan, and reviewing the "expert" psychiatric testimony, Dr. Simpson discussed his findings with the prison's chief psychiatrist, Dr. David G. Schmidt. Together they concluded that their findings did not confirm "but, in fact, were strictly in conflict" with the findings reported at Sirhan's trial.

"Nowhere in Sirhan's test response," Dr. Simpson said in the affidavit, "was I able to find evidence that he is a 'paranoid schizophrenic' or 'psychotic' as testified by the doctors at the trial . . . The fact is, paranoid schizophrenics are almost impossible to hypnotize. They are too suspicious and do not trust anybody, including friends and relatives, not to speak of a hypnotist from, for him, the most hated race. Psychotics in general are among the poorest subjects for hypnosis. They cannot concentrate, they do not follow instructions and basically do not trust. Sirhan, however, was an unusually good hypnotic subject. Sirhan asked me to hypnotize him, which I did not do, in order not to contaminate my test findings with fantasies. He himself had manufactured a hypno-disk, and was practicing self-hypnosis in his cell, an activity requiring considerable self-control which no psychotic has. The fact that Sirhan was easy to hypnotize, as testified by Dr. Diamond, proves he was not a paranoid schizophrenic.

"Dr. Diamond," Simpson continued, "used hypnosis in six sessions out of eight with Sirhan. What was the purpose of it? To plant ideas in Sirhan's mind, ideas that were not there before? To make him accept the idea that he killed Robert F. Kennedy?

"When Dr. Diamond was unable to get Sirhan to admit that he wrote the notebooks, he testified: '. . . so I undertook some experiments on possible hypnotic suggestion.' This admission strongly suggests the possibility of hypnosis being used for implanting hypothetical ideas in Sirhan's mind, rather than uncovering facts . . . A lie detector, not hypnosis, should have been used in finding out whether Sirhan killed Robert Kennedy.

"Why was a lie detector not used? It should have been, as it is much more reliable than hypnosis, which often provided contaminated results . . . Dr. Diamond's testimony is wrong, as he states: 'I have very little or no faith in the accuracy [of a lie detector].' The truth is, the polygraph exceeds in accuracy certain techniques, such as hypnosis, that tend to fuse and contaminate experiences from past and present and also can be influenced significantly by the operator [hypnotist]; it makes a significant difference who the hypnotist is. . ."

In 1975 when the California investigation into the RFK killing was briefly reopened, the public learned that crucial physical evidence, such as ceiling tiles from the hotel pantry and bullet fragments, had been destroyed or lost by the LAPD. And, as in the Oswald case, critical testimony had been ignored. [The above testimony, of Dr. Simpson, pointed to the possibility that Sirhan was a hypno-programmed assassin.]

Also in 1975, seven years after the crime, former high-ranking U.S. intelligence officer and one of the developers of the PSE Charles McQuiston analyzed recordings of Sirhan's interview with psychiatrists in San Quentin.

Sirhan said, "To me, sir, he [Kennedy] is still alive . . . I still don't believe what has happened . . . I don't believe that he is dead. I have no realization still that I killed him, that he is in the grave." McQuiston's PSE analysis showed that on this statement Sirhan exhibited very little stress.

"After analyzing the tapes," McQuiston said, "I'm convinced that Sirhan wasn't aware of what he was doing. He was in a hypnotic trance when he pulled the trigger and killed Senator Kennedy . . . Everything in the PSE charts tells me that someone else was involved in the assassination—and that Sirhan was programmed through hypnosis to kill RFK. What we have here is a real live 'Manchurian Candidate.' "[4]

After examining Sirhan's PSE charts, Dr. John W. Heisse, Jr., president of the International Society of Stress Analysis, agreed with McQuiston. Dr. Heisse, who had studied hundreds of people under hypnosis using the PSE, said, "Sirhan kept repeating certain phrases. This clearly revealed he had been programmed to put himself into a trance. This is something he couldn't have learned by himself. Someone had to show him and teach him how.

"I believe Sirhan was brainwashed under hypnosis by the constant repetition of words like 'you are nobody, you're nothing, the American dream is gone' until he actually believed them. At that stage someone implanted an idea, kill RFK, and under hypnosis the brainwashed Sirhan accepted it."

Dr. Herbert Spiegel, who wrote the introduction to *The*

Control of Candy Jones, has been billed as one of the country's leading medical experts on hypnosis. Spiegel said of Sirhan's case: "It's very possible to distort and change somebody's mind through a number of hypnotic sessions. It can be described as brainwashing because the mind is cleared of its old emotions and values which are replaced by implanting other suggestions . . . This technique was probably used with Sirhan. From my own research, I think Sirhan was subjected to hypnotic treatment."

Even in the early days of the investigation, there were those who found it easy to believe the hypno-programming theory. Among them was writer Truman Capote, who had for a long while been a friend of Jacqueline Kennedy and her sister, Lee Radziwill. After writing his best seller *In Cold Blood,* Capote was regarded as something of an expert on murder. On the NBC "Tonight" show Capote suggested that Sirhan and his accomplices had been intensively trained and brainwashed trigger men. Their purpose, Capote proposed, was to drive the United States to its knees by assassinating all its leaders.

According to Robert Blair Kaiser, "With a little more diligence than they exercised, and a great deal more intelligence than they had, the police might have established links between Sirhan and the underworld, between Sirhan and the right wing, between Sirhan and the left wing, between Sirhan and the Al Fatah. . ."[5]

But neither the police nor the FBI showed any interest in Sirhan's "connections"—perhaps because there were so many. Like Lee Harvey Oswald, Sirhan was a contradiction. He could be linked to many different groups, all of which could easily have had a political motive to kill Robert Kennedy. So the LAPD did the same thing the Warren Commission did; it took what evidence it needed to prove its case for a "lone nut" and ignored the rest.

Defense director Diamond, subsequently explaining his tactics in Sirhan's trial, said he was surprised when he first tried to hypnotize Sirhan. "Most people may take an hour or more to go under hypnosis the first time," Diamond said. "A schizophrenic usually takes much longer, if he goes under at all. But it took less than ten minutes for Sirhan to go into a deep authentic sleep."

Sirhan, Dr. Diamond concluded, had obviously had experience with hypnosis before. He found that Sirhan was reluctant to speak under hypnosis but that he could easily write without being posthypnotically blocked. "Writing under hypnosis is called automatic writing," Diamond said, "and the term aptly describes the way Sirhan would write like a robot and keep on repeating a word or phrase until I stopped him."

Taking a sheet off a legal pad lying nearby, Diamond asked Sirhan to write his answers to the questions put to him in the hypnotic trance. He showed Sirhan a sample of his diary page.

"Is this crazy writing?" Diamond asked.

"YES YES YES," Sirhan wrote.

"Are you crazy?" Diamond asked.

"NO NO," Sirhan wrote.

"Well, why are you writing crazy?" Diamond asked.

"PRACTICE PRACTICE PRACTICE," Sirhan responded.

"Practice for what?" Diamond asked.

"MIND CONTROL MIND CONTROL MIND CONTROL" is what Sirhan wrote.[6]

Perhaps now, looking back, we can understand more about Sirhan from David. David was a good Air Force candidate for mind-control: He was an obedient soldier, penitent, and patient. His amnesia, you'll recall, was so total, so complete, that it took years of psychotherapy to restore his memory. This is what he had to say on the subject of forgetting and remembering:

"The air force used hypnosis for opening up my subconscious mind. It's the subconscious mind that remembers everything. That was the way it was explained to me. The subconscious mind must trust the person who is conditioning it. So if a person gets another's subconscious mind to trust them, then that subconscious mind will tell them everything that it has seen or heard from the day it was born even back to when it was in its mother's womb.

"So under a voice or word command the information can be brought out once the subconscious has been conditioned to respond to the right command. It might respond to one voice or a group of voices. I'd be given a certain cue and I would remember what I was supposed to remember. I was tested constantly. And then, when the meeting was over, I would be unable to remember, and automatically my subconscious would close.

"The cue command would be at the beginning of a meeting. I don't think you need a dual command. I think you need only a command to start, then once something is finished, the process stops automatically. During the training period I'd do whatever I wanted for a couple of days, then go back and the next thing I knew I was remembering the computer numbers again. A word would be said and I'd just begin remembering. They'd give a command, and if your subconscious has really trusted the person conditioning you, that triggers the memory. I don't know who the person I trusted was, because I was usually only talking to the tape recorder. I was actually thinking I was talking to someone that was very close. That would be the person who'd listen to the tape, I guess.

"Really I was talking to myself, but behind this was that person—no name, no face, just that friendly, trustworthy person who had conditioned me. And at the same time it was myself. Who would I trust more than myself?

"They must have told me that after I got out of the service I'd be unable to remember anything of a sensitive nature. I suppose they told me in a way that made it acceptable. But I don't think I ever thought I would have the problems which resulted from loss of my memory . . . When you can't remember things in sequence about your life, you have no idea what that does to you. It interferes with your whole identity."

Considering the connections between Cuba or Cubans and Lee Harvey Oswald, Jack Ruby, James Earl Ray's Latin accomplice 'Raoul,' and Luis Castillo's Cuban intelligence training one cannot help but wonder whether a variation on a scenario written in 1943 by hypnotist George Estabrooks wasn't being played out in the assassinations.

In his book *Hypnotism,* Estabrooks outlined a plan in which suddenly the Cubans had become belligerent and were "building a great naval base at Havana, an obvious menace to our overseas trade." He suggested that a Cuban oil executive be hypno-programmed to spy on the Cuban government. "Neither he nor the group in question (his oil company) need know anything of the arrangements. The instructions to his unconscious in hypnotism are very definite. Find out everything possible about the naval base. He is shown maps of this before he goes and coached as to just what is important. Nor is he ever allowed to submit written reports. Everything must be handed on by word of mouth to one of the very few individuals who are able to hypnotize him . . . Under these circumstances we may count on this man doing everything in his power to collect the information in question."

Estabrooks explained: "There are certain safeguards if we use hypnotism. First, there is no danger of the agent selling out, but this would probably not be of great importance in this particular case. More important would be the conviction of innocence which the man himself had, and this is a great aid in many situations. He would never 'act guilty' and if ever accused of seeking information would be quite honestly indignant. This conviction of innocence on the part of a criminal is perhaps his greatest safeguard under questioning by authorities. Finally, it would be impossible to 'third degree' him and so pick up the links of a chain. This is very important, for the most hardened culprit is always liable to 'talk' if the questioners are but ruthless enough."

Then Estabrooks expanded his point: "Far more useful than the foregoing purpose, however, would be that for a counterespionage service, built along the same lines. This would require both care and time to perfect, but once working it might prove extremely effective. Here the best approach would probably be through those of enemy alien stock within our own gates. Once again let us choose the aggressive Cubans as examples. In the event of war, but preferably well before the outbreak of war, we would start our organization. We could easily secure (say) one hundred or one thousand excellent subjects of Cuban stock who spoke their language fluently, and then work on these subjects.

"In hypnotism we would build up their loyalty to this country; but out of hypnotism, in the 'waking' or normal state we would do the opposite, striving to convince them that they had a genuine grievance against this country and encouraging them to engage in 'fifth column' activities. Here we would be coming very close to establishing a case of 'dual personality.' There is nothing at all impossible in this. We know that dual, and even multiple, personality can be both caused and cured by hypnotism. Moreover, that condition, the Dr. Jekyll and Mr. Hyde combination, is a very real one once it is established.

"They would, as we before said, be urged in the waking state to become fifth columnists to the United States, but we would also point out to them in hypnotism that this was really a pose, that their real loyalty lay with this country, offering them protection and reward for their activities. Through them we would hope to be kept informed of the activities of their 'friends,' this information, of course being obtained in the trance state."

As to the possibility of hypno-programming assassins, Estabrooks wrote: "Strange to say, most good subjects will commit murder. In the writer's opinion there can be very little doubt on this score. They commit a legal, but not an ethical murder, so to speak. For example, we hypnotize a subject and tell him to murder you with a gun. We hand him a loaded revolver. In all probability he will refuse. Frankly for very obvious reasons, the writer has never made the experiment. Corpses are not needed in psychological laboratories."

That, Estabrooks suggests, best be left to the intelligence agencies.[7]

Chapter Seventeen
THE PATRIOTIC ASSASSIN

All the assassins in the cryptocracy's army of hit men are not, by any means, programmed. There are other ways besides mind control to motivate the commission of murder.

In 1298 Marco Polo returned from his Asiatic travels with a tale of assassins who were motivated by an unusually clever technique. Polo described a fortress he had visited in the valley of Alamut in Persia. He said the valley was the headquarters of a notorious group known as the *Ashishin*, from which the word "assassin" evolved.

Polo's story echoed numerous legends about an "Old Man of the Mountain," named Allahudin, who used subtle and elaborate psychological tricks to motivate simple country boys to undertake fearless acts of murder. The Old Man had created an inescapable valley between two mountains by building up high walls at both ends. He turned the valley into a beautiful garden, the largest and most beautiful that had ever been seen. In this valley he planted every kind of fruit tree and built several elaborate, ornamented pavilions and palaces which were said to be of such elegance they could not be described in words. Everything that could be, was covered with gold. The buildings housed the most exquisite collection of paintings and sculpture in the known world. Man-made streams flowed wine, milk, honey, and water.

Also in the Old Man's garden was a harem of the most beautiful houris in the world, trained to play all manner of instruments, and to sing and dance in the most sensuous and seductive manner. All had also been highly trained in the fine art of lovemaking, and were reputed to know every possible way in which to make a man happy.

The garden was well fortified, and there was no way to get in or out of it except through the Old Man's castle. None were allowed to enter the Old Man's Garden except those who had been selected to be among the *Ashishin.*

Youths from the countryside were attracted to the Old Man's court, lured by tales of the fantastic paradise. They believed that the Old Man was one of God's elect, and that angels did his bidding. Only those ranging in age from twelve to twenty years who displayed a taste for soldering and were in prime physical condition were admitted to the *Ashishin.*

The Old Man's garden duplicated every detail of Paradise as described in the Koran by the Prophet Mohammed. A young man selected for the *Ashishin* would soon come to believe in the Old Man just as he already believed in Mohammed.

After the proper indoctrination was completed, the Old Man would have his candidate drugged with a mysterious potion that would cast him into a deep sleep. Once asleep, the candidate would be lifted and carried into the garden and would wake up to find himself in a place he was certain must be Paradise.

As time went on, he'd become more and more convinced that he was in Paradise. Ladies offered everything a young man could want, beyond even the wildest expectations of these simple folk. After only a few days in this garden, no young country boy would have left of his own accord.

When the Old Man wanted to send one of his young *Ashishin* on a mission, he would again have him given the mysterious potion, and carried in his sleep from the garden to the castle. There the youth would be dressed in his old clothes and placed into the original position in which he'd fallen asleep before being taken into the Garden.

Upon awakening to "reality" he would experience a great sense of loss at finding that he was no longer in Paradise. Then, as if meeting this young man for the first time, the Old Man would ask him where he had come from. Usually the youth would reply that he had just come from Paradise, and in great excitement explain that it was exactly as Mohammed had described it in the Koran. This would, of course, give eavesdroppers an even greater desire to get there, and the strongest among them would, days later, wake up in the arms of the houris of paradise.

When the Old Man wanted a rival prince killed, he would command such a youth who'd just returned from Paradise, "Go thou and slay So-and-so; and when thou returnest my angels shall bear thee back into Paradise. But shouldst thou die in the process, nevertheless, even so will I send my angels to carry thee back into Paradise."

With this psychological ruse the Old Man would motivate youths to transcend the fear of death. Usually there was no order that a young *Ashishin* would not obey, no peril he would not risk, so great was his desire to get back to Paradise.

In this manner the Old Man got his *Ashishin* to murder anyone he named. He inspired such dread in the princes of other kingdoms that they offered tribute to him in order that they might live in peace.

Marco Polo's story of early mind control has elements which bear a striking similarity to today's modern *Ashishin* of the cryptocracy.

In the 1950s the CIA smuggled a captive Soviet Air Force officer to the United States for interrogation. He was taken from a West Berlin prison to the CIA's Langley, Virginia, "farm" where he was interrogated at length. Once he'd begun to fear for his life, the CIA men showed him clemency. They took him to New York, where he attended a baseball game, and enjoyed a full sampling of the nectar of freedom. He was plied with wine, women, song, and, in the true American tradition, hot dogs.

After a few weeks of high living, the officer was returned to the West Berlin prison, where he was thrown into a dark cell. At an opportune moment he was allowed to escape. After the CIA had established that he was back at his post, flying the kind of aircraft they needed, they placed an ad in a Western paper which was circulated in the underground behind the Iron Curtain. The ad said that a certain group, not identified with the CIA, would pay $100,000 and arrange for political asylum for any pilot who would deliver the specified Soviet aircraft to the West.

A few days after reading the ad, the Soviet officer flew his plane to the West, collected his $100,000, gained political asylum, and entered the "paradise" he had glimpsed for only two weeks.

It should come as no surprise that many men will murder for simple, old-fashioned motives: sex, love, or money. One psychologist found that a sizable percentage of Americans would be willing to kill another human being if they were offered enough money and assured they would never be caught.

In 1976 a Pasadena, California, psychologist, Dr. Paul Cameron, put the murder-for-pay question to 452 persons. Those questioned were divided into two groups. The first group included those who had already deliberately killed or attempted to kill another human being—usually in military service. The second group consisted of those who had never attempted to kill another person.

The question was: "What is the least amount of money you would take to push a button to kill a person inside a black box—if no one would ever know what you did?"

To Cameron's surprise, 45 percent of those who had killed before said they would be willing to push the black box button for an average price of only $20,000. Twenty-five percent of those who'd never killed said they'd be willing to commit murder for an average price of $50,000, about the price of a house in the suburbs.

Mind control is not needed to motivate assassins; it is, however, most useful to protect assassins and their employers from their own incriminating memories.

In the course of researching this book I talked with a number of retired intelligence personnel (from various government agencies) who had either committed assassination or admitted having heard tales of assassins in their work. Few had heard of an assassin being mind-controlled. One man I consulted, however, took a special interest in the stories of David and Castillo. A chemist who had worked for one of the intelligence research labs, he developed new ways for killing quickly and quietly. And he had met several of the killers who were to use his formulas.

Over a three-year period I talked with this chemist on a number of occasions. He came to trust that I would reveal no names and endanger no lives in telling the story of mind control. After hearing details of my research, he offered to introduce me to a man he had met while working at the lab. This man had been a high-ranking officer in the military, retired after thirty years of service. He had served as an officer in World War II and Korea. During the Vietnam conflict because of his special knowledge of "black science," he was induced to sign on after he retired from military service as a private contractor for the cryptocracy. During the next eighteen years, he accepted several simple assassination jobs. He told the chemist about some of his friends having come back from similar missions with "holes in their memories."

The chemist had arranged a meeting in a noisy public restaurant in a small New Mexico town. Having promised to take no notes, I had secreted in my pocket the smallest tape recorder made, which allowed me to record three hours of the assassin's talk, amid clanking glasses and the general restaurant noise.

When I finally sat across from him, my heart raced. The retired assassin was a sixty-year-old man, gray-haired, but as strong as a man twenty-five years his junior. He had a .357 magnum revolver strapped to his side, as did the man he introduced as his bodyguard. As a cover for the guns, he and the bodyguard both wore National Rifle Association patches sewn prominently to the pockets of their crisply pressed khaki clothes.

The chemist had already informed his friend about the book I was researching. As we sat down and were introduced by first names only, I told the assassin I was especially interested in finding out why men had been returned to civilian life with amnesia.

I mentioned the ad I had placed and the number of men who had responded. I mentioned also that the majority of those who responded, and who had reason to believe their minds had been tampered with, had been enlisted men.

Career officers, he explained, were legally bound by security oaths and economically dependent upon pensions and the privileges of rank, but enlisted men, while perhaps bound by an oath, were likely to separate from the service knowing more than they needed to know. Somebody had to man the high-technology instruments of war and those who were merely computer fodder had to be protected against their knowledge—they could not be trusted. Patriotism, especially during the Vietnam era, was a waning motivation. Their memories had to be erased. But, he explained, mind control was not needed to make a killer. Professionals didn't usually need to be motivated. Most members of search-and-destroy or "executive action" teams were already willing to kill—men, women, or children—if their superiors ordered it.

I concluded that he meant a career killer didn't need to be debriefed by mind control. When I said that, he contradicted me. "You want to bet?" he said. "They'd all kill, but they might not be able to keep the secret. It would depend entirely upon what activities they were involved in, whether the assignment was combat, mop-up, search-and-destroy, political assassination, or whatever . . .

"This debriefing is done in such a way, in many cases, as to cause actual memory damage. As things have gone along and progressed, the techniques have been smoothed out, but memory damage still occurs. In certain cases memory recall is so critical that they bend over backwards to be damned sure that you can't remember.

"Many of the things that occur are not as pretty as you'd like the public to think," he said.

"So you've witnessed many atrocities of war?" I asked.

"I don't call them atrocities," he countered. "I call them military actions. There's a lot of conflict of interest there—the politicians against the military . . ."

I let him rail a while about the evils of the government and then brought him back to my point of interest. "OK, who killed JFK, RFK, King, and who was behind Bremer?" I asked. He didn't remember who Bremer was, so I explained that he was the man who'd shot Wallace.

"Oh, yeah," he said. "Bremer was just a kook. Wallace was shot just by a kook. But whoever got the Kennedys and King probably got a gold medal.

"We were set up to wipe Castro out. Kennedy interfered at the last minute. You want to take a guess at who killed him? . . . Oswald was just a patsy. I've fired the same kind of rifle Oswald was supposed to have used. You can't rapid-fire that thing like he was supposed to have done. Now who do you suppose killed Kennedy?

". . . Don't kid yourself. This country is controlled by the Pentagon. All the major decisions in this country are made by the military, from my observations on the clandestine side of things.

"The CIA's just the whipping boy. NSA [the National Security Agency] are the ones who have the hit teams. Look into their records—you won't find a thing. Look into their budget—you can't. For the life of you, you can't find any way they could spend the kind of money they've got on the number of people who're supposed to be on their payroll. Even if they had immense research and development programs, they couldn't spend that kind of money.

"The CIA's just a figurehead. They are more worldwide—like the FBI is. They're accountants, lawyers, file clerks, schoolboys. They are information gatherers. They've pulled a lot of goddamned shenanigans, I'm not going to deny that, but as far as intelligence goes the NSA's far, far superior to them—far in advance in the 'black arts.'

"The CIA gets blamed for what NSA does. NSA is far more vicious and far more accomplished in their operations. The American people are kept in ignorance about this—they should be, too."

"In other words," I responded, "what you're saying is that the military is more dangerous to our democracy than the CIA or other intelligence groups?"

"The CIA gathers information, but the military heads the show. Look at how many former military officers work for the CIA. Look at how many former high-ranking military officers work for the multinational corporations. Can't you figure it out?"

"What are you suggesting, that there is an invisible *coup d'état* which has occurred in the United States?" I asked.

"OK. There is a group of about eighteen or twenty people running this country. They have not been elected. The elected people are only figureheads for these guys who have a lot more power than even the President of the United States."

"You mean that the President is powerless?" I asked.

"Not exactly powerless. He has the power to make decisions on what is presented to him. The intelligence agencies tell him only what they want to tell him, however. They don't tell him any more than they have to or want to.

"You have to wonder at American stupidity. How much does it take to get people to wake up to what has happened? It's public knowledge that the CIA has falsified documents and given Presidents fake intelligence reports so that he can only arrive at one conclusion—the conclusion they want them to arrive at. The Pentagon Papers revealed that fact.

"What people don't know is that the global corporations

have their own version of the CIA. Where they don't interface with the CIA, they have their own organizations—all CIA-trained. They also have double agents inside CIA and other intelligence organizations who are loyal to those corporations—I mean where's the bread buttered? Would you rather take the government pensions, or would you rather work a little for the corporation on the side and get both government pensions and corporate benefits after you retire? Most men retire after twenty years, and they're only in their mid-forties . . . then they go to work for the corporation they've been working for while they were in government service. They get both the pension and the corporate paycheck that way!

"Together with what the corporations do on their own, they have a worldwide espionage system far better than the CIA's. There is a network of what amounts to double agents—they do work for the government, and may appear to be government agents, but they are first loyal to the corporations. They report to those corporations on the government and on what foreign governments might be planning which would interfere with those corporations foreign investments. These guys are strictly free enterprise agents."

"You call these guys contract agents?" I wondered.

"Oh, no, no, no . . . Take, for example—we develop a new death ray. We've got all the security the government can think of on it. We've got the best security in the United States on it, which is tied for second place for the best security in the world. Tied for first place are the Russian and Chinese security systems.

"Now even with all this security, before FACI [First Article Configuration Inspection, the government's checking system on the manufacturing of military hardware] on a government contract—that death ray is up for grabs in every nation in the world. Any amount of military security can't keep it secret."

"What you're saying," I interrupted, "is that American people are selling secrets, wholesale, to the highest bidder? That is to say, I assume, if the highest bidder is an American company?"

"And even if it's not," he said. "Usually it is another nation. I've dealt with weapons and usually the nation that wants it most will pay the most for it. Once in a while these companies, these government contractors, will find that someone has stolen one of their secrets and there'll be a big flap. But the big boys that are in the military are an entirely different ball of wax . . . the big guys get away with it.

"When one of these companies finds someone inside it that's selling secrets, they take him on a fishing trip, a boat ride, and get rid of him. It's quite common," he said. "For example, if I was tied in with one of these companies where money is no object, and they wanted me to get rid of you, I'd obtain a passport or a duplicate passport with your smilin' face on it. After I'd obtained it, I'd put whoever's face on it I wanted. Then after we dumped you, that 'someone' whose face was on your passport would take a trip to Australia.

"Later your friends or family would notice you were missing and people would begin to inquire as to your whereabouts. Eventually they'd check with the Australian customs who'd say, yes, this guy entered the country on such and such a date. By then the guy who'd traveled over there on your passport would have already come back on his own, and as far as the best detective could tell you've gone to Australia and you've never come back."

"What do you know about the military or the intelligence agencies' use of pain-drug hypnosis?" I asked.

"They used several different things. I've seen, actually seen, guys coming back with blanks only in certain places of their memory. Let's say that I know positively, not by hearsay, that it's done."

"You've seen it?" I asked.

"You'll never get me to admit it," he grinned.

"Well, how is it done?" I asked.

"They use hypnosis and hypnotic drugs. They also use electronic manipulation of the brain. They use ultrasonics, which will boil your brain. When they use hypnosis, they'll at the same time be using a set of earphones which repeat 'You do not know this or that,' over and over. They turn on the sonics at the same time, and the electrical patterns which give you memory are scrambled. You can't hear the ultrasonics and you can't feel it, unless they leave it on—then it boils your gray matter."

Unless the assassin had done the same research I had, he could only have known this through firsthand experience. The CIA documents released in 1976 revealed that ultrasonic research was undertaken for a period of more than twenty years. But the documents said that the research had stopped, so I asked him about that.

"Yeah. The *research* has stopped. They've gone operational. It ain't research any more. They know how to do it," he said.

"Do you mean that it is your *opinion* that it hasn't stopped, or do you mean that you *know* it hasn't stopped?" I asked.

"I mean I *know* it hasn't stopped," he said. "For example, suppose that a dictator in some South American country is setting up real problems and we try to kick him out. We call in some of my former group and say, 'Look, the bastard has got to have a fatal accident, and it's gotta look good—like he fell on a bar of soap and broke his neck in the bathtub or something.' So we go down there and get the job done.

"But it could be quite embarrassing if any of the guys were cross-examined about where they'd been and what they'd done . . . So the guys who were in on the job suddenly have a cold or something, and they are put in a hospital for maybe just a routine checkup. They come out of the hospital in about fifteen days. They're alive. They're well. They're healthy. And they're happy, too. Lots of luck if you question them: *they don't remember anything.*

"That's one way it's used. The other way is to use it to improve memory—say, with couriers. You want a secret message carried, outside the chain of command—there's no need to have it carried by a person if it's a legal message, because the military's got a thousand ways of sending messages which are unbreakably secret. But if it's *outside* the chain of command, as so many things are these days, if it's an illegal message, and our Constitution doesn't permit us to do much that is legal—then you have a hypno-programmed guy carry the message. You improve his memory so that he can carry an entire coded book of what appears to be gibberish, and when he's got it down you give him amnesia and seal off that message by a posthypnotic code word, and whammo! You got a real good secret courier, because he can be tortured to death but he can't remember. *Unless* the proper cue is uttered.

"Then if the courier's going to operate against the enemy, who might have the techniques of hypnosis down, you give him several layers of post hypnotic command. In the first layer, he'll confess a false message. In the second layer, he'll confess another different false message. Finally, maybe on the fourth or fifth layer is the real message.

"Our guy who is supposed to get the message knows that the first three cues, say, are fake, and he gives the fourth cue and out comes the correct message. If the courier was in enemy hands he could be there for years before anybody will figure out where he was in all those layers . . . Each identity will probably be that of a real 'cut out'—a person enough like him, so that the enemy will think that they've got the real guy.

"Many of the men in my unit were given assignments, after which they were so 'persuaded' that they didn't remember anything. I mean to say, they'd gone in believing that the only thing in life that meant anything to them was completing the assignment—to get it done, and when they got done with it they couldn't remember anything about it."

"Could these guys have been that way without hypnosis?" I asked.

"Well, they could have believed that their mission in life was that particular assignment. They usually had no family affiliations, no friends, nothing but their careers. But I don't think they'd have forgotten about those kind of assignments. Not without a little help, let us say."

"What was the conditioning that these guys had, was it drugs, hypnosis, or something else?" I wanted to know.

"Hypnosis, electro therapy, programming them by tapes, by voice-over earphones, awake or in trance, or asleep. By a number of methods."

"How widespread was this mind control?" I asked.

"Well, it was—well, that is something I can't really answer. I know of several different groups upon whom it was used. I know that it was used in some of the hairier areas of Korea and Vietnam, and it was started in World War Two, but it has been refined far more since then. How much of it was used, I don't know. I know of several groups that I was affiliated with that had it used on them."

"Would you say this kind of thing did not exist before World War Two?" I asked.

"Oh, it did. But it was not in such a sophisticated form. It's as old as man, but now it is refined to an art. Before it was torture and psychological pressure—that can accomplish a lot. We've been trained to use it in primitive field situations. But now it's done with the idea that the mind can be put under complete control. Just like they used to use rubber hoses at the police stations. They don't do that anymore. Well, rubber hoses still work, but they don't work as well as some other things which the police now have."

"Are you saying that the police also use mind control?" I asked.

"At the highest levels, yes. The FBI certainly uses it, and they, of course, give a lot of help to the local police. There are certain areas of the brain which control your inhibitions. When they control those centers, then the subject will go on with his assignment, regardless. I've seen men whose mother could be sitting there having coffee, and if they'd been instructed to kill her, they'd walk right in and shoot her, and it wouldn't even upset their appetites for supper. They were conditioned to do it in such a way that they have no guilt. They wouldn't have guilt because after they were through they wouldn't even remember it.

"Let me tell you something: the cheapest commodity in the world is human beings. Most assassins don't need to be programmed to kill. They're loyal to command. They're conditioned, first by the circumstances of their own early life, then by a little 'loyalty training.' The command is their only justification for living. It is also their only protection once they're into it . . .

". . . When I came out of the service and went to work for the government, I had a colonel assigned to me as a bodyguard. When he retired I hired *him,*" he said, pointing to his bodyguard. "He's still with me, and that's why we have these . . ." He pointed to the .357 magnum—the most powerful handgun in the world—strapped to his side in plain sight.

"Who're you worried about? The Russians? The Chinese?"

"Well, I'll tell you. You can damned near put a pin in the map anywhere you want. I got into military security before the Second World War. I was just a kid. Over the years I was assigned to thirty two different countries. So you can draw your own conclusion."

"But what you've been talking about is a political action,

not a military one. How, then, as a military security man did you get involved in political actions?"

"Well, suppose there were countries that were doing technological research on things which could be injurious to the welfare of the United States. I'd be one of the guys assigned to destroy those scientists who were involved in the research. That was with friendly *and* unfriendly governments. So, naturally, if they found out that I was in on it, even now, they'd come after me.

"In other cases I was involved in knocking off some dictators. Then we'd change the people's voting ideas when they had to elect someone."

I returned to the main thread of our conversation, "OK now, since we have this mind-control technology, what is to keep the guys in the cryptocracy or the military, as you maintain, from programming Presidents as soon as they take office, or immediately after they get elected?"

"I have always wondered about Nixon," he mused. "He was very pro-military. He gave them just about everything they wanted in the world. But he wanted to create a monarchy with himself as king. And, slowly but surely, he tried to take over the military and the CIA through subordinate officers who were loyal to him only.

"All you hear about are left-wing conspiracies to overthrow our government. You never hear about right-wing conspiracies.

"Well, some of these right-wing groups are far more dangerous than the left wing. The left wing's mostly kids with dreams. The right wing is usually retired military. They're hard. They're trained. They've got arms. But if the right wing took over right now, there would be just a military dictatorship, and the military would find that its best plans were not upset at all. I'm saying *if* a dictatorship took over. Hell, we've got one right now, but it ain't overt, it's subtle."

"You mean those twenty men you were talking about?" I asked.

"Yeah . . . if the people of this country actually knew that, they would say 'no' the next time they were asked to go to Vietnam. We need the people behind us to fight a war, and if they knew the true facts, who's running things, there wouldn't be the following we'd need to defend the country. That fact alone keeps the sham of politics and 'free elections' going."

"If that is the case, then the results would be different?"

"Yes. If people knew they had a dictatorship. Have you ever heard of a factory slowdown, a strike? Well, Russia has run up against the problem, and so have we in supporting the foreign dictators we support. The American people, like most people, have to feel that they have some right, that they're the 'good guys.' This is the reason we have never lost a war and have never won a peace.

"You've got to maintain the sham of freedom, no matter what. It wouldn't make any difference what party is in charge or whether it was the elected government or what you call the cryptocracy running it; from an operational sense, the government would operate as it presently is. From the point of view of people paying taxes and defending their country, well, we found in Latin America that people won't fight if they think that they have a dictator who is just as bad as the enemy who is attacking.

"That's probably why it would be fairly easy to take over the Soviet Union, short of nuclear war. The Soviets could probably be convinced by psychological warfare that their government is certainly a lot more evil than ours. And if we went to war with them we could eventually win . . . that is until the H-bomb started to fall, then nobody'd be the winner."

Changing the subject I asked, "What area of the military were you involved in?"

"I don't think I ought to answer that. Let's say there was a group which first sought to solve problems politically. If that didn't work, then there was another group which went in and tried to buy solutions. If that failed, then my group was sent in to be damned sure things were accomplished the way we wanted them to be."

"So you were operational, and not research at all?" I asked.

"No. I had been in the lab for a long time. The knowledge I developed was very valuable in an operational sense. I was put into the field because of this knowledge."

"You're talking about pretty sophisticated equipment, not commando stuff?"

"Right. For example, I won't say the name of the country, but it was a South American country. We had a leader that we had supported there who suddenly got the idea that he was going to go off on his own. They tried to reason, negotiate, buy off his affections. When all that failed, my team was sent in to correct the situation.

"We went in very quietly and left very noisily. We went in as tourists, but the important material we brought in was the turning point. Let's say we couldn't reason with the man anymore. We were there about six days, and the problem disappeared. Not many bodies, just the important ones."

The assassin was very specific telling about some of the jobs he'd accomplished. Several included actions taken against a well-known political figure—that, the assassin said, was the only assassination he'd ever "blown." His rifle malfunctioned at the critical moment when he had his target in the crosshairs of his sight.

I cannot say that I had originally believed the assassin's claims, but after running the Psychological Stress Evaluator on all the critical portions of his interview, and finding no areas which unexpectedly or inexplicably produced stress, I believed that the assassin was telling the truth. The newspaper office he had mentioned *was* bombed when he said it was, but he could have gained knowledge of that from newspaper reports. The target of his unsuccessful hit was subsequently "taken care of" in another way which did not cost him his life.

The assassin concluded the interview with a chilling prophecy. Jimmy Carter was then a candidate for the presidency.

"I'll tell you something right now," the assassin said. "You've got a man running for office that is expressing the same goddamned philosophy John Kennedy had. Now he could be saying this stuff just to get elected. Matter of fact, if you look into his background, you find that he was a good naval officer. He had top security clearance. He was trained by Admiral Rickover who, he said, had a strong influence on his life. Taking this into consideration, you can assume that he's a loyal member of the old boy net, so he probably will make a good figurehead president for those in power.

"But if he *ain't* an old boy and if he does believe all those things he's been telling the voters—if he tries to implement those reforms he's talking about, well, it's not a question of whether he's going to be snuffed, it's only a question of when or where."

* * *

The assassin confirmed many of my own conclusions which had been based only on research: that an invisible *coup d'état* had taken place in the United States; that the CIA is only the tip of the cryptocracy iceberg; and that ultrasonic and electrical memory erasure was used to protect "search-and-destroy" operators from their own memories. I had some indication that the cryptocracy had investigated such techniques (a 1951 CIA document had briefly cited the need for such research), but the assassin's disclosure that the cryptocracy had developed invisible forms of sonics and electronic stimulation of the brain for mind control sent me back to the libraries.

Chapter Eighteen
DEEP PROBE

Jose Delgado stood sweating in the center of a bull ring in Madrid. He was steaming from the heat of the sun reflected on the sand. He felt a twinge of natural fear as the door at one end of the walled ring swung open, and a huge black bull lunged forth from the darkness into the *plaza de toros*.

This was a very good bull, one the best *matador* would have desired. It charged as if on rails, straight at Delgado. In front of a ton of black beef two sharp horns aimed to gore the vital parts of his body.

Delgado stood face to face with the charging Andalusian *toro*. But Delgado was no *matador*. He stood in the ring alone in his shirtsleeves. He wore no "suit of lights" and he carried no cape. Instead of a sword, he held only a little black box.

He wanted to wait until the last possible moment, but he could not contain his fear. When the bull was thirty feet away he pressed the button on the box. The bull immediately quit his attack and skidded to a halt. *Toro* looked right, then left, then, as if bewildered, he turned his broad side toward Delgado and trotted away.

From the stands it was difficult to see the metal box between the horns which held that small radio receiver which picked up Delgado's signal and transmitted it as an electric impulse through a probe inserted into the center of the bull's brain. Delgado was not living out the boyhood fantasy of being a *matador*, nor was he demonstrating his bravery. He was demonstrating his faith, as a scientist, in the power of electronic brain stimulation.

Jose Delgado was a neurophysiologist at the Yale University School of Medicine. By 1964, when he made his dramatic demonstration with the bull, he had already been experimenting with electronic stimulation of the brain (ESB) for nearly two decades. His work, supported by the Office of Naval Research, had been inspired by the Spanish histologist Santiago Ramon y Cajal, who said that knowledge of the physiochemical basis of memory, feelings, and reason would make man the true master of creation. Cajal suggested that man's most transcendental accomplishment would be the conquest of his own brain, and upon this premise Jose Delgado began his relentless quest to make his mentor's dream come true.

"From ancient times," Dr. Delgado said, "man has tried to control the destiny of other human beings by depriving them of liberty and submitting them to obedience. Slaves have been forced to work and to serve the caprices of their masters; prisoners have been chained to row in the galleys; men were and still are inducted into the armed forces and sent thousands of miles away to create havoc, take lives, and lose their own.

"Biological assault has also existed throughout recorded history. In ancient China, the feet of female children were bound to reduce their size. In many countries thieves have been punished by having their hands cut off; males have been castrated to inhibit sexual desire and then placed as eunuchs in charge of harems; and in some African tribes it was customary to ablate the clitoris of married females to block their possible interest in other men and insure their fidelity."[1]

The Spanish-born Delgado believed that, thanks to electronic brain stimulation, science was at last on the verge of "a process of mental liberation and self-domination which is a continuation of our evolution." He believed that through the direct manipulation of the brain, society could produce "more intelligent education, starting from the moment of birth and continuing throughout life, with the preconceived plan of escaping from the blind forces of chance."

Delgado believed that by direct influence of the cerebral

mechanisms and mental structure it would someday be possible to "create a future man . . . a member of a psycho-civilized society, happier, less destructive, and better balanced than the present man."

In 1969 Dr. Delgado pleaded that the U.S. government increase research into ESB in order to produce the fundamental information which would give birth to a "psycho-civilized society." He said that the needed research could not be "generated by scientists themselves, but must be promoted and organized by governmental action declaring 'conquering of the human mind' a national goal at parity with conquering of poverty or landing a man on the moon."[2]

Delgado insisted that brain research was much less expensive than going to outer space and would produce benefits to society equal to, if not greater than, those produced by space technology.

By the time Delgado's remarks were published, the cryptocracy had already come a long way in developing the techniques to create the "psycho-civilized society" Delgado dreamed of. Delgado himself had been funded by grants from the cryptocracy but, like other researchers, was kept isolated and compartmented. He had no way of knowing about the other government-directed brain control research that was going on simultaneously with his own. A number of government agencies were actually at work on projects similar to Delgado's, and through these projects the cryptocracy had gained the technology for direct access to the control of the brain and through it, the mind.

In 1949, Dr. Irving Janis of the Rand Corporation had recommended that the air force undertake a study of the "effects of electricity on the brain." His report said that, in research based on the literature of the 1940s, there were at least some indications that electric shocks to the brain might be conducive to mind control.

Janis wrote: "Many studies have shown that there is a temporary intellectual impairment, diffuse amnesia, and general 'weakening of the ego' produced during the period when a series of electroshock convulsions is being administered."

Dr. Janis was not talking about electronic brain stimulation; he was referring to electro-convulsive therapy (ECT), a crude treatment for schizophrenia originated in Hungary in the 1930s, which consisted of passing a strong electrical current through the entire brain at once.

Unlike ESB, ECT was not aimed at the microscopic neural centers of the brain. It was just one large jolt of electricity, which produced, rather than a specific neural event, a massive convulsion. Electrical current administered in such a way temporarily affected the electrical properties of all the neurons in the brain. It produced sharp biochemical changes in the levels of glucose, oxygen consumption, protein synthesis, and other functions. It also produced amnesia, sometimes temporary, sometimes permanent.

As biochemist Steven Rosen said, "The [ECT] treatment is analogous to attempting to mend a faulty radio by kicking it, or a broken computer by cutting out a few of its circuits."[3] Often the extreme convulsions induced by ECT produced such strong muscular contractions that the bones of the subject's body snapped like breadsticks.

But Dr. Janis did not seem to think it too severe a treatment for use in mind control. "From my own and others' investigations of the psychological effects of such treatments," he wrote, "I would suspect that they might tend to reduce resistance to hypnotic suggestions. It is conceivable, therefore, that electroshock treatment might be used to weaken difficult cases in order to produce a hypnotic trance of great depth."[4]

Meanwhile, astonishing discoveries were being made which indicated that the use of electronic stimulation of the pleasure center of the brain as a reward for performance could be used to enhance learning. Experiments conducted at the end of World War II showed that rats learned to run around mazes and perform in Skinner boxes better after they had received properly applied electronic stimulation of their brains. Repeated experiments showed that when animals were rewarded with electricity applied to the pleasure center of the brain, they learned much more rapidly than did animals who were conditioned by rewards of food. One Department of Defense project graphically illustrated the use of such pleasure stimulation conditioning.

The Sandia Corporation in New Mexico was asked by the Department of Defense to set up a demonstration of ESB and film the results. Sandia produced a striking film which showed electrodes being implanted into the brain of an army mule. After the mule recovered from surgery, a brain stimulator was placed in a pack on its back, along with a prism and mirror which were arranged so that they operated a photocell when the animal was facing directly toward the sun. When sunlight struck the photocell, it turned on a brief burst of electricity which was sent along wires into the pleasure center of the mule's brain. When the mule turned away from the sun, the stimulation stopped. But when the mule faced the sun again, the pleasurable stimulation resumed.

So wired, the mule marched over hill and dale across the barren land of New Mexico, always facing the sun. Finally it came to the boundary of the property, where a scientist was waiting. The mirror was reversed and then the mule retraced its steps by keeping its back to the sun. Mules are not noted for being cooperative beasts, but this electrically stimulated mule traced and retraced its path without deviation, just as long as the stimulation continued.

Sandia's mule film created a great deal of enthusiasm at the Pentagon. Quickly, the officers saw the military significance of the experiment: mules could be made to clear minefields! They could be used to deliver explosives to assigned targets, much as the Russians had used trained dogs to carry explosives against German tanks during World War II! And what mules could accomplish on land, porpoises, with much greater intelligence, could accomplish in the sea!

It soon became clear to the cryptocracy that electronic brain stimulation held the greatest promise for specific, selective mind control. The usefulness of drugs in manipulating human behavior had been limited by the inability of researchers to control either the desired or the undesired effects of the drugs with any precision. ESB, however, used in conjunction with psycho-surgery and behavior modification, offered unlimited possibilities. After experiments on laboratory animals met with success, human experimentation was enthusiastically undertaken in quest of the most reliable and absolute method of *remote* control of the mind.

Because human behavior is influenced by many more variables, experimentation on humans proved to be more complex than with animals. Experimenters were constantly reaching false conclusions. Often the observed effects of stimulating certain areas of the brain turned out to be only indirectly related to the stimulation.

For example, a fifty-year-old female mental patient was stimulated in what was thought to be her pleasure center. She had been an extremely withdrawn and melancholy person whose expression always seemed impassive and dour. When electronic stimulation was applied at irregular intervals and different times of day, she would laugh or smile. The scientists concluded that they were stimulating a strong pleasure region in her brain and grew confident that they had found a way to cure the woman of her melancholia. They began to discuss their findings openly in her presence, until one day she became angry and told them she did not enjoy the experiments at all. She explained to the scientists that the stimulus was not giving her pleasure, it was creating a rhythmic contraction of certain pelvic muscles. She had smiled and laughed from being tickled!

After many years of experimentation, it is still unknown just exactly which effects of electronic brain stimulation are psychological, which are physical, and which are psychophysical. For every experiment suggesting that a particular behavior change is due to the direct effect of electricity applied to a center of the brain, there are others which suggest that the effect is a result of some psychological response to the initial stimulus.

From the Brain Research Institute at the University of California came a report by Dr. Mary Brazier that one patient continued to "self-stimulate even after electricity was turned off and there was no more current in the electrode." Others gave similar reports, saying that some subjects continued to press a lever which had rewarded them with pleasurable stimulation long after the current was cut off. These subjects pushed the lever hundreds of times when they were receiving no stimulation at all, and kept on doing it until the experiment was terminated.

Several experimenters reported that ESB elicited sexual feelings and in some cases orgasms. In a report summarizing seven years of research with ESB, Dr. R. G. Heath told of one melancholic patient who had attempted suicide a number of times. When all else failed to elevate his mood, doctors resorted to ESB. An electrode implanted in his hypothalamus was activated and the subject smiled. After the experience he said, "I feel good. I don't know why, I just suddenly felt good." Upon further questioning the patient admitted that there might have been sexual overtones in his experience. He said, "It's like I had something lined up for Saturday night . . . a girl."

Heath reported that in several instances ESB led to orgasm. While orgasms may have been caused by genital sensations created when certain areas of the brain were stimulated, Heath said that he did not believe that genital sensations had to be present for orgasm to occur. He observed that self-stimulation usually stopped after orgasm was reached. He concluded that stimulation of the orgasm center of the brain, if that was what had produced the orgasms, appeared to be no more compelling than masturbation.

From the Soviet Union came a report typical of many of the surprising results of ESB. A thirty-seven-year-old woman suffering from Parkinson's disease was given ESB treatments to alleviate the effects of palsy. The stimulation evoked sexual sensations which eventually led to orgasm. The woman then began to hang around the laboratory. She would initiate conversation with aides and assistants whenever she could. She even waited for them in the hospital corridors and the garden trying to find out when the next session was scheduled. She was especially affectionate toward the doctor who was throwing the switch to activate the probes in her brain. When she was finally told that there would be no more stimulation, she displayed extreme dissatisfaction.

Strangely, the stimulation did not give the woman any sexual pleasure until her menstrual cycle, which had been absent for eight years, resumed as a result of the stimulation. Soviet investigators expressed their belief, based on studies such as this, that the motivational consequences of ESB are subject to conscious control. This conclusion is supported by the results of many experiments in the West as well.

In 1964 Richard Helms reported to the Warren Commission (see Appendix A) that the trend in the Soviet Union was to build "the New Communist/Man" through cybernetics (the use of machines as control/mechanisms). Helms quoted an unidentified Soviet author saying: "Cybernetics can be used in 'molding of a child's character, the inculcation of knowledge and techniques, the amassing of experience, the establishment of social behavior patterns . . . all functions which can be summarized as control of the growth process of the individual.' " The Helms memo indicated that the Soviets did not possess any knowledge which the West did not have, and in some areas even lagged far behind U.S. research. The tone of his memo seemed to suggest that the U.S. cryptocracy was also interested in creating a "new man"—a cyborg.

The term "cyborg" was coined in the mid-sixties by C. Maxwell Cade. It was first used to describe a human body or other organism whose functions are taken over in part by various electronic or electromechanical devices. But true man-machine interface will not exist until the machine becomes an extension not of a man's hands but of his brain. When the machine responds directly to thought, just as an arm or hand does, then the cyborg will be among us. Electronic brain stimulation is the first real step toward the creation of a true cyborg.

ESB has, meanwhile, been strikingly successful in other areas. It has been used to modify mental mechanisms, to produce changes in mood and feelings, to reinforce behavior both positively and negatively. It has been used to activate sensory and motor regions of the brain in order to produce elementary or complex experiences or movements, to summon memories, and to induce hallucinations. It also has been used to suppress or inhibit behavior and experience and memory—outside of the conscious control of the owner of the brain.

ESB has inhibited the intake of food. It has inhibited aggressiveness and even the maternal instinct. It has been widely used in medical research to help stroke victims recover from paralysis and to block epileptic convulsions. It has proved to be an aid to paraplegics in controlling their bladders and it has helped certain kinds of paralysis victims to walk again. It has been found to be effective in blocking even the most severe pain.

ESB has been used by psychiatrists to improve mood, increase alertness, and produce orgasm. It has been used as a conditioning tool to "cure" undesirable social behavior such as homosexuality. And, in 1974, the first victim of Parkinson's disease treated by ESB walked gracefully out of a San Francisco hospital under his own power, thanks to portable ESB. He had a "stimoceiver" implanted in his brain which he could activate from a battery-powered device in his belt. The "stimoceiver," which weighed only a few grams and was small enough to implant under his scalp, permitted both remote stimulation of his brain and the instantaneous telemetric recording of his brain waves.

Ten years before, Dr. Delgado had foreseen the day when a psycho-civilized society would resort to the use of such stimoceivers for control of the masses. He had said, "A two-way radio communication system could be established between the brain of a subject and a computer. Certain types of neuronal activity related to behavioral disturbances such as anxiety, depression, or rage could be recognized in order to trigger stimulation of specific inhibitory structures . . ."[15] What he was describing was a society kept under emotional control by electronic brain manipulation. Rather than have man control a machine with his brain, Delgado wanted the control of man by machine.

The present state of Western technology enables man to open garage doors, fly model airplanes, and change television channels by remote control. The government communicates via telemetry with satellites far out in the solar system. Medical scientists monitor heartbeats and vital functions of patients in hospitals and astronauts on the moon. And by the late 1960s, the "remote control" of the human brain—accomplished *without* the implantation of electrodes—was well on its way to being realized.

A research and development team at the Space and Biology Laboratory of the University of California at the Los Angeles Brain Research Institute found a way to stimulate the brain by creating an electrical field completely outside the head. Dr. W. Ross Adey stimulated the brain with electric pulse levels which were far below those thought to be effectual in the old implanting technique.

In one experiment, Dr. Adey analyzed the brain waves of chimpanzees who were performing tasks that involved learning. He established that there were two very distinct brain-wave patterns which accompanied correct and incorrect decisions. Building on this, Dr. Adey attempted to control the rate at which the chimps learned by applying force fields to the outside of the head to alter behavior, moods, and attention. Dr. Adey's research indicated that his subjects were able to remember new information faster and better with stimulation.

In the vanguard of brain technology, Dr. Adey worried about misuse of ESB when applied to humans. "My personal concern," he said, "is that we do it well. That if we decide that this manipulation is feasible, that we do it in ways that are socially acceptable."[6]

In 1975 a primitive "mind-reading machine" was tested at the Stanford Research Institute. The machine is a computer which can recognize a limited amount of words by monitoring a person's *silent thoughts*. This technique relies upon the discovery that brain wave tracings taken with an electroencephalograph (EEG) show distinctive patterns that correlate with individual words—whether the words are spoken aloud or merely subvocalized (thought of).

The computer initially used audio equipment to listen to the words the subject spoke. (At first the vocabulary was limited to "up," "down," "left," and "right.") At the same time the computer heard the words, it monitored the EEG impulses coming from electrodes pasted to the subject's head and responded by turning a camera in the direction indicated. After a few repetitions of the procedure, the computer's hearing was turned off and it responded solely to the EEG "thoughts." It moved a television camera in the directions ordered by the subject's thoughts alone!

This "mind-reading machine" was the creation of psychologist Lawrence Pinneo and computer experts Daniel Wolf and David Hall. Their stated goal was eventually to put a highly skilled computer programmer into direct communication with the computer. Their research indicated that a nonsymbolic language—brain-wave patterns—did exist. By teaching computers this language, the time-consuming practice of speaking or writing computer instructions could be abandoned. Faster programming would result in an information explosion whose effects could cause a transformation of our civilization unlike anything that has happened since the Industrial Revolution.

Many beneficial effects of the Stanford "mind-reading machine" may eventually accrue. Physically handicapped people may be able to use mini-computers to interpret signals from their environment and compensate for the loss of some bodily functions. The deaf may be able to hear; the blind to see; the paralyzed to walk.

Military applications of a "mind-reading machine" will someday allow faster computer input and output of information, remote control of war machines, and even the creation of animal or human robots to do the bidding of the military.

Norbert Wiener, the "father of cybernetics," once said that the human brain, while functioning in a manner parallel to the computer, actually imitates only *one run* of it. Rudolph Flesch clarified Wiener's statement, adding that it was the computer which had the advantage since it had the ability to store memory away until needed for the consideration of a new problem. He said that while the machine starts each new problem from scratch, man carries his past with him until he dies.

One young scientist at Rockefeller University, Dr. Adam Reed, is working under a Department of Defense contract to change all that. At a 1976 symposium of the American Association for the Advancement of Science, Dr. Adam Reed said, "Ideally, the computer of the future should be an electronic extension of the natural brain functioning in parallel with some of the existing brain structures and using the same program and data languages."

According to Dr. Reed, within two decades it will be possible to encode and transmit brain waves from a small device implanted inside the skull. It will be linked by radio control to a large computer with a huge memory bank which, he said "will have stored in it everything you might want to know about foreign languages, mathematics, music, history—and any other subject you would want to add. You'll enjoy instant recall. The information stored in your own memory cells and in your computer will be readily accessible. You won't be able to forget things . . . You'll also be able to calculate even the most complicated problems with split-second speed."

But Dr. Reed admitted that there were very real dangers to mental freedom posed by the brain technology now being developed. "It is essential that people be able to use them [the computers] for their own purposes rather than for purposes imposed on them by the political structure."

While Dr. Reed conceded that it was "conceivable that thoughts could be injected" into a person's mind by the government, he indicated that he did not believe it had already been done. "If the political system changes and massive abuses appear likely," he said, "that would be the time to disappear from the society."

Dr. Lawrence Pinneo at the Stanford Research Institute also discouraged the idea of a conspiracy to create a "psycho-civilized," mind-controlled society. When asked if there weren't a real and present danger of government control of the thoughts of citizens posed by brain-computer technology, Pinneo told a San Francisco reporter, "Anything is possible. But government could lock us all up today, so this sort of thing doesn't really change that possibility. It is really up to us to be vigilant against misuse."[7]

Typically, the scientists have not been vigilant enough, for the cryptocracy already has developed remote-controlled men who can be used for political assassination and other dangerous work, as is the cyborg in the "Six Million Dollar Man"—but for less noble purposes. Cyborgs—altered and controlled humans—are far less expensive than fully mechanical robots. Due to the high cost of technology men are cheaper than machines, and much more expendable.

Chapter Nineteen

FROM BIONIC WOMAN TO STIMULATED CAT

In 1967 a writer named Lincoln Lawrence published a book which asked the question: Was Lee Harvey Oswald a robot-assassin programmed by a sophisticated technique known as RHIC–EDOM? The letters stood for Radio Hypnotic Intra-Cerebral Control–Electronic Dissolution of Memory.

Lawrence speculated that Oswald had been behavior-controlled and prepared during his "defection" to the Soviet Union as a "sleeper" agent programmed to return to the United States and murder on cue. It was the Manchurian Candidate theme, with one exception. Lawrence insisted that the Russians had not masterminded the RHIC–EDOM plan. It had been masterminded, he thought, by an international cartel of commodities merchants who sought to make millions by driving the market down with the assassination of a president—any president.

Lawrence wrote, "Lee Harvey Oswald was to be utilized as . . . (and now you must clear your brain and put aside your preconceived notions of what espionage and sabotage are *today*) . . . an RHIC controlled person . . . somewhat like a mechanical toy. An RHIC controlled person can be processed (as Oswald was in Minsk), allowed to travel to any country . . . and be put to use even years later by the application of RHIC controls. In short, like the toy, he can in a sense be 'wound up' and made to perform acts without any possibility of the controller being detected.

"Under RHIC, a 'sleeper' can be used years later with no realization that the 'sleeper' is even being controlled! He can be made to perform acts that he will have no memory of ever having carried out. In a manipulated kind of kamikaze operation where the life of the 'sleeper' is dispensable, RHIC processing makes him particularly valuable because if he is detected and caught before he performs the act specified . . . *nothing* he says will implicate the group or government which processed and controlled him."[1]

Mr. Lawrence used as evidence the official Russian records that Oswald had been admitted to the hospital in Minsk at 10 A.M. on March 30, 1961. The records state that he was admitted with complaints about suppuration from the right ear and a weakening in hearing. Lawrence said that this was a cover-up for "the real reason for Oswald's stay—but there was one slight oversight. He was hospitalized for eleven days for an 'adenoid' operation. Eleven days for an adenoid removal is, or course, preposterous. In austere Soviet Russia it was particularly ridiculous!"

What really happened, according to Lawrence, was that during the operation a small electrode was implanted inside Oswald's mastoid sinus. The electrode responded to a radio signal which would make audible, inside Oswald's head, certain electronic commands to which he had already been posthypnotically conditioned to respond. (The autopsy report in Dallas noted that there was a small scar on the mastoid sinus behind Oswald's ear.)

In 1967 the idea sounded utterly preposterous. Mr. Lawrence's book, *Were We Controlled?*, found only a minuscule audience. Lawrence, on the other hand, may have had much more evidence than he was allowed to present. His credentials indicated that he had been "working in liaison with the department of defense."

In 1975 the RHIC–EDOM story surfaced again. This time a Tennessee journalist said he had been given top-secret documents by two former CIA officials whom he would not identify. The journalist, James L. Moore, said that the papers in his possession described the details of "a military technique of mind-control called Radio-Hypnotic Intra-Cerebral Control—Electronic Dissolution of Memory."

Moore described the RHIC–EDOM file as a 350-page scientific report, which was prepared by the CIA immediately after the murder of President John F. Kennedy. He said it described a way of turning men into electronically controlled robots programmed to kill on command.

According to Moore, in the initial (RHIC) stage of programming the prospective killer is put into a deep hypnotic trance, and conditioned to go into trance at the sound of a specific tone. "A person may be placed under this control with or without his knowledge, programmed to perform certain actions and maintain certain attitudes" whenever he hears the tone. "Effective for a lifetime," Moore said, "control may be triggered weeks, months, or even years after the first 'hypnosis' and programming."

"Medically," Moore continued, "these radio signals are directed to certain parts of the brain. When a part of your brain receives a tiny electrical impulse from outside sources, such as vision, hearing, etc., an emotion is produced—anger at the sight of a gang of boys beating an old woman, for example. This same emotion of anger can be created by artificial radio signals sent to your brain by a controller. You could instantly feel the same white hot anger without any apparent reason."

The second part of the process, electronic dissolution of memory (EDOM), Moore said, is more complex. "In the brain is a chemical called acetylcholine, which carries electrical impulses from the eyes, ears, nose, nerve endings, etc., to the part of the brain where memory is located. Memory is nothing more than the recording of these electrical impulses, and acetylcholine is the path (or 'wire') that connects the inner brain to the nerves of your eyes and ears . . . By electronically jamming the brain, acetylcholine creates static which blocks out sights and sounds. You would then have no memory of what you saw or heard; your mind would be a blank."

Moore said that according to CIA documents, this method can be used either to block the memory completely, or to slow it down so that events seem to have happened later than they actually have. "According to a knowledgeable CIA source, this is what happened in Dallas and later in Los Angeles," Moore stated.

Moore quoted his unidentified source as saying, "That was the first thought to hit us at CIA. It's pretty obvious that Ruby was programmed to kill Oswald, even by Ruby's own words . . . As for Sirhan, there is no other explanation; it's a proven fact that his memory has been completely erased."

"The assassination of John Kennedy," Moore said "was carried out by disgruntled CIA and FBI personnel, using Mafia and Cuban exile flunkies."[2]

The claims of James L. Moore would sound fantastic were it not for the abundance of information to support the possibility of their validity.

The Helms memo to the Warren Commission mentioned something called "biological radio communication." Although the term was not fully explained, Helms related it to ESB: "Current research indicates that the Soviets are attempting to develop a technology for control in the development of behavioral patterns among the citizenry of the USSR in accordance with politically determined requirements of the system. Furthermore, the same technology can be applied to more sophisticated approaches to the 'coding' of information for transmittal to population targets in the 'battle for the minds of men.' "

It seems entirely possible that the "radiomagnetic waves" Moore referred to and the "biological radio communication" Helms referred to may be one and the same. Both terms probably describe waves radiated in the electromagnetic spectrum. Both sound waves and radio waves have been studied for their coercive effect on the mind. Ultrasonics are sound waves, traveling in a medium different from the radio medium.

A 1951 MKULTRA CIA memo also described what could be related to RHIC–EDOM. "There is no reason to believe that Russia and some of the satellites have not investigated the effects of ultrasonics on man, perhaps to the extent of its possible use in the future for interrogation purposes. We have no reports which indicate past use of ultrasonics on prisoners for this purpose, but its possible use should be taken into consideration."

Meanwhile, ultrasonics research was underway. Drs. W. Fry and R. Meyers of the University of Illinois used focused ultrasonic waves to make brain lesions of a very controlled size. Their research, conducted in 1961, demonstrated the great advantage of ultrasonics over the psychosurgical techniques which implanted electrodes in the brain. By using low-energy sound beams, Fry and Meyers stimulated or destroyed neural tissue at the point of focus of the beams without cutting or drilling into the brain.

A few years later Dr. Peter Lindstrom at the University of Pittsburgh used a single unfocused sonic beam to destroy fiber tracts without damaging the nerve cells next to them. Lindstrom used this "prefrontal sonic treatment" as a substitute for lobotomy, to destroy fiber tracts in the frontal lobes of patients who had either untreatable pain or severe psychiatric disorders.

The cryptocracy's secret funds and guidance directed a number of research projects into the effects on the brain of various vibrations beyond the perception of ordinary human senses. In one experiment recommended by Norbert Wiener, a sheet of tin was suspended from the ceiling and connected to a generator working at ten cycles per second. When large field strengths of one or two volts per centimeter (a very minute amount) were oscillating at the alpha frequency of the human brain, extremely unpleasant sensations were reported by the volunteer subjects.

Scientists at the Brain Research Institute of the University of California took up the investigation of the effects of oscillating fields on human behavior. They experimented with field strengths of not more than a few hundredths of a volt per centimeter. After fifteen minutes of exposure to such oscillating fields, subjects showed measurable degeneration in performance of simple tasks.

These and other experiments led the cryptocracy to study the effects of very-low-frequency sound (VLF)—the opposite of ultrasonics—as an instrument of war. Research revealed that there is a natural wave guide between the ionosphere and the earth which could be used to propagate very-low-frequency radiation and guide it to selected locations on the earth. Studies showed that this low-frequency sound subtly affected the electrical behavior of the brain in much the same way that Dr. Adey's studies had shown.

The alpha-wave frequency of the human brain is from eight to twelve hertz (cycles per second). The ionospheric wave guide oscillates at eight hertz, making it a good harmonic carrier of low-frequency sound (LFS) waves. These are such long waves that they are virtually impossible to detect. Pentagon reports apply LFS to demobilizing the productive capacity of a civilian population in time of war.

Dr. Frank Barnaby, Director of the Stockholm International Peace Research Institute, suggested what the cryptocracy already knew: "If methods could be devised to produce greater field strengths of such low-frequency oscillations, either by natural (for example, lightning) or artificial means, then it might become possible to impair the performance of a large group of people in selected regions over extended periods."[3]

Since Anton Mesmer's early experiments with animal magnetism, Western scientists have known that monotonous rhythms produce drowsiness and open the individual to hypnotic induction. Scientists found that flashing a strobe light at a certain frequency could induce epileptics to have seizures. Subjected to ultrasonic or very-low-frequency sound in harmony with alpha rhythms, an entire population might be lulled into a state of drowsiness by the unperceived waves, and radio and television—the normal channels of mass hypnosis—could implant suggestions to control the behavior of entire nations.

Soviet scientists have used electronic fields applied outside the head to induce and enhance the qualities of sleep. Their most widely publicized device is the "electrosone." It permits low-frequency pulses to be applied to the cerebral cortex through mild electrical stimulation—electrical current sent through electrodes placed on the eyelids and behind the ears. The Soviets claim that this technique, called electronarcosis, can give the benefits of a full night's sleep in only two or three hours. The sleep is induced rapidly and is so deep that the subject wakes up as fully refreshed and invigorated as if he had slept an entire night.

Radiation has also leapt into the vanguard of mind-control technology. The Soviets have been studying the effects of microwave radiation since 1933. They have found that, among other things, microwaves can affect the central nervous system. They have also discovered that microwave radiation, even of low intensity, can seriously alter the normal rhythm of brain waves, causing hallucinations and drastic perceptual changes, including a loss of the *sense of time*. In biological studies, they found that exposure to microwaves causes changes in protein composition and in white blood cells. A number of endocrine responses are also altered by microwave radiation, including the activities of the thyroid and other glands. And, lastly, microwaves can cause maternal lactation to cease and, in some cases, male sterility.

In 1962 when the CIA discovered that the U.S. Embassy in Moscow was being irradiated with mocrowaves, the cryptocracy reacted with silence. For years the U.S. government knew about the Russian research but appeared to ignore it. Perhaps they feared that any claim that microwave radiation could affect human behavior would bring great restrictions on the use of radar, microwave relays, and on booming microwave oven sales. But a less obvious reason suggests itself: the cryptocracy did not want to draw attention to its own use of radiation in mind control.

In May, 1968, General Electric announced that it was recalling 90,000 color TV sets which were emitting excessive amounts of dangerous X-rays. This set the gears in motion for Senate hearings on the problem of radiation effects. But the cryptocracy still protected its interests; the Defense Department sent two high-ranking medical officers from each branch of the armed forces to assure the senators that safeguards to military-sponsored research into the biological effects of radiation had been adequate. They testified that nobody in the armed forces was being exposed to hazardous amounts of radiation.

Meanwhile, the microwave bombardment of the U.S. embassy continued, and the CIA acted as if it knew nothing at all about radiation effects, denying that there was even a problem.

Yet in 1964, when Dr. Milton Zaret, an ophthalmologist at New York University's Bellevue Medical Center, published a paper reporting that there were harmful biological and behavioral effects to micro-radiation, the CIA immediately came around to ask Zaret some questions.

They wanted to know whether he thought that electromagnetic radiation beamed at the brain from a distance could affect the way a person might act. Dr. Zaret told the CIA that from what he'd read in the Soviet literature on the subject it seemed quite conceivable that microwaves could produce behavioral changes. On another occasion, Zaret said, a CIA doctor inquired of him if he thought that microwaves could be used to "facilitate brainwashing."

In early 1965 the CIA informed Dr. Zaret that the Russians had been irradiating the American embassy. Later Zaret was called to attend a special meeting at the Institute for Defense Analysis in Arlington, Virginia. There he met a number of people from the Defense Department's Advanced Research Projects Agency who were also working on the problem of radiation.

Subsequently Dr. Zaret and others set out to duplicate the conditions of micro-radiation in the embassy. "I remember that in one experiment we succeeded in replicating a Czechoslovakian study of behavioral effects in rats, but also observed some unique convulsions in these animals prior to death." When Dr. Zaret relayed that information to Washington he received a telegram from the CIA ordering him not to pursue the investigation any further.[4]

In May, 1972, Jack Anderson broke the "Moscow Signal" story, which had been kept secret for ten years: the Russians were bombarding the American embassy in Moscow with micro-radiation. Anderson speculated that the CIA had been trying to cover up the fact that the Russians were trying to brainwash American diplomats by microwave bombardment. He implied (probably correctly) that the CIA had created the cover-up to protect its own secrets of mind control by irradiation.

After the disclosure, Anderson came under heavy attack from representatives of both the military and industry. There were loud protests from the microwave oven manufacturers, but no one refuted the brainwashing angle of micro-radiation. The story lay dormant until June of 1977, when it was announced that teams of scientists at the University of Utah and the University of Washington had received grants from the National Institute of Environmental Health Sciences to study the effects of chronic low-level microwave exposure. Dr. Om P. Gandhi, professor of electrical engineering and bioengineering at Utah, said, "Most U.S. scientists are still quite skeptical of the Soviet studies."

As hypnotists had done over the years, many scientists express doubt that electronic, sonic, or radiation techniques would ever be used for such purposes.

"The reports of new technical developments for brain stimulation have led to a concern that it will be used as the basis of an 'electroligarchy' where people could be virtually enslaved by controlling them from within their own brains . . . there is actually little foundation for the belief that brain stimulation could be used as a political weapon," Dr.

Elliot S. Valenstein said. "It doesn't make sense. Anyone influential enough to get an entire population to consent to having electrodes placed in its head would already have his goal without firing a single volt."[5]

Dr. Willard Gaylin agreed, saying, "Electrode implantation or surgical ablation of brain sections as a direct means of political control seems unlikely—much less a threat, for example, than drugs. Such an individualized and dramatic procedure hardly seems suited to the enslavement of populations or the robotization of political leaders. Drugs, brainwashing by control of the media, exploitation of fears through forms of propaganda, and indoctrination through the sources of education, particularly if preschool education or neonatal conditioning . . . becomes an approved practice, all seem more likely methods of totalitarian control."[6]

The British biochemist Dr. Steven Rose issued a similar objection: "Unlike ancient maps marked 'here be monsters,' there will not be . . . brains transplanted into bodies or bottles, thought, memory or mind control, telepathic communication or genetic engineering, artificial intelligence or robots . . . I believe them impossible—or at least improbable; more importantly because scientific advance and its attendant technology only comes about in response to social constraints and social demands. Because there are at present no or few social demands in the direction of these lurid potential developments, they do not represent, in a world beset with crises and challenges to human survival, serious contenders for our concern."[7]

Of course, when science is developed in a piecemeal, compartmentalized fashion, as it is under the direction of the cryptocracy, then no social constraints come into play. Where the public is kept ignorant, and where scientists themselves are manipulated by the grant system, the balance upon which Dr. Rose relies is absent.

On the other hand, for every scientist who denies that mind control exists or will ever exist, there is one who sees it as a *desirable* form of social control. Social psychologist Kenneth B. Clark appears to be one of those men.

Expressing the fear of the nuclear age, and the group paranoia of the Cold Warriors, Clark said, "Given the urgency of the immediate survival problem, the psychological and social sciences must enable us to control the animalistic, barbaric and primitive propensities in man and subordinate these negatives to the uniquely human moral and ethical characteristics of love, kindness, and empathy . . . We can no longer afford to rely solely on the traditional prescientific attempts to contain human cruelty and destructiveness."

Clark suggested that behavior control requirements be imposed on all "power-controlling leaders," and even those who aspire to such leadership. He would require them to accept and submit to "biochemical intervention which would assure their positive use of power and reduce or block the possibility of using power destructively.

"It would assure," Clark said, "that there would be no absurd or barbaric use of power. It would provide the masses of human beings with the security that their leaders would not sacrifice them on the altars of their personal ego."[8]

But if there were a mind-controlled President in the White House, what guarantee would we have that the cryptocracy would not use such access for purely selfish motives? Obviously, submission to any form of mind control by politicians could lead to Clark's "masses of human beings" being sacrificed not on the altars of personal ego but on the altars of national security.

There seems to be a good deal of cultural momentum leading toward a cybernetic anthill society. If we can draw any inference from the numerous predictions made by men of accomplishment in our society, it is that direct brain-computer interface, the cyborg, and the resulting mass mind control are on the horizon.

D. G. Brennan, member of the Hudson Institute, mathematician, and expert on national security problems, predicted: "Computers as sophisticated as the human brain will be small enough to be carried in a shoe box."[9]

Arthur C. Clarke, science-fiction writer, predicted: "The first intelligent computer will be the last machine man will need to make—and quite possibly the last that he'll be permitted to make."[10]

Gerald Feinberg, professor of physics at Columbia University, predicted: "It will be possible to tinker with the brain—to make the human memory more reliable and accessible at the expense, say, of breadth in sensory responses."[11]

Olaf Helmer, founding member of Institute for the Future, predicted: "Slave robots are likely to appear. It may also be possible to devise a way for a disembodied brain to be kept alive so that it can give instruction to a robot which will act as its body."[12]

Stephen Rosen, a research scientist at IBM, predicted the unification of physical medicine (like drugs and organ transplants) with behavioral techniques (like biofeedback, cybernetic learning, and psychology).

And there is Jose Delgado, who predicted—among other things—the coming of a psycho-civilized society. Delgado also said that the fundamental question of the future would be "who is going to exert the power of behavior control?" And even Delgado, a true believer in ESB, issued a warning that in the future the cryptocracy would have to be curtailed. "It is . . . essential that relevant information not be restricted to a small elite, but be shared by all."[13]

Whether created by the use of hypnosis, drugs, behavior modification, electronic or sonic brain stimulation, or through a combination of these tools of psycho-science, the cyborg is stalking us in our dreams. And just as life imitates art, men live out their dreams in their waking state.

The dream, expressed by the prophetic visions of men from all walks of life, is of a time when the machine or the drug will take over and relieve man of his difficult burden of self-responsibility. For better or worse, self-responsibility—where each individual acts consciously, and accepts the consequences of his own actions—is the stuff of which freedom is made.

The prophecies of poets, writers, scientists, and futurists express what can be considered a regressive, devolutionary myth. Sprung from the complexity of technological life, where self-responsibility is largely directed by propaganda and indoctrination, where an ignorant rather than an enlightened public is desired, the majority of responsibile actions can result only in cultural disaster. This, in turn, adds to the frustration of the individual who, weighing all the facts—or what were presented as facts—thought he had made the best choice possible. When these decisions, based on false information, are shown to result in negative effects, the frustration of the individual grows. Weariness eventually sets in, and the individual becomes willing to surrender his self-responsibility and eagerly awaits his liberation by some authoritarian figure.

In the past such people as Hitler, Lenin, or Mao Tse-Tung were high-profile father figures who inspired trust and surrender by the masses. In the modern technological miasma, a nameless, faceless cryptocracy is manipulating world politics.

The cryptocracy supports only those foreign and domestic leaders who are sycophants of secrecy. Of necessity keeping a low profile, the cryptocracy can inspire neither the allegiance nor the surrender which was inspired by the previous exploiters of the cult of personality. Thus, with no human image representing benevolent authority, the masses embrace a substitute father figure—technology. The dream of test tube babies, genetically engineered children, and electronically controlled parents visits the collective unconscious and manifests itself in the way we see the future and in the mysticism of the day.

Even Uri Geller, the Houdini of parapsychology, seems to be expressing this very myth. His supposedly occult powers, he says, come from contact with beings who present themselves as "deliverers" from outer space. With superior intelligence, they manifest all forms of telepathy, telekinesis, and teleportation, and have told Mr. Geller that they are pure mind, maintained throughout eternity by machines which traverse the universe and transcend time and space.

As the psychologist Erich Fromm said, "A specter is stalking in our midst whom only a few see with clarity. It is not the old ghost of communism or fascism. It is a new specter: a completely mechanized society, devoted to maximal material output and consumption, directed by computers; and in this social process, man himself is being transformed into a part of the total machine, well fed and entertained, yet passive, unalive, and with little feeling. With the victory of the new society, individualism and privacy will have disappeared; feelings toward others will be engineered by psychological conditioning and other devices, or drugs."[14]

Fromm is talking about the new myth, which anticipates a time when the machine or the drug will manipulate the human mind and relieve man of his difficult burden of freedom. From the new mythology comes the public tolerance of the cryptocracy as well as the hero worship of such figures as James Bond, the Six Million Dollar Man, and the Bionic Woman. Everywhere in modern literature and art, and in the mass entertainment media, one can see the expressions of the modern myth of techno-eroticism and the dark shadow of the priesthood of secrecy. There is so much of it in the media, in fact, one has to suspect that the American public is deliberately being desensitized to the concept of mind control and the "psycho-civilized" society.

The cryptocracy has gone to absurd lengths to develop remote-controlled beings. Victor Marchetti revealed that the CIA had once tried to create a cyborg cat. He said that the Agency wired a live feline for sound in an attempt to use the pet for eavesdropping purposes. The cat was first altered electronically so that it would function as a listening device in areas where potential enemy agents would be discussing covert plots.

But problems developed, Marchetti said, and the cat had to be rewired. The cat would wander away from its target area, as cats will, looking for food. The CIA fixed that by inserting wires directly into the hunger center of the cat's brain. The wires were attached to a radio receiver which would suppress the hunger pangs by remote control. But once that problem was solved, the CIA found that the kitty needed more circuitry in its brain to control its natural urges. After the hunger center was turned off the cat still would wander away, this time following the sex instinct. The CIA planted more electrodes into the sex center of the cat's brain.

After the electronic feline was at last ready for its assignment, it was turned loose on the street and was followed by a CIA support van loaded with electronic monitoring gear. Before any conversations could be picked up, however, Marchetti said, "the poor thing got run over by a taxicab."

The future should come as no surprise, now that *Science Digest* has reported that as of 1976 there has been a robot population explosion in the United States, with some 6,000 mechanical humanlike machines performing simple human tasks. According to the publication, within the next thirty years there will be more robot than human workers in America.

The typical state of robotdom is still very expensive. Today the average robot costs about $50,000. Most use television to "see" and to review their work. A number of the 6,000 robots in service are busy building other robots. A Robot Institute of America is already in existence.

Even situation comedies such as the television show about the robot cop Holmes and Yoyo embody the myth and condition the individual to accept the day when wires will enter his brain—wires hidden inside the skull: clandestine circuitry for covert cyborgs. The myth of surrender to control by technology is being glorified as the highest aim of the twentieth century version of the American Dream.

The American Dream is turning into a cybernetic nightmare. As poet Richard Brautigan said, trying to find hope in their myth, one day we may all be "watched over by machines of loving grace."

Chapter Twenty
THE ENGINES OF SECURITY

> The gases of technology fuel the engines of security. New terrifying technology created secret systems to conceal its potential for devastation. Those systems, in turn, proliferated into an industry of secrecy. That industry turned its vast potential to research and development to create a science of secrecy—mind control—a science unto itself.

The cryptocracy has used mind control for the past thirty years. It has used it on its own agents and employees, on enemies and friends alike. It has used it on thousands of Americans without their knowledge or consent. The CIA has programmed assassins and couriers by it. The CIA has even openly confessed to its conspiracy of mind control.

Many people will believe that since the CIA has publicly disclosed its interest in mind control, it has now ceased its activities. The earlier CIA records, however, contain a number of termination dates for aspects of Operation Mind Control, yet evidence clearly suggests that it continued past those dates.

In 1975, following the release of the Rockefeller Commission Report and the subsequent investigations by Senator Church's and Congressman Pike's committees, a public accounting was given and apologies were made. The intelligence community was reprimanded and small changes made.

But then in July, 1977, following a wave of resignations in the CIA's clandestine services, CIA Director Adm.

Stansfield Turner informed the Senate Intelligence Committee that the whole story had not been told, even though the case had been put to rest. Turner informed the committee and the White House that additional information had been "found" that proved the CIA had given a number of mind-controlling drugs to untold numbers of Americans, including alcoholics, drug addicts, and terminal cancer patients. A CIA spokesman questioned by reporters could say no more than he did not know how many persons were tested or whether any harm resulted, but that the new records indicated that there had been cases in addition to those revealed in the previous congressional hearings.

The result was headlines in the press about the CIA and drugs (the two words were now commonly linked), but few newsmen made the connection between drug tests and behavior control or mind control.

Recent history documents the fact that the CIA, as the whipping boy of the cryptocracy, covers up and routinely lies about its activities, heaping one lie on another, in a labyrinthine network of falsehood. It stretches credibility to believe, therefore, that the CIA and especially lower-profile members of the cryptocracy have terminated the mind-control research and development that has been going on for thirty years. While it may be true that the pain-drug-hypnosis aspects of mind control have been stopped, one cannot believe that it has ceased because it is thought illegal or immoral. If it has ceased, it has ceased only because it is obsolete and the new technology of radiation and electronic brain stimulation has given the cryptocracy a more powerful form of control. What is likely is that the cryptocracy is moving from the control of an individual's mind and body to the control of the masses.

There is usually a twenty-year lag between the laboratory development of new technology and its application at large. For example, the techniques of audio-visual desensitization were developed at Stanford University in the mid-fifties by Volpe and Lazarus. Working under government contracts at the time, they discovered how a person could be cured of phobic fears (such as the fear of flying), alcoholism, drug addiction, homosexuality, and other "social illnesses" that were previously thought incurable. While Volpe and Lazarus thought that they were merely trying to develop a technique to help people, the government kept a watchful eye on their research. As we discovered by the confession of Commander Narut, the navy used audio-visual desensitization for its own purposes in the mid-seventies, exactly twenty years after its original development. The techniques of narco-hypnosis were developed before World War II and became widely applied in the early sixties. The next stage of mind control is based on radiation which can stimulate the brain for the purpose of remote control. This technology already exists today and is in the experimental stage. We can be assured that inside twenty years it will be used widely by people outside the government.

The problem of mass manipulation is much easier to solve than individual manipulation. A number of studies have demonstrated that people behave in groups much differently then they do alone. One navy study showed that the most potent modifier of behavior is peer-group pressure. This same pressure comes into play in crowd psychology. By controlling the leaders of a crowd, the entire crowd can be controlled through simple suggestion. It has been demonstrated that the cryptocracy has the desire and the technology to control us all.

The cryptocracy's desire for control comes from the desire for national security. National security has been the excuse for illegal U.S. activities everywhere in the world. National security has made a mockery of the Geneva Convention as well as the Constitution of the United States. It has become the fool proof cover not only for authorized foreign activities but also for unsanctioned deeds of both cryptocrats and politicians. It has been the main instrument for the manipulation of public opinion. The primary target against which the national security managers have waged their psychological war has been the people of the United States.

Secret government cannot function in a climate of free speech, open criticism, and public exposure. The question comes down to one of democracy: are the American people willing to give up their democratic principles in exchange for this elusive national security?

In his book *Roots of War,* retired cryptocrat Richard Barnet wrote: "[The] great root of war is the vulnerability of the public to manipulation on national security issues. People do not perceive where their true interests lie and hence are easily swayed by emotional appeals to support policies that cost them their money, their sons, and their own lives. Because they have been willing to accept uncritically the myth of the national interest—i.e., the definition advanced by the national security managers—they exercise almost no control over the commitments the managers make in their name. Supposedly [they are] the beneficiaries of national security policy which really protects the interests of all Americans only if those interests are articulated in the political process."

Even Gen. Maxwell Taylor has lamented the corruption of the national security premise: "National security," he said, "once a trumpet call to the nation to man the ramparts and repel invaders, has fallen into disrepute, a victim of complications arising from the Vietnam syndrome and from its own internal contradictions, excessive defense budgets and collusive dealings with the military-industrial complex. Watergate revelations have fueled suspicions that it may be little more than a cover for executive encroachments upon civil liberties and a free press."[1]

While propaganda, disinformation, misinformation, and assassination have all played an important role in bringing the American democracy to heel, mind control holds its future. It is not surprising that under the label of national security the cryptocracy should seek to control minds. Nor can it come as a surprise that the cryptocracy (always in the vanguard of technology) should develop efficient methods of mind control. But that the legal machinery of the Constitution of the United States should become so fouled by the practitioners of psycho-politics can be experienced only with the outrage one feels at a case of rape, for it not only represents the rape of law and democratic values, but also the rape of heretofore inviolate recesses of man—his mind and soul.

America's form of government was created by men who clearly saw that those in power, no matter how well meaning, could unwittingly endanger the liberties of individuals. The Bill of Rights was incorporated in the Constitution to ensure liberty. Most important, it set limits on what the government *could not do* to its citizens, even with the approval of the majority. The constitutional protections were largely effective until they were circumvented by the technological revolution and the National Security Act of 1947.

By that one act, the safeguards of privacy which had protected U.S. citizens for nearly two centuries were dissolved by a President and approved by a Congress which emerged into a Cold War paralyzed by fear of the new death-dealing technology the cryptocracy had created.

The National Security Act is Catch-22. It grants the National Security Council sweeping and virtually unlimited powers to integrate all policies of government and coordinate all agencies, both foreign and domestic. And just what is "national security"? Presidents, secretaries of state and defense, and scholars have been trying to define it since the term was coined.

According to Frank N. Trager and Frank L. Simonie, in their book *National Security and American Society,* national security is "the part of government policy having as its objective the creation of national and international conditions favorable to the protection or extension of vital national values against existing and potential adversaries."

Over the years we've seen the "adversaries" defined as home-grown Communists, critics of government policy, and all those who marched to end the Vietnam conflict, and eventually anyone Richard Nixon thought did not agree with his political outlook. We've seen "vital national values" defined as those values which work for the interests of corporate oligopolies, regardless of their effects on the national economy or the best interests of the people of the United States.

Rather than live by the principles of democracy, and demonstrate to the totalitarian countries the dynamics of freedom, the cryptocrats resorted to the practice of tyrants. In so doing they damaged their own cherished institutions, and lost time, money, and lives in the useless and poorly conceived Cold War campaign.

Since its beginning the cryptocracy's Cold War against communism has been a losing battle. In the postindustrial world, politics and nationalism were replaced by economics as the motivating force of modern society. The U.S. cryptocrats seemed not to believe in the strength of the "free enterprise" system. They ignored the fact that the world had become more than anything else an economic battleground.

Despite the realities of modern global politics, the U.S. cryptocracy has continued to assert that secrecy is its most vital weapon against the Communists. On this point the argument goes: "In our open society with its free press, it is very difficult to win against a closed Communist world. We must assume the cloak of secrecy, like the Communists, in order to hold our own against them."

The "national security" mentality, while manifesting a paranoid need for secrecy and control, was not the major cause of the growth of cryptocracy. The wonders of the post industrial age were the real cause for the erosion of freedom and privacy. The creation of new weapons of terrible proportions created a nuclear medusa complex; all who looked upon the bomb were turned to stone by their fear. The growth of the "soft" social sciences made possible an invisible totalitarianism. These "humanist" sciences became new tools for studying and labeling individual behavior. They came to be applied to create boundaries of conformity. Further, the desire for conformity created the need for the surveillance of individual behavior.

The growth of government and the creation of large industry inevitably gave birth to bureaucracy. Bureaucracy with the aid and encouragement of the educational establishment created files, and cryptocracy created super secret psychological files. With advancements in electronic technology—increasingly sophisticated microphones, transmitters, and surveillance devices—the erosion of privacy becomes a mudslide.

Although the most often invoked justification for secrecy is to keep technology from falling into enemy hands, history has shown that secrecy is, at best, only a delay to public access. Since modern technologies have been developed from a pool of common scientific knowledge, they cannot be kept secret for long. Eventually, all the fruits of the empirical pool slip from specific control and find their way into general use as independent discoveries take place.

Mind control, as it exists today, will certainly become available within twenty years to anyone who desires it and can afford it.

Equally to blame with the cryptocracy for the development of mind control are the psycho-sciences. Here are educated men and women who have spent many hours in study, preparing (supposedly) for years of service to their fellow men. They have high standing in the society and are well paid. They are the priests of a new religion.

The psycho-scientists who have allowed their research to

be used against humanity should be known. They must be held ethically accountable for their research into coercive mind control. Psychology itself is not entirely made up of cryptocrats and people who seek control over others. There are "humanist" psychologists who seek only to help people. But to behaviorists humanistic psychology seems to be not much more than a fad. And if a fad it is, it will probably fade into history, leaving behind the Skinnerian kind of psychology, the kind that now dominates American college classrooms, the only really reliable psychology, the psychology of conditioning—behaviorism. And from behaviorism comes behavior modification.

Mind control remains above United States law, making it a most attractive tool for clandestine operators. U.S. courts, and even the majority of the psychiatric profession, will not admit that it is possible to take over someone's memory and willpower by mind control. Until now, there has been little to prove the case.

In several foreign democracies, however, cases have come to trial which involved hypnotists who had their subjects commit crimes while acting under posthypnotic suggestion. The "criminals" robbed banks or committed murders without being conscious of their crimes. In these cases the foreign courts placed the burden of blame on the mind controllers. The hypnotists, received the stiff sentences, while the "trigger persons" were either allowed to go free or given greatly reduced terms. In the United States no such precedent exists. When it has come up in a trial, the question has been ducked, since it would require lengthy testimony by psycho-scientific experts, few of whom seem able to agree on the subject.

The closest the courts have come to considering the case of mind control was in the Patty Hearst case, but F. Lee Bailey at the last minute backed away from his planned "brainwashing" defense. One of the witnesses for the defense was Dr. Martin T. Orne. Dr. Orne testified at the trial that Patty Hearst had indeed been "brainwashed" by the SLA. Orne should have known whether or not Patty was brainwashed since, as the head of the Office of Naval Research's Committee on Hypnosis, he helped develop the coercive use of hypnotic mind control for the cryptocracy. Despite Orne's expert testimony Ms. Hearst's plea of duress was ignored and she was imprisoned subject to psychiatric review. A close examination of her trial records may shed a great deal of light on the problem an individual faces in pleading "mind control."

There is no one who dispenses freedom, but there are many who would take it away. Freedom is not free; it must be won. The individual must stand with others against even the smallest tyranny. The price of freedom is eternal vigilance.

Former CIA official Victor Marchetti put it plainly when he told Freedom News Service what he thought ought to be done.

When pressed for concrete examples of what a citizen can do to curb secrecy, dismantle the cryptocracy, and return democracy to the people, he said, "You know, you just can't beat it. The only way you're going to clean up some of these outfits would be if a President came in there and said, 'Well, I'm just not going to tolerate some of this stuff.' And even then it would be difficult for the President because this bureaucracy is so entrenched and so fortified that it has connections all over in our society.

"The CIA and the FBI do not completely control the office of the President obviously, but they have an awful lot of influence in that office. Their influence derives from their capabilities and the fact that they operate in secrecy . . . They are not really concerned with the public interest. They always hide behind such things as 'national security' and they say that their activities are in the 'national interests' but the record doesn't substantiate that.

"You may stem the tide, and then begin to push it back, but you're not going to change it overnight. This thing was building for thirty-five years. . . . These guys aren't going to just change. They're going to go down swinging; we've seen that already."

In July, 1977, President Carter appointed his former Annapolis classmate, Adm. Stansfield Turner, to head the entire intelligence community. In so doing he gave him sweeping powers which no other intelligence director in the history of the United States has ever possessed. With one quick stroke of the pen Carter created America's version of Lavrenti Beria, the late chief of the Soviet secret police. This was Carter's promised reorganization of the intelligence community. Appearing to reorganize it under Turner, he merely strengthened its totalitarian potential.

Only days before Turner was made intelligence czar, as director of CIA he testified before the Senate Intelligence Committee investigating MKULTRA. Turner told the senators that the CIA had stopped all drug testing. He was not asked nor did he volunteer information about new technologies of mind control. He did not say the mind-control operations had stopped, only that the experiments had stopped.

While the CIA has been severely criticized, and some of its activities appear to have been apparently curtailed, so unfettered is the cryptocracy that some other, as yet unnamed, agency may be right now consolidating power and extending the ruthless and subtle psychological war against democracy.

The individual can do little to stop the use of psychopolitics, the cryptocracy's most important weapon, against him. But individuals working together can be effective. Americans are a people with a tradition of freedom—as always, paid for in blood. Regardless of how difficult life becomes in the complex modern world, men must not give up their freedom to think for themselves. From that freedom springs all others. But we must not be naive. To attempt to stop mind control is to confront the cryptocracy in its lair. Without mind control how can the cryptocracy be certain it will be able to keep its secrets?

Operation Mind Control will not be exposed by the work of an honest security guard and diligent reporters, as was the case with Watergate. It will take nothing less than a concerted effort on the part of an informed and outraged public, their legal representatives, and the press to uncover even the beginning of the trail to the identity of the elite core of the secret government which rapes the human mind. And, in the process of uncovering the cabal of mind controllers, the entire fabric of the United States government may well come unraveled.

To stop the cryptocracy, the Congress and the people will have to wage a ceaseless campaign to dismantle and reorganize the entire intelligence community from the ground up under some law other than the ill-defined National Security Act. Congress has taken only token steps in this direction, having embraced the myth of National Security. The campaign to stop the cryptocracy will require the same sacrifice, the same endurance, the same expression of national group feeling that it took to end the Vietnam conflict. In one way the fight is the same—the enemy is within.

Somewhere within the United States the technology for the creation of the perfect slave state is being perfected. Whether or not the mind-controlled state becomes a reality depends not so much upon the efforts of the cryptocrats, but upon the free will, determination, and strength of character of the American people.

Appendix A

MEMORANDUM

SUBJECT: Soviet Research and Development in the Field of Direction and Control of Human Behavior

1. There are two major methods of altering or controlling human behavior, and the Soviets are interested in both. The first is psychological; the second, pharmacological. The two may be used as individual methods or for mutual reinforcement. For long-term control of large numbers of people, the former method is more promising than the latter. In dealing with individuals, the U.S. experience suggests the pharmacological approach (assisted by psychological techniques) would be the only effective method. Neither method would be very effective for single individuals on a long-term basis.

2. Soviet research on the pharmacological agents producing behavioral effects has consistently lagged about five years behind Western research. They have been interested in such research, however, and are now pursuing research on such chemicals as LSD-25, amphetamines, tranquillizers, hypnotics, and similar materials. There is no present evidence that the Soviets have any singular, new, potent drugs, or that they are particularly expert in the use of such drugs to force a course of action on an individual. They are aware, however, of the tremendous drive produced by drug addiction, and perhaps could couple this with psychological direction to achieve control of an individual.

3. The psychological aspects of behavior control would include not only conditioning by repetition and training, but such things as hypnosis, deprivation, isolation, manipulation of guilt feelings, subtle or overt threats, social pressure, and so on. Some of the newer trends in the USSR are as follows:

a. The adoption of a multidisciplinary approach integrating biological, social and physical-mathematical research in attempts better to understand, and eventually, to control human behavior in a manner consonant with national plans.

b. The outstanding feature, in addition to the interdisciplinary approach, is a new concern for mathematical approaches to an understanding of behavior. Particularly notable are attempts to use modern information theory, automata theory, and feedback concepts in interpreting the mechanisms by which the "second signal system," i.e., speech and associated phenomena, affect human behavior. Implied by this research was the hope for a technology for controlling behavior via the "second signal system," using information inputs as causative agents rather than chemical agents, electrodes or other more exotic techniques applicable, perhaps, to individuals rather than groups..

c. This new trend, observed in the early Post-Stalin Period, continues. By 1960 the word "cybernetics" was used by the Soviets to designate this new trend. This new science is considered by some as the key to understanding the human brain and the product of its functioning--psychic activity and personality--to the development of means for controlling it and to ways for molding the character of the "New Communist Man". As one Soviet author puts it: Cybernetics can be used in "molding of a child's character, the inculcation of knowledge and techniques, the amassing of experience, the establishment of social behavior patterns...all functions which can be summarized as 'control' of the growth process of the individual." 1/Students of particular disciplines in the USSR, such as psychologists and social scientists, also support the general cybernetic trend. 2/

4. In summary, therefore, there is no evidence that the Soviets have any techniques or agents capable of producing particular behavioral patterns which are not available in the West. Current research indicates that the Soviets are attempting to develop a technology for controlling the development of behavioral patterns among the citizenry of the USSR in accordance with politically determined requirements of the system. Furthermore, the same technology can be applied to more sophisticated approaches to the "coding" of information for transmittal to population targets in the "battle for the minds of men." Some of the more esoteric techniques such as ESP or, as the Soviets call it, "biological radio-communication", and psychogenic agents such as LSD,

are receiving some overt attention with, possibly, applications in mind for individual behavior control under clandestine conditions. However, we require more information than is currently available in order to establish or disprove planned or actual applications of various methodologies by Soviet scientists to the control of actions of particular individuals.

References

1. Itelson, Lev, "Pedagogy: An Exact Science?" USSR October 1963, p. 10.

2. Borzek, Josef, "Recent Developments in Soviet Psychology," Annual Review of Psychology, Vol. 15, 1964, p. 493-594.

CENTRAL INTELLIGENCE AGENCY
WASHINGTON 25, D.C.

19 JUN 1964

Commission No. 1131

MEMORANDUM FOR: Mr. J. Lee Rankin
General Counsel
President's Commission on the
Assassination of President Kennedy

SUBJECT: Soviet Brainwashing Techniques

1. Reference is made to your memorandum of 19 May 1964, requesting that materials relative to Soviet techniques in mind conditioning and brainwashing be made available to the Commission.

2. At my request, experts on these subjects within the CIA have prepared a brief survey of Soviet research in the direction and control of human behavior, a copy of which is attached. The Commission may retain this document. Please note that the use of certain sensitive materials requires that a sensitivity indicator be affixed.

3. In the immediate future, this Agency will make available to you a collection of overt and classified materials on these subjects, which the Commission may retain.

4. I hope that these documents will be responsive to the Commission's needs.

DECLASSIFIED
By C. I. A.
letter of

Richard Helms
Deputy Director for Plans

Attachment

CD 1131

WARNING NOTICE
SENSITIVE SOURCES AND METHODS INVOLVED

Appendix B

LIST OF DRUGS TESTED BY CIA in Projects Bluebird, Artichoke, MKULTRA, and MKDELTA:

1. Adrenalin
2. Aktetron
3. Alcohol
4. Amphetamine
5. Amphetamine sulphate
6. Analasine
7. Anhalamine
8. Anhalidine
9. Anhaline
10. Anhalonidine
11. Anhalonine
12. Anhalonium
13. Aphyllidine
14. Aphyllin
15. Atropine
16. Atrosine
17. Bambusa
18. Banisterine
19. Barbiturate
20. Belladonna
21. Benzidrene
22. Bendocaine
23. Bromoharmine
24. Bulbocapnine
25. Butyl-bromallyl-barbituric acid
26. Caffeine
27. Caffeine sodium
28. Cannabidiol
29. Cannabinol
30. Cannabis
31. Cannabol
32. Carboline
33. Caroegine
34. Chloral hydrate
35. Cocaine
36. Coffee
37. Coramine
38. Delvinyl sodium
39. Di benzo pyran derivatives
40. Dicain
41. Dramamine
42. Ephedrine
43. Ephetamine
44. Epinephrine
45. Ergot
46. Ergotamine
47. Ethyl harmol
48. Eucaine
49. Eucodal
50. Eukotal
51. Eunacron
52. Epicane

53. Escrine
54. Ether
55. Evipal
56. Evipan
57. Evipan sodium
58. Genoscopolomine
59. Harmaline
60. Harmalol
61. Harman
62. Harmine
63. Harmine methiodide
64. Harmol
65. Heroin
66. Hexacol
67. Histadyl
68. Hydractine
69. Hypoloid soluble hexabarbitone
70. Icoral
71. Indole
72. Indole methyllarmine
73. Insulin
74. Lophop-nine
75. Lyscorbic acid
76. (illegible)
77. (illegible)
78. (illegible)
79. (illegible)
80. Methy-cocaine
81. Metra-ol
82. Morphine
83. Morphine hydrochloride
84. Narco-imal
85. Nambutal
86. Nicotine
87. Nitrous oxide
88. Novacaine
89. Nupercaine
90. Pantocaine
91. Pantopone
92. Parahyx
93. Pellotine
94. Pentobarbitol sodium
95. Pentothal acid
96. Pentothal sodium
97. Percaine
98. Pernoston
99. Peyotl
100. Pheactin
101. Phenamine
102. Pehyl-thio-urethanes
103. Picrate
104. Picrotoxin
105. Procaine
106. Pulegone-orcinol
107. Pulegone-olivetol
108. Pyrahexyl
109. Pyramidon
110. Quinine
111. Salsoline
112. Scopolomine
113. Scopolomine aminoxide hydrobromide
114. Scopolomine-phetamine-eukotal
115. Sodium amytal
116. Sodium barbital
117. Sodium dlelvinal
118. Sodium evipal
119. Sodium pentobarbital (nembutal)
120. Sodium pentothal
121. Sodium phenobarbital
122. Sodium rhodanate
123. Sodium soneryl
124. Sodium thioethamyl
125. Somnifen
126. Stovaine
127. Strychnine
128. Styphnic acid
129. Sympatol
130. Synhexyl
131. Telepathine
132. Tetra-hydro-cannabinol acetate
133. Tetra-hydro-harman
134. Tetra-hydro-harmine
135. Tropacocaine
136. Tropenone
137. Yageine
138. Yageine
139. Yohimbine sulphate

1. Sodium succinate (77)
2. Nikthemine (narcotic)
3. Calcium chloride (35)
4. Caramine (narcotic)
5. Evipan sodium (35)
6. Sodium______(62)
7. Manganese chloride (35)

Notes

Chapter 1

1. Joost A.M. Meerloo, *The Rape of the Mind* (New York, Crowell, 1956)

Chapter 3

1. George E. Smith, *P.O.W.* (Berkeley, Ramparts Press, 1971)
2. Edward Hunter, *Brainwashing in Red China*, 3d ed. (New York, Vanguard, 1971)
3. Robert Jay Lifton, *Thought Reform and the Psychology of Totalism* (New York, Norton, 1961)
4. William J. Bryan, *City News Service*, September, 1960.
5. Francis Gary Powers, *Operation Overflight* (New York, Holt, 1970)
6. Allen Dulles, *The Craft of Intelligence* (New York, Harper, 1963)
7. Albert Biderman and Herbert Zimmer, eds., *The Manipulation of Human Behavior* (New York, Macmillan, 1961)
8. Edgar Schein, *Journal of World Politics*, April, 1959.
9. Eugene Kinkead, *In Every War but One* (New York, Norton, 1959)

Chapter 4

1. George Estabrooks, *Argosy*, February, 1950.
2. Estabrooks, *Hypnotism*, 3d ed. (New York, Dutton, 1944)
3. Bernard C. Gindes, *New Concepts in Hypnosis* (Wilshire Books, N. Hollywood, Cal., 1973)
4. Wesley Wells, *The Journal of Psychology*, 1941.
5. Milton Erickson, *Journal of Biology and Pathology of Interpersonal Relations*, August, 1939.

6. Estabrooks, *Hypnotism.*
7. Seymour Fisher, *The Use of Hypnosis in Intelligence and Related Military Situations.*

Chapter 5

1. L. Ron Hubbard, *The Science of Survival* (Church of Scientology, L.A. Cal., 1951)
2. Louis Gottschalk, *The Use of Drugs in Information-Seeking Interviews.*
3. Albert Hofmann, *High Times,* July, 1976.
4. *Ibid.*
5. Gottschalk, *op. cit.*
6. Alfred W. McCoy, Cathleen B. Reed, and Leonard P. Adams, *The Politics of Heroin in Southeast Asia* (New York, Harper, 1973)
7. Victor Marchetti, Freedom News Service, August, 1976.
8. Solomon Snyder, Zodiac News Service, July 29, 1975.
9. *Washington Post,* July 25, 1975.
10. Gottschalk, *op cit.*

Chapter 6

1. Mary Ray, Documentary, "Guinea-Pig Soldiers," Granada Television, Ltd.

Chapter 7

1. Jessica Mitford, *Kind and Unusual Punishment* (New York, Knopf, 1974)

Chapter 8

1. Donald Bain, *The Control of Candy Jones* (Chicago, Playboy Press, 1976)

Chapter 9

1. Miles Copeland, *Beyond Cloak and Dagger: Inside the CIA* (New York, Simon & Schuster, 1975)
2. Anthony Cave Brown, ed., *The Secret War Report of the OSS* (New York, Berkeley, 1976)
3. *Ibid.*
4. *Ibid.*
5. *Ibid.*
6. *Ibid.*
7. *Ibid.*
8. R. Harris Smith, *OSS: The Secret History of America's First Central Intelligence Agency* (Berkeley, University of California Press, 1972)

9. Townsend Hoopes, *The Devil and John Foster Dulles* (Boston, Atlantic Monthly Press, 1973)
10. David Wise and Thomas Ross, *The Invisible Government*, 5th ed. (New York, Random House, 1964)
11. Harry Rositzke, *CIA's Secret Operations* (New York, Reader's Digest Press, 1977)

Chapter 10

1. John B. Watson, *Behaviorism*, rev. ed. (New York, Norton, 1930)
2. B. F. Skinner, *Beyond Freedom and Dignity* (New York, Knopf, 1971)
3. Interview. Name withheld by request.
4. Skinner, *op. cit.*
5. Lewis M. Andrews and Marvin Karlins, *Requiem for Democracy?* (New York, Holt, 1971)
6. Philip J. Hilts, *Behavior Mod* (New York, Harper, 1976)
7. David Rorvich, *Behavior Control: Big Brother Comes*, Intellectual Digest, Jan. 1974.
8. Leo Hollister, letter to Thomas Clauson, July 3, 1973.
9. Hilts, *op. cit.*
10. James McConnel, *Psychology Today*, May, 1970.
11. Andrew Salter, *Conditioned Reflex Therapy* (New York, Creative Age Press, 1949)
12. Hilts, *op. cit.*

Chapter 11

The full story of Narut and related events can be found in Peter Watson's book *War on the Mind: The Military Uses and Abuses of Psychology* (Basic Books, 1978)

Chapter 12

The full story of Luis Angel Castillo will be told in a forthcoming book, *The Zombie Killer*, by Richard Popkin, Jeff Cohen, and others.

Chapter 14

1. Willem Oltmans, *Atlas*, May, 1977.

Chapter 16

1. Robert Blair Kaiser, *R. F. K. Must Die*, 2d ed. (New York, Dutton, 1970)
2. *Ibid.*
3. *Ibid.*
4. Charles McQuiston, *National Enquirer*, October 20, 1975.

5. Kaiser, *op. cit.*
6. Bernard Diamond, *Psychology Today*, September, 1969.
7. Estabrooks, *Hypnotism.*

Chapter 18

1. Jose Delgado, *Physical Control of the Mind* (New York, Harper, 1969)
2. *Ibid.*
3. Steven Rosen, *Future Facts* (New York, Simon & Schuster, 1976)
4. Irving Janis, *Are the Cominform Countries Using Hypnosis Techniques to Elicit Confessions in Public Trials?*
5. Delgado, *op. cit.*
6. Fred Warshofsky, *The Control of Life: The 21st Century* (New York, Viking, 1969)
7. Lawrence Pinneo, *San Francisco Chronicle*, June 28, 1974.

Chapter 19

1. Lincoln Lawrence, *Were We Controlled? The Assassination of President Kennedy* (New York, University Books, 1967)
2. James Moore, *Modern People*, August 18, 1975.
3. Frank Barnaby, *New Scientist*, June 17, 1976.
4. Paul Brodeur, *The New Yorker*, December 13, 1976.
5. Elliot Valenstein, *Brain Control* (New York, Wiley, 1973)
6. Willard M. Gaylin, Joel S. Meister, and Robert C. Neville, eds., *Operating on the Mind* (New York, Basic Books, 1975)
7. Steven Rose, *The Conscious Brain* (New York, Knopf, 1976)
8. Kenneth Clark, *American Psychological Association Monitor*, October, 1971.
9. David Wallechinsky and Irving Wallace, *The People's Almanac* (Doubleday, 1975)
10. *Ibid.*
11. *Ibid.*
12. *Ibid.*
13. Delgado, *op. cit.*
14. Erich Fromm, *The Revolution of Hope* (Harper, 1968)

Chapter 20

1. Maxwell Taylor, *Foreign Affairs*, April, 1974.

Bibliography

ASSASSINATION

Abrahamsen, David, *The Murdering Mind.* New York, 1973.

Assassination Information Bureau, *Government by Gunplay.* Edited by Sid Blumenthal and Harvey Yazijian, New York, 1976.

Brener, Milton E., *The Garrison Case: A Study in the Abuse of Power.* New York, 1969.

Byas, Hugh, *Government by Assassination,* New York, 1942.

Condon, Richard, *The Manchurian Candidate.* New York, 1958.

Freed, Donald, and Lane, Mark, *Executive Action.* New York, 1973.

Hartogs, Renatus, and Freeman, Lucy, *The Two Assassins.* New York, 1965.

Hurwood, Bernhardt J., *Society and the Assassin.* New York, 1970.

Joesten, Joachim, *Oswald: Assassin or Fall Guy?* New York, 1964.

Kaiser, Robert Blair, *"R. F. K. Must Die!"* 2d ed., New York, 1970.

Knight, Janet M., ed., *3 Assassinations: The Deaths of John and Robert Kennedy and Martin Luther King.* New York, 1971.

Lawrence, Lincoln, *Were We Controlled? The Assassination of President Kennedy.* New York, 1967.

Leek, Sybil, and Sugar, Bert R., *The Assassination Chain.* New York, 1976.

McMillan, George, *The Making of an Assassin.* New York, 1976.

Model, Peter F., and Groden, Robert J., *JFK: The Case for Conspiracy.* New York, 1976.

Newman, Albert H., *The Assassination of John F. Kennedy: The Reasons Why.* New York, 1970.

Noyes, Peter, *Legacy of Doubt*. New York, 1973.

Oglesby, Carl, *The Yankee and Cowboy War*. Kansas City, 1976.

Oltmans, Willem, "New Mysteries in the Kennedy Assassination," *Atlas,* trans. from *Nieue Review,* Amsterdam, May, 1977.

O'Toole, George, *The Assassination Tapes*. New York, 1975.

Sparrow, Gerald, *The Great Assassins*. New York, 1969.

U.S. Congress, Senate, Select Committee to Study Government Operations, Intelligence Activities, United States Senate, *Alleged Assassination Plots Involving Foreign Leaders,* 94th Cong., 1st Sess., 20 November 1975.

U.S. Congress, Senate, Select Committee to Study Government Operations, Intelligence Activities, United States Senate, *The Investigation of the Assassination of President John F. Kennedy: Performance of the Intelligence Agencies,* 94th Cong., 2d Sess., 23 April 1976.

Warren Commission, Report of the, *The Assassination of President Kennedy*. New York, 1964.

BRAINWASHING

Biderman, Albert D., *March to Calumny*. New York, 1963.

Biderman, Albert D., and Zimmer, Herbert, eds., *The Manipulation of Human Behavior*. New York, 1961.

Brownfield, Charles A., *Isolation*. New York, 1965.

Cohen, Stanley, and Taylor, Laurie, *Psychological Survival*. New York, 1974.

Deane, Phillip, *I was a Captive in Korea*. New York, 1953.

Group for the Advancement of Psychiatry, *Factors Used to Increase the Susceptibility of Individuals to Forceful Indoctrination: Observations and Experiments*. Symposium no. 3, New York, 1956.

Hansen, Kenneth K., *Heroes Behind Barbed Wire*. New York, 1957.

Hubbard, L. Ron, *The Science of Survival,* Church of Scientology, L.A. Cal., 1951.

Hunter, Edward, *Brainwashing,* 3d rev. ed., New York, 1962.

Hunter, Edward, *Brainwashing, from Pavlov to Powers*. Linden, New Jersey, 1960.

Hunter, Edward, *Brainwashing in Red China*. 3d ed., New York, 1971.

Kinkead, Eugene, *In Every War but One*. New York, 1959.

Lifton, Robert Jay, *Thought Reform and the Psychology of Totalism*. New York, 1961.

Loh, Robert, and Evans, Humphrey, *Escape from Red China*. New York, 1962.

Meerloo, Joost A. M., *The Rape of the Mind*. New York, 1956.

Pasley, Virginia, *21 Stayed*. New York, 1955.
Sargant, William, *Battle for the Mind*. New York, 1957.
Schein, Edgar H., "The Chinese Indoctrination for Prisoners of War," *Psychiatry*, vol. 19, no. 2, May, 1956.
TSD Tech. Report, *Communist Control Techniques: An Analysis of the Methods Used by Communist State Police in the Arrest, Interrogation, and Indoctrination of Persons Regarded as "Enemies of the State."* S44. 2 April 1956, Declassified by authority of 187475, 14 November 1975.
U.S. Dept. of Army, *Communist Interrogation, and Exploitation of Prisoners of War*. Dept. of the Army Pamphlet no. 30101, May 1956.
U.S. Congress, Committee on Internal Security, House of Representatives, *Hearings Regarding H.R. 16742: Restraints on Travel to Hostile Areas*. 92d Cong., 2d Sess., 19 and 25 September 1972.
U.S. Dept. of Navy, Naval Training Command, *Human Behavior and Leadership*. NAVTRA 10058A, 1973.
White, William Lindsay, *The Captives of Korea*. New York, 1957.
Wolff, Harold G., "Every Man Has His Breaking Point(?): The Conduct of Prisoners of War," *Military Medicine*, vol. 125, no. 2, February, 1960.

CRYPTOCRACY

Ackley, Charles Walton, *The Modern Military in American Society*. Philadelphia, 1972.
Adorno, T. W., Frenkel-Brunswik, Else, Levinson, Daniel J., and Sanford, Nevitt R., eds., *The Authoritarian Personality*. New York, 1969.
Agee, Philip, *Inside the Company: CIA Diary*. Harmondsworth, 1975.
Ashman, Charles, *The CIA-Mafia Link*. New York, 1975.
Ayers, Bradley, Earl, *The War That Never Was*. New York, 1976.
Beaumont, Roger A., *Military Elites*. New York, 1974.
Berding, Andrew H., *Dulles on Diplomacy*. Princeton, New Jersey, 1965.
Blackstock, Nelson, *Cointelpro*. New York, 1975.
Blackstock, Paul W., *The Strategy of Subversion*. Chicago, 1964.
Borosage, Robert L., and Marks, John, eds., *The CIA File*. New York, 1976.
Brown, Anthony Cave, *Bodyguard of Lies*. New York, 1975.
Brown, Anthony Cave, ed., *The Secret War Report of the OSS*. New York, 1976.
Burchard, John, *Q.E.D.: M.I.T. In World War II*. New York, 1948.

Commission on CIA Activities, *The Nelson Rockefeller Report to the President*. New York, 1975.
Copeland, Miles, *Beyond Cloak and Dagger: Inside the CIA*. New York, 1975.
Deindorfer, Robert G., ed., *The Spies*. Greenwich, Conn., 1949.
Dulles, Allen, *The Craft of Intelligence*. New York, 1963.
Dulles, Allen, ed., *Great True Spy Stories*. New York, 1968.
Cox, Arthur Macy, *The Myths of National Security*. Boston, 1975.
Delarue, Jacques, *The Gestapo*. New York, 1964.
Donovan, James A., *Militarism, U.S.A*. New York, 1970.
FitzGibbon, Constantine, *Secret Intelligence in the Twentieth Century*. New York, 1976.
Gehlen, Reinhard, Irving, David, trans., *The Service*. New York, 1972.
Gramont, Sanche de, *The Secret War*. New York, 1962.
Halperin, Morton H., Berman, Jerry L., Borosage, Robert L., and Marwick, Christine M., eds., *The Lawless State*. New York, 1976.
Hamilton, Andrew, *The Helpless Giant, a Metaportrait of the Defense Budget*. New York, 1972.
Hammer, Richard, *The Court Martial of Lieutenant Calley*. New York, 1971.
Hoopes, Townsend, *The Devil and John Foster Dulles*. Boston, 1973.
Hunt, E. Howard, *Under Cover*. Berkeley, 1974.
James, Peter N., *The Air Force Mafia*. New York, 1975.
Kaufman, Richard F., *The War Profiteers*. New York 1972.
Kirkpatrick, Lyman B., Jr., *The Real CIA*. New York, 1968.
Kirkpatrick, Lyman B., Jr., *The U.S. Intelligence Community*. New York, 1973.
Linedecker, Clifford L., *Psychic Spy*. New York, 1976.
McGarvey, Patrick J., *C.I.A., The Myth and the Madness*. Baltimore, 1972.
Marchetti, Victor, and Marks, John D., *The CIA and the Cult of Intelligence*. New York, 1974.
Miale, Florence R., and Selzer, Michael, *The Nuremberg Mind*. New York, 1975.
Mintz, Morton, and Cohen, Jerry S., *America, Inc*. New York, 1973.
Orlov, Alexander, *Handbook of Intelligence and Guerrilla Warfare*. New York, 1972.
Parenti, Michael, *The Anticommunist Impulse*. New York, 1969.
Payne, Robert, *The Corrupt Society*. New York, 1975.
Penkovskiy, Oleg, *The Penkovskiy Papers*. Rev. ed., New York, 1966.
Prouty, L. Fletcher, *The Secret Team*. New York, 1973.

Ransom, Harry Howe, *The Intelligence Establishment.* Cambridge, Mass., 1970.
Rodberg, Leonard S., and Shearer, Derek, eds., *The Pentagon Watchers.* New York, 1970.
Rositzke, Harry, *CIA's Secret Operations,* New York, 1977.
Schiller, Herbert I., and Phillips, Joseph D., eds., *Super*State.* University of Illinois Press, Chicago, 1972.
Schwien, Edwin E., *Combat Intelligence,* Washington, D.C., 1936.
Silk, Leonard, and Vogel, David, *Ethics and Profits.* New York, 1972.
Smith, Harris R., *OSS, The Secret History of America's First Central Intelligence Agency.* Berkeley, 1972.
Smith, Joseph B., *Portrait of a Cold Warrior.* New York, 1976.
Steele, Alexander, *How to Spy on the U.S.* New York, 1974.
Toledano, Ralph de, *Spies, Dupes and Diplomats.* New York, 1967.
Tully, Andrew, *CIA, The Inside Story.* New York, 1962.
Tully, Andrew, *The Super Spies.* New York, 1969.
Tully, Andrew, *White Tie and Dagger.* New York, 1968.
Ungar, Sanford J., *FBI.* Boston, 1976.
U.S. Congress, Senate, Subcommittee on Intergovernmental Relations of the Committee on Government Operations and the Subcommittees on Separation of Powers, and Administrative Practice and Procedure of the Committee on the Judiciary, United States Senate, *Executive Privilege Secrecy in Government Freedom of Information,* 93d Cong., 1st Sess., April 10, 11, 12; May 8, 9, 10, 16; June 7, 8, 11, 26, 1973.
U.S. Congress, Senate, Subcommittee on Intergovernmental Relations of the Committee on Government Operations, United States Senate, *Government Secrecy,* 93d Cong., 2d Sess., May 22, 23, 29, 30, 31; June 10, 1974.
U.S. Congress, Senate, Subcommittees on Administrative Practice and Procedure and Separation of Powers of The Committee on the Judiciary, United States Senate, and the Subcommittee on Intergovernmental Relations of the Committee on Government Operations, *Freedom of Information Executive Privilege Secrecy in Government,* 93d Cong., 1st Sess., June 7, 8, 11, 26, 1973.
U.S. Congress, Senate, Hearings Before the Select Committee to Study Governmental Operations with Respect to Intelligence Activities, *Intelligence Activities Senate Resolution 21,* 94th Cong., 1st Sess., Huston Plan, September 23, 24, 25, 1975.
U.S. Congress, Senate, Hearings Before the Select Committee to Study Governmental Operations with Respect to Intelligence Activities, *Intelligence Activities Senate Resolution 21,*

94th Cong., 1st Sess., Vol. 3, Internal Revenue Service, October 2, 1975.

U.S. Congress, Senate, Hearings Before the Select Committee to Study Governmental Operations with Respect to Intelligence Activities, *Intelligence Activities Senate Resolution 21*, 94th Cong., 1st Sess., Vol. 5, The National Security Agency and Fourth Amendment Rights, October 29, and November 6, 1975.

U.S. Congress, Senate, Hearings Before the Select Committee to Study Governmental Operations with Respect to Intelligence Activities, *Intelligence Activities Senate Resolution 21*, 94th Cong., 1st Sess., Vol. 6, Federal Bureau of Investigation, November 18, 19, December 2, 3, 9, 10, and 11, 1975.

U.S. Congress, Senate, Hearings Before the Select Committee to Study Governmental Operations with Respect to Intelligence Activities, *Intelligence Activities Senate Resolution 21*, 94th Cong., 1st Sess., Vol. 7, Covert Action, December 4, 5, 1975.

Winterbotham, F. W., *The Ultra Secret*. New York, 1974.

Wise, David, *The Politics of Lying*. New York, 1973.

Wise, David, and Ross, Thomas B., *The Espionage Establishment*. New York, 1967.

Wise, David, and Ross, Thomas B., *The Invisible Government*. 5th ed., New York, 1964.

COLD WAR

Fontaine, André, *History of the Cold War: From the October Revolution to the Korean War 1917–1950*. New York, 1968.

Fontaine, André, *History of the Cold War: From the Korean War to the Present*. New York, 1969.

Hale, Julian, *Radio Power*. Philadelphia, 1975.

Hermes, Walter G., *Truce Tent and Fighting Front*. Washington, D.C., 1966.

La Feber, Walter, *America, Russia, and the Cold War, 1945–1966*, New York, 1967.

Lukacs, John, *A History of the Cold War*. Rev. ed., New York. 1962.

Lukacs, John, *A New History of the Cold War*. 3rd ed., New York, 1966.

O'Ballance, Edgar, *Korea 1950–1953*. London, 1969.

Powers, Francis Gary, *Operation Overflight*. New York, 1970.

Stone, I. F., *The Haunted Fifties*. New York, 1969.

Stone, I.F., *The Hidden History of the Korean War*. New York, 1952.

DRUGS

Brecher, Edward M., and the Editors of *Consumer Reports, Licit and Illicit Drugs*. Boston, 1972.

Candlin, Stanton A.H., *Psycho-chemical Warfare*. New York, 1973.

Group for the Advancement of Psychiatry, *Pharmacotherapy and Psychotherapy: Paradoxes, Problems and Progress*. Vol. IX, Report no. 93, March, 1975.

Hersh, Seymour M., *Chemical and Biological Warfare*. New York, 1969.

McCoy, Alfred W., with Read, Cathleen B., and Adams, Leonard P., II., *The Politics of Heroin in Southeast Asia*. New York, 1973.

Newsday, The Heroin Trail. New York, 1974.

U.S. Congress, Senate, Subcommittee to Investigate the Administration of the Internal Security Act and Other Internal Security Laws, *Marihuana-Hashish Epidemic and Its Impact on United States Security*, 93d Cong., 2d Sess., May 9, 16, 17, 20, 21, and June 13, 1974.

THE EROSION OF PRIVACY

LeMond, Alan, and Fry, Ron, *No Place to Hide*. New York, 1975.

Miller, Arthur R., *The Assault on Privacy*. Ann Arbor, Mich. 1971.

Rosenberg, Jerry M., *The Death of Privacy*. New York, 1969.

Sobel, Robert, *The Manipulators, America in the Media Age*. New York, 1976.

U.S. Congress, Senate, Joint Hearings Before the Ad Hoc Subcommittee on Privacy and Information Systems, of the Committee on Government Operations, Subcommittee on Constitutional Rights, Committee on the Judiciary, United States Senate, *Privacy: The Collection, Use, and Computerization of Personal Data*, 93d Cong., 2d Sess., June 18, 19, 20, 1974.

MIND CONTROL

Arons, Harry, *Hypnosis in Criminal Investigation*. Springfield, Ill., 1967.

Bain, Donald, *The Control of Candy Jones*. Chicago, 1976.

Block, Eugene B., *Hypnosis: A New Tool in Crime Detection*. New York, 1976.

Blythe, Peter, *Hypnotism, Its Power and Practice*. New York, 1972.

Brenman, Margaret, "Experiments in the Hypnotic Production of Anti-Social and Self-Injurious Behavior," *Psychiatry*, Vol. 5, 1942.

Bryan, William J., *The Legal Aspects of Hypnosis*. Springfield, Ill., 1962.

Calder, Nigel, *The Mind of Man*. New York, 1973.

Delgado, Jose M. R., *Physical Control of the Mind*. New York, 1969.

Estabrooks, G. H., *Hypnotism*. 3d ed., New York, 1944.

Ferguson, Marilyn, *The Brain Revolution*. Rev. ed. New York, 1975.

Fisher, Seymour, *The Use of Hypnosis in Intelligence and Related Military Situations*, Study SR 177-D, Contract AF 18(600) 1797 Tech Report #4 December 1958.

Fromm, Erika, and Shor, Ronald E., *Hypnosis: Research Developments and Perspectives*. Chicago, 1972.

Gaylin, Willard M., Meister, Joel S., and Neville, Robert C., eds., *Operating on the Mind*. New York, 1975.

Gindes, Bernard C., *New Concepts of Hypnosis*. North Hollywood, CA., 1973.

Gottschalk, Louis A., *The Use of Drugs in Information-Seeking Interviews*, Study SR 177-D, Contract AF 18(600) 1797, Tech Report #2, December, 1958.

Hilgard, Ernest R., and Hilgard, Josephine R., *Hypnosis in the Relief of Pain*. Los Altos, CA., 1975.

Janis, Irving L., *Are the Cominform Countries Using Hypnosis Techniques to Elicit Confessions in Public Trials?*, U.S. Air Force Project Rand Research Memorandum, R.M.-161, April, 1949.

Kline, Milton V., ed., *Hypnodynamic Psychology*. New York, 1955.

LeCron, Leslie M., ed., *Experimental Hypnosis*. Secaucus, N.J., 1972.

LeCron, Leslie M., *Self Hypnotism*. Englewood Cliffs, N.J., 1964.

Marcuse, F. L., *Hypnosis*. Rev. ed., Baltimore, 1966.

Marcuse, F.L., *Hypnosis Throughout the World*. Springfield, Ill., 1964.

Pines, Maya, *The Brain Changers: Scientists and the New Mind Control*. New York, 1975.

Rhodes, Raphael H., ed., *Therapy Through Hypnosis*. Hollywood, CA., 1972.

Roetter, Charles, *The Art of Psychological Warfare*. New York, 1974.

Roruich, David, *Behavior Control: Big Brother Comes*. Intellectual Digest, Jan. 1974.

Rose, Steven, *The Conscious Brain*. New York, 1976.

Russo, Salvatore, and Kuhn, Lesley, eds., *Modern Hypnosis.* New York, 1947.
Salter, Andrew, *What Is Hypnosis?* 3d ed., New York, 1965.
Valenstein, Elliot S., *Brain Control.* New York, 1973.

PROPAGANDA

Baker, Robert K., and Ball, Sandra J, *Violence and the Media.* Washington, D.C., 1969.
De Dubnic, Vladimir Reisky, *Communist Propaganda Methods.* New York, 1960.
Ellul, Jacques, *Propaganda: The Formation of Men's Attitudes.* New York, 1973.
McQuail, Denis, ed., *Sociology of Mass Communications.* Baltimore, 1972.
Mitchell, Richard H. *Thought Control in Prewar Japan.* Ithaca, New York, 1976.
Packard, Vance, *The Hidden Persuaders.* New York, 1973.
Smelser, Neil J., *Theory of Collective Behavior.* New York, 1967.

PSYCHO-POLITICS

Brandt, Anthony, *Reality Police: The Experience of Insanity in America.* New York, 1975.
Eysenck, H. J., *Uses and Abuses of Psychology.* Rev. ed., Baltimore, 1962.
Friedrich, Otto, *Going Crazy.* New York, 1975.
Harper, Robert A., *The New Psychotherapies.* Englewood Cliffs, New Jersey, 1975.
Hoffer, Eric, *The True Believer.* New York, 1966.
Hunter, Edward, ed., *Tactics.* Vols. II–XII, Arlington, Va., 1965–75.
Jonas, Gerald, *Visceral Learning.* New York, 1973.
Leach, Gerald, *The Biocrats.* New York, 1970.
Maltzman, Irving, and Cole, Michael, eds., *A Handbook of Contemporary Soviet Psychology.* New York, 1969.
Overstreet, Bonaro W., *Understanding Fear in Ourselves and Others.* New York, 1971.
Schiller, Herbert I., *The Mind Managers.* Boston, 1974.
Scientific American, Readings from, *Frontiers of Psychological Research.* San Francisco, 1948.
Shapiro, David, Barber, T. X., Dicara, Leo V., Kamiya, Joe, Miller, Neal E., and Stoyva, Johann, *Biofeedback and Self-Control.* Chicago, 1972.
Szasz, Thomas, *Heresies.* New York, 1976.
Szasz, Thomas, *The Manufacture of Madness.* New York, 1970.

Warshofsky, Fred, *The Control of Life: The 21st Century*. New York, 1969.

Wiener, Norbert, *The Human Use of Human Beings*. Cambridge, Mass., 1950.

Winn, Ralph B., trans. and ed., *Psychotherapy in the Soviet Union*. New York, 1962.

Wright, Derek, *The Psychology of Moral Behavior*. Baltimore, 1971.

PSYCHO-SCIENCE

Andrews, Lewis M., and Karlins, Marvin, *Requiem for Democracy?* New York, 1971.

Berne, Eric, *A Layman's Guide to Psychiatry and Psychoanalysis*. New York, 1947.

Berne, Eric, *Transactional Analysis in Psychotherapy*. New York, 1961.

Bindra, Dalbir, and Stewart, Jane, eds., *Motivation*. 2d ed., Baltimore, 1968.

Boyers, Robert, ed., *Psychological Man*. New York, 1975.

Deibert Alvin N., and Harmon, Alice J., *New Tools for Changing Behavior*. Champaign, Ill., 1973.

Dunlap, Knight, *Habits: Their Making and Unmaking*. New York, 1972.

Fromm, Erich, *May Man Prevail?* New York, 1971.

Gentry, Doyle W., ed., *Applied Behavior Modification*. St. Louis, 1975.

Goldenson, Robert M., *Mysteries of the Mind*. New York, 1974.

Group for the Advancement of Psychiatry, Committee on Mental Health Service, *Drug Misuse: A Psychiatric View of a Modern Dilemma*, Vol. VII, Report no. 80, New York, June, 1971.

Group for the Advancement of Psychiatry, *Medical Uses of Hypnosis*. Symposium no. 8, New York, April, 1962.

Group for the Advancement of Psychiatry, Committee on Psychiatry and Law, *Misuse of Psychiatry in the Criminal Courts: Competency to Stand Trial*, Vol. VIII, Report no. 89, New York, February, 1974.

Group for the Advancement of Psychiatry, *Pavlovian Conditioning and American Psychiatry*. Symposium no. 9, New York, March, 1964.

Group for the Advancement of Psychiatry, Committee on Therapy, *Psychotherapy and the Dual Research Tradition*. New York, October, 1969.

Group for the Advancement of Psychiatry, Committee on Research, *Some Observations on Controls in Psychiatric Research*. Report no. 42, New York, May, 1959.

Group for the Advancement of Psychiatry, Committee on Government Agencies, *The VIP With Psychiatric Impairment.* Vol. VIII, Report no. 83, New York, January, 1973.
Hilts, Philip J., *Behavior Mod.* New York, 1976.
Hook, Sidney, ed., *Dimensions of Mind.* London, 1969.
Jacoby, Russell, *Social Amnesia.* Boston, 1975.
Lilly, John C., *Programming and Metaprogramming in the Human Biocomputer.* New York, 1974.
Maslow, Abraham H., *Motivation and Personality,* 2d ed., New York, 1970.
Milgram, Stanley, *Obedience to Authority.* New York, 1975.
Mitford, Jessica, *Kind and Unusual Punishment.* New York, 1974.
Moustakas, Clark, *Creativity and Conformity.* New York, 1967.
Pavlov, I. P., *Conditioned Reflexes.* New York, 1960.
Rachman, S., and Teasdale, J., *Aversion Therapy and Behavior Disorders: An Analysis.* Coral Gables, Fl. 1970.
Rokeach, Milton, *The Open and Closed Mind.* New York, 1960.
Ruesch, Jurgen, *Disturbed Communication.* New York, 1957.
Salter, Andrew, *Conditioned Reflex Therapy.* New York, 1949.
Sansweet, Stephen J., *The Punishment Cure.* New York, 1975.
Sarason, Seymour B., *Psychological Problems in Mental Deficiency.* New York. 1949.
Shostrom, Everett L., *Man, the Manipulator.* New York, 1968.
Siegel, Ronald K., and West, Louis Jolyon, eds., *Hallucinations.* New York, 1975.
Siegler, Miriam, and Osmond, Humphrey, *Models of Madness, Models of Medicine.* New York, 1974.
Skinner, B. F., *About Behaviorism.* New York, 1976.
Skinner, B. F., *Beyond Freedom and Dignity.* New York, 1971.
Skinner, B. F., *Science and Human Behavior.* New York, 1965.
Taylor, John G., *The Shape of Minds to Come.* Baltimore, 1971.
Tennov, Dorothy, *Psychotherapy: The Hazardous Cure.* New York, 1975.
Thomson, Robert, *The Psychology of Thinking.* Baltimore, 1959.
U.S. Congress, Senate, The Staff of the Subcommittee on Constitutional Rights, Committee on the Judiciary, *Individual Rights and the Federal Role in Behavior Modification,* 93d Cong., 2d Sess., Nov., 1974.
Watson, John B., *Behaviorism.* Rev. ed., New York, 1930.
Watzlawich, Paul, Weakland, John, and Fisch, Richard, *Change.* New York, 1974.
Wickham, Harvey, *The Misbehaviorists.* Toronto, 1928.

Wyrwika, Wanda, *The Mechanisms of Human Behavior.* Springfield, Ill., 1972.

TOTALITARIANISM

Arendt, Hannah, *The Origins of Totalitarianism.* New York, 1972.
Huntford, Roland, *The New Totalitarianism.* New York, 1972.

TECHNO-TOTALITARIANISM

Allardice, Corbin, and Trapnell, Edward R., *The Atomic Energy Commission.* New York, 1974.
Baker, Samm Sinclair, *The Permissible Lie.* Cleveland, 1968.
Barber, Bernard, *Science and the Social Order.* New York, 1970.
Boffey, Philip, *The Brain Bank of America.* New York, 1975.
Calder, Nigel, ed. *Unless Peace Comes.* New York, 1968.
Ellul, Jacques, *The Technological Society.* New York, 1964.
Ferkiss, Victor C., *Technological Man: The Myth and the Reality.* New York, 1969.
Foreign Policy Association, ed., *Toward the Year 2018.* New York, 1968.
Friedman, Maurice, *The Hidden Human Image.* New York, 1974.
Gabor, Dennis, *Innovations, Scientific, Technological and Social.* London, 1970.
Hahn, Walter F., and Neff, John C., *American Strategy for the Nuclear Age.* New York, 1960.
Kahn, Herman, and Wiener, Anthony J., *The Year 2000.* New York, 1968.
Kemeny, John G., *Man and the Computer.* New York, 1972.
Koestler, Arthur, *The Ghost in the Machine.* New York, 1968.
Lambright, Henry W., *Governing Science and Technology.* New York, 1976.
Medawar, P. B., *The Future of Man.* New York, 1961.
Orwell, George, *1984.* New York, 1961.
Nieburg, H. L., *In The Name of Science.* Chicago, 1969.
Prehoda, Robert W., *Designing the Future.* New York, 1967.
Rosen, Steven, *Future Facts.* New York, 1976.
Wilson, Andrew, *The Bomb and The Computer.* New York, 1968.

VIETNAM

Fall, Bernard B., *The Two Viet-Nams.* New York, 1967.
Hubbell, John G., *P.O.W.* New York, 1976.
Johnson, Lyndon Baynes, *The Vantage Point.* New York, 1971.
Lane, Mark, *Conversations with Americans.* New York, 1970.

Lifton, Robert Jay, *Home from the War*. New York, 1974.
Random House, ed., *The Vietnam Hearings*. New York, 1966.
Sheehan, Neil, Smith, Hedrick, Kenworthy, E.W., and Butterfield, Fox, *The Pentagon Papers*. New York, 1971.
Smith, George E., *P.O.W.*, Berkeley, 1971.

WATERGATE

Chester, Lewis, McCrystal, Cal, Aris, Stephen, and Shawcross, William, *Watergate*. New York, 1973.
Hunt, E. Howard, *Give Us This Day*. New York, 1973.
Hutschnecker, Arnold A., *The Drive for Power*. New York, 1976.
Schell, Jonathan, *The Time of Illusion*. New York, 1976.
Wills, Garry, *Nixon Agonistes*. New York, 1971.

INDEX

Understanding American Politics

R. V. Denenberg

In this concise guide to American politics, R. V. Denenberg offers an up-to-the-minute account of the workings, functions and relations of American institutions, from the Constitution and the Presidency, through Congress and the Supreme Court, to the bureaucracy and the mass media.

'Three cheers . . . for this brief, lucid, accurate and exceedingly informative study of a difficult and important subject.'

Hugh Brogan, *New Society*

'. . . a splendid introduction which avoids the patronizing tone that experts often assume when describing an unfamiliar political system, and also succeeds in being humorous without cynicism – not always an easy task.'

Sunday Telegraph

'. . . a quick, illuminating and often edgy account of some of the things in danger of falling apart.'

Martin Hillman, *Tribune*

Problems of Knowledge and Freedom

Noam Chomsky

This book contains the revised text of the two Bertrand Russell Memorial Lectures which Chomsky delivered at Trinity College, Cambridge, in 1971. The lectures reflect his concern with some of the problems that Russell investigated and the causes to which he devoted himself.

The first discusses how, through the study of language, Russell's thinking can be taken further. The second develops Russell's ideas on freedom and human nature, and on social and political issues, into an outline of Chomsky's own views on these matters.